D1391363

TEACH YOURSELF BOOKS

CHESS

This book is intended both for those who know nothing of Chess but wish to learn and for those who are experienced in the game and can benefit from a scientific analysis of its many aspects. It is accordingly carefully graduated: Part I introduces the chess pieces, describes their powers and values, and explains the elementary endgame; Part II deals with the middle game, and tactics and strategy; and Part III discusses the openings and some refinements in the endgame, and includes a selection of illustrative games. It aims to teach the reader to think like a chess player, to see moves for himself rather than relying on his memory.

"A thorough study of this work should indeed give the student an adequate grounding in the art of chess."

The Guardian

TEACH YOURSELF BOOKS

CHESS

GERALD ABRAHAMS
M.A. (Oxon.), BARRISTER-AT-LAW

TEACH YOURSELF BOOKS

ST. PAUL'S HOUSE   WARWICK LANE   LONDON EC4

First Printed 1948
New Edition 1953
This Impression 1971

ISBN 0 340 05544 8

*Made and Printed in Great Britain for The English Universities Press, Ltd., London
by C. Tinling & Co. Ltd., London and Prescot*

PREFACE TO FIRST EDITION

The philosopher Mendelssohn gave up Chess because he found it too serious to be a game and not serious enough to be an occupation. If, in disregard of that great example, the reader desires to immerse his mind in this scientific Lido, then the author undertakes in these pages to prevent him from drowning, and so to exercise him that his general mentality will be strengthened rather than weakened by his new pursuit. And in these pages swimming lessons are also available to those who have long disported themselves in the water.

In other words, the author has endeavoured, in this book, to produce something that shall be useful to many classes of persons interested in Chess, ranging from those who know nothing at all about it but wish to learn, to those who are experienced in the game and can benefit (as who cannot?) from a scientific analysis of its many aspects.

The book sets out from the belief that there are many readers completely ignorant of Chess but possessed of a fair intelligence and a desire to learn. It is believed that the number of people desirous of learning Chess is increasing. It is important that these shall learn the moves, but not stop at that; and this book is written on the assumption that such readers not only want to know the moves, but wish for an education in the game that shall bring them to a stage at which they are participating in an undertaking of skill and not a mere game of chance.

The book is accordingly graduated; graduated according to the expectation that, at any point after the earliest pages, the reader will have improved as a Chess player through having mastered what has gone before. He is expected to absorb and understand—and practise—what he reads; not to learn it by heart. If he understands what he reads, then, as he works his way through the second chapter, he will find himself acquiring a certain capacity to think for himself about moves. After the second chapter he may even be thinking like a Chess player. From that stage on, the book should be of some interest even to players of considerable experience. In this respect, *inter alia*, it is claimed that this book differs in its method and purpose from other books available to beginners.

Naturally, such an undertaking—the undertaking to educate in Chess, rather than to equip with minimal knowledge —has been incompatible with the simultaneous or continuous presentation of all aspects of the game at the same level. But, in the author's view, the Chess mind does not require such a preliminary presentation of knowledge before it can

PREFACE

be educated. Also it fortunately happens that Chess is sufficiently organic a science for the reader who is struggling with the rudiments of the game to be made aware of processes that he will have to study at a later stage.

In his ordering of the book in the light of these purposes the author has used a method that is original without being heretical. For many reasons the book does not commence with the openings, though indications of the nature of the openings present themselves on early pages. In the author's view, the learning of opening variations immediately after the learning of the moves is a quite false approach to the game. Most of the present masters were good players before they learned any opening variations. A move in an opening, like a move at any other stage, is a good, bad, or indifferent move. There are very few moves recommended in the openings which are not independently recognisable as reasonably good moves. Now the important thing about Chess is the need for seeing good moves at every moment of time when it happens to be the player's turn to move. There is no stage of the game at which this capacity is not the factor of highest importance. If a student sets out with the idea that he will be materially assisted by learning a series of moves by heart, then he is the victim of at least one fallacy. He is doing precisely what a traveller would do if he tried to make a phrase-book act as a substitute for the knowledge of a language. Phrases are important to those who already have a grasp of a language. In the same way Chess learning is only useful to those who can already play. That is why the proper place for a study of the openings is at the end of a Chess book, not at the beginning.

Again, since the author is convinced that intelligence and imagination, rather than memory, are the qualities of mind to be developed in Chess, he has abstained from the presentation of large numbers of opening variations. What he has undertaken is to give to the reader some conception of the strategic purposes that are expressed in the various openings. If the reader becomes able to see a move, and gains some notion of what is important strategically, then he will not go seriously wrong either in the openings or at any other stage of the game.

And there is a final thought that is worth elaborating. The book is subordinate to the game. The game dwarfs all the advice that is given about it. A book, therefore, should not recommend moves, only say: thus and thus try to find the best move. Moreover, few games are lost through the failure at any particular moment to find the very best move. Often the very best move does not exist. Besides, there is such an elasticity in Chess that advantages are easily reduced, and resources are usually available. At all stages the player is advised to look for the best that he can see, and not regard himself as controlled by any convention. To achieve that state of mind he must play—play hard and think much—rather than read. When he reads, let his reading be subordinate to what he is discovering in play. Whatever learning (whether from books or from other players) a student of Chess acquires is only valuable in the degree that it makes his mind receptive to the possibilities of the board, to the ideas and the notions that pervade the board, and in so far as it widens and deepens his awareness of a rich and enjoyable field of experience.

The author wishes to express his appreciation of the invaluable help given to him at proof stage by Mr. J. H. Williams, the tireless librarian of the Manchester Chess Club.

PREFACE TO 1962 EDITION

Much Chess has been played since there was delivered to me at a London Tournament in 1948, amid cries of "too late", the advance copy of *Teach Yourself Chess*.

But Chess is timeless. In the 13 and more years that have elapsed since the book was written, new figures have ascended the high places of the Chess world—and some have descended again—but the game is still fought along the same lines: if I may say so, along the lines of thought that I described in the first edition.

There have been changes of fashion in opening play, and these continue to occur, as do fashions in lady's hats; but "time writes no wrinkles" on Caïssa's brow. I think her smile that favoured Botwinnik in 1961 is the same that favoured him in 1948; and is, indeed, the same that was seen by all the earlier generations of great players.

To the student of Chess, then, there is no need for any restatement of any truths that are basic in the game. Nor would later instances and examples improve on earlier ones, whether as sources of instruction or as sources of pleasure.

Apart, then, from a few alterations of phrase, in order to excise possible ambiguities, I have found nothing to alter in this book. All I had to take away was the dated word "recent." All I could have added—had there been space—was quantity.

GERALD ABRAHAMS

CONTENTS

PART I

THE ELEMENTS

CHAPTER

PRELIMINARY

INTRODUCING THE CHESS MEN: THEIR FUNCTIONS AND VALUES: THE SCIENCE OF CHESS

In the diagram on this page the reader will see a Chess Board with the Pieces, or Men, set up in the position they occupy at the beginning of an ordinary game of Chess.

(BLACK)

(WHITE)

The Board and Men at the commencement of a game.

The Board has been compared to a battle field, and the two sets of Pieces (White and Black) to contending armies. That comparison is a useful one to bear in mind because, in learning Chess, the average reader will find himself in contact with players and writers who think in terms of attack and defence, threats, manœuvres for position, captures, ambushes (traps as they are sometimes called), and many other terms suggesting combat. Eventually he will himself absorb, and act upon,

A*

notions which are of the first importance in war and other modes of activity, as well as in Chess : for example, the notion of strategy, and the related notion of tactics. From elementary ideas such as capturing and recapturing, advance and retreat, he will proceed to think in terms of strong-points, blockade, tempo and general development. In the light of these accumulating notions he will be able to assess the real forces underlying threats and parades of strength. While doing this he will gradually be acquiring a control over affairs, and learning that the real opposition consists in nothing other than the limits of the material and his own limitations —his lack of confidence or of capacity ; and at the end of his development he will discover, as every good General does, that he has mastered not only an opponent, but a Science.

Perhaps the best standpoint that the reader can adopt if he wishes to justify to himself the expenditure of time on Chess, is that he is studying a Science ; not a Science as exact as Pure Mathematics, but a relatively unpredictable system of Dynamics analogous to the Dynamics of War. With the material available one has to set about achieving an ultimate object—the capture of the King. That involves scientific planning, and calls for the capacity to appreciate future developments. Moreover, Chess is scientific in that those who understand it find their operations determined, not by their own tastes, but by the limits and the possibilities of the material in which they are working. Chess has its beauties, but its essence is mental discipline such as only a Science can give. And Chess has the further advantage that its rules are universal—a fact which distinguishes it from the many games with which it is sometimes classified.

History

Chess, moreover, being well established in time, enjoys a considerable history and literature. Its earliest history is of antiquarian interest. Having originated in some part of Asia as a war game—claims have been made for India, China and Persia*—it seems to have become crystallized in its present form at the time when books were first written about the subject ; that is to say, in Spain during the period of the mediaeval Arab culture. Since the invention of printing

---

*There is evidence of an early Indian game (3rd century C.E.) called Chaturanga (four corners). The accepted theory (based on the scanty contemporary literature) is that this is the original game of Chess ; and that Chinese and Persian forms of the game are later derivatives from it.

there has been no important change—save that the popularity
of the game has moved northward from Iberia to modern
Siberia. After the decline of the Moors, the game continued
to flourish in Spain—the prolific Ruy Lopez having con-
tributed to Chess as well as to literature—and became popular
also in Italy and France.

In England, Chess was well known in Shakespeare's day.
It may be inferred (from *The Tempest*) that the game was
popular in Court circles. But before that time, Chaucer
knew Chess well—and there is a Ballad of some Chess interest.

Caxton, one of the first English printers, has provided us
with an excellent book descriptive of Chess in its modern form.
But it was not till the nineteenth century that England,
and the northern nations, Germany and Russia, took over
the initiative in the development of Chess. In these countries,
and cognate America, the leadership of Chess has now rested
for a century. Meanwhile in Asia the development of the game
—more or less standardized by the Arabs—has lagged a
little behind the European development ; but the modern
Indian game (there is an old form, Desi) differs in so little from
the European game (the Pawn's first move, and a limitation on
promotion) that in this century a native Indian found himself
able to win the British Championship. To all intents and
purposes it may therefore be said that Chess has the advantages of age and universality over most other games; and the
rules set out herein are applicable wherever it is played.
Finally, being describable in notation, Chess is completely
communicable, and a player in any part of the world can
follow developments in any other part of the world.

THE BOARD AND MEN

The Board on which Chess is played is a chequered Board—
i.e., divided into 64 squares of alternating colour—and is the
same board as that required for the modern form of Draughts.*

*Although the two games have a scientific character in common, they
are of different origin. Chess is Asiatic ; Draughts appears to have
originated in the Mediterranean lands. Perhaps that explains its less
dynastic appearance. The chequered board seems to have been known
all over the world. For English readers it may be interesting to observe
that this Board is the ultimate origin of the title "Exchequer." It may
also be interesting to notice that the name Bishop for one of the Pieces
is indigenous to England—which suggests the conjecture that this name
was given at a time when Ecclesiastics controlled the Exchequer. On the
continent, the Piece we call Bishop is described as " le fou," or " laüfer."
These words, which suggest " Court Jester," or " Courier," are probably
corruptions of the Arabic Alfil (Elephant), the Moorish name for the Piece,
adopted in Spanish. (cf. Italian Alfieri.) The Russian name is Slon
(Elephant).

On this Board all the moves are from square to square and only one Piece is allowed to remain on any one square at any given time.

The Board is set out with a Black corner square at each player's left hand side. The Chess Men of each colour—two complete sets of 16 White and 16 Black Men respectively being involved—are arrayed along the two back " ranks " nearest the player who is handling that particular colour. Referring to the first diagram, and reading from left to right, they are : White's back row ; Rook, Knight, Bishop, Queen, King, Bishop, Knight, Rook. (Those which the Queen separates from the King are called Queen's Rook, Queen's Knight, Queen's Bishop, to distinguish them from King's Rook, King's Knight, King's Bishop : this nomenclature is for the purpose of notation and does not correspond to any difference of powers.) Along the front rank (second row) stand the Pawns. The corresponding Black Men are directly opposite ; King (fourth from Black's left) facing King, Queen facing Queen, etc., etc.

Thus it will be seen that each player has, at the outset, two Rooks, which stand on the corner squares, and are, of course, equal to each other in value, two similarly equivalent Knights, which stand on the squares next to the Rooks, two Bishops, again equivalent to each other, but with the difference that one is confined to the Black squares and the other to the White squares ; these flank the King and Queen respectively. Also one Queen, which always starts the game on a square of its own colour (White Queen on White square, Black Queen, opposite, on Black square) ; one King, the only Piece on the Board which dare not be lost, and which stands next to the Queen, i.e., always on a square of its opposite colour; finally, eight Pawns, which stand along the second rank.

The Chess Men, or Pieces, of opposite colour move alternately, i.e., White, Black, White, Black, White having the not negligible privilege of the first move ; and each player must move at his turn to move. The Pieces proceed from their original positions, according to their powers and when they are not obstructed, along the " files " (vertical lines), " ranks " (horizontal lines), and diagonals ; and, with the exception of the promoted Pawn, they retain their original and normal powers of movement throughout the game.

They can all capture hostile Pieces (not more than one per move). This they do, not, as Draughtsmen, by jumping over the victim, but by occupying (except in one very special case) the square of the hostile occupant. The latter is automatically removed from the Board for the duration of the game, unless and until the promotion of a Pawn, in an appropriate case, recalls it. Conversely, subject to one restriction, the Pieces can all be captured.

The restriction on capturability is that the capture of the King is the end of the game. Whoever loses his King, or finds himself so placed that his King must be lost before his opponent's, loses the game. This is another way of saying that *the object of a game of Chess is the capture of one's opponent's King.*

The tactical and strategic consequences that follow from the special character of the King—the divinity which hedges it—will be considered after we have dealt with the geometric moves of the Pieces. Here, suffice it to mention two terms which are of the first importance. (1) When the King is attacked—in the sense that an opponent threatens to capture it next move by bringing a Piece to occupy its square —there is in being a situation which is called *Check*. It is usually said that the King is in Check.* (2) When the King is in Check, and there is no way of terminating the Check, the King is *Check-Mate* or *Mate*. (Check is a corruption of Shah : Mate is a Semitic word, meaning dead.)

These cannot be illustrated conveniently until the reader has learnt the moves (which follow). It is also important for the reader to learn the notation, which enables Chess players to read Chess as musicians read music. Incidentally, it will be necessary to know the notation in order to read this, or any other, Chess book. The notation is given at the end of the Chapter.

THE MOVES

The powers of the Pieces, as distinct from their tactical and strategical importances and their relative values, are quite easily described and grasped.

On the battle field which is the Chess Board there are three obvious directions—as it were, three sets of ready-made roads—along which Pieces can operate, viz. the ranks, the files, and the diagonals. The powers of five, out of the six, functionally different units—that is to say the powers of Rook, Bishop, Queen, King and Pawn—can be simply

*It is customary, but not obligatory, to announce Check orally. This is, however, unrequired, albeit not discourteous, when one's opponent is a good player. On the other hand there is no custom of announcing an attack on the Queen or any other Piece. Such an announcement is " not done."

described as specific movements in these various directions. Rooks move on ranks and files, Bishops on diagonals, Pawns on files (with capturing power on the diagonals), King and Queen along ranks, files and diagonals. The sixth mode of movement, that of the Knight, which, being the Cavalry of the game, seems to make its own special path across the Board, can also be grasped without much difficulty in terms of the same geometry.

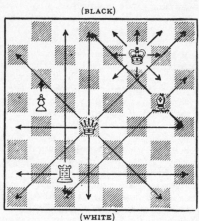

(BLACK)

(WHITE)

Paths of 5 pieces.

THE ROOK (French, Tour; German, Turm; Russian, Ladj; English notation R).*

The Rook has a relatively simple linear move along any rank or any file. That is to say, it can move as few or as many squares as are desired and are available along any rank or file on which it happens to find itself at the moment of moving. Along a file it can move backwards or forwards, i.e., towards or away from its own side of the Board. From any square on an empty Board the Rook has a range of 14 possible moves, and can, in one move, "cover" any other square of the 64.

*The term Rook, if it were derived, as some think, from the Italian Rocca, or the French Roche, would—like the archaic name Castle—do no credit to this Piece's mobility. Its function suggests the Tank rather than the Fortress. But the real origin of the word Rook, the Persian Rukh, meaning a wind or a spirit, does express the notion of mobility. In the Persian game the Rook was, indeed, the most mobile and powerful of the Pieces. That was before the powers of what is now the Queen were increased to their modern magnitude.

THE BISHOP (French, Fou ; German, Laüfer ; Russian, Slon ; English Notation, B).

The Bishop moves as few or as many squares as are desired and available, backwards or forwards, along any diagonal on which it finds itself at the moment of moving. Since that square will be either a Black square or a White square and since each set of diagonals is monochrome, it follows that the Bishop starting on a White square stays on White squares, so long as it is on the Board. If it were not such a militant Piece, one might say that each Bishop is confined to its own diocese. From a centre square the scope of either Bishop is 13 possible moves.

THE QUEEN (French, Dame ; German, Dame ; Russian, Firze ; English Notation, Q)*.

The Queen, which is the most powerful, though, as we have seen, not the most important, Piece on the Board, combines the powers of the Rook and the Bishop ; more accurately, the Powers of the Rook and either Bishop, because by virtue of her linear movement, she can find herself on either diagonal —so is not confined to one. Briefly then, the Queen can move as many òr as few squares as are desired and available along any rank or along any file or along any diagonal ; and, in the case of movement along the files or diagonals she can move backwards or forwards. From a centre square, the Queen has a range of 27 squares out of the 64†.

*Nobody knows exactly when, or why, the most powerful piece on the Board became called the Queen. The name was probably adopted earlier than the period of the great Catherines and Elizabeths—but the famous Isabella may be the responsible influence. A Hebrew poem, attributed to Ibn Ezra (12th century), but probably later (because it refers to the modern Pawn move), describes the Queen or Consort as a Piece having a range of three squares in any direction. Certainly, in the original Indo-Chinese game, no Piece had such great power as the modern Queen, and in those days the King is believed to have been at least as powerful as its neighbour. The earliest Moorish records describe a Piece somewhat less powerful than the modern Queen as the Vizier. Vizier has, since the invention of printing crystallized the rules of Chess, become generally known in Europe as the Queen or Lady. An interesting relic of the Mediaeval name is that in Russia the Queen is called Firze, which is derivative from Vizier. Students of English literature may be re-minded of the old Romance of the Rose : " When he took my Fers away, then I could no longer play." In the days of Elizabeth I the Queen had developed her present powers—" checking the world."

†AVAILABLE SQUARES AND CAPTURES. At this point, having dealt with the long range Pieces, it may be convenient to point out to any reader who has not already inferred it, that, in Chess, Pieces only travel over empty squares. With three exceptions, which are either apparent only, or else specially explicable, the Chess Pieces do not jump. The exceptions are : the Knight's move (which is only apparently exceptional

THE KNIGHT (French, Chevalier ; German, Springer ; Russian, Konj ; English Notation, Kt ; sometimes S, or N, in order to avoid possible confusion with K).

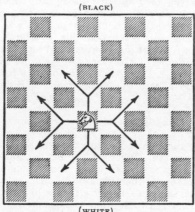

(BLACK)

(WHITE)

THE KNIGHT

Geometrically, the Knight's move may be described as the shortest possible move in which a Piece can change both its rank (or file) and its diagonal. An easier description is to say that the Knight moves from corner to corner of any rectangle three squares by two, of which its own square is a corner square. More easily, for the purpose of visualizing, one can because the Knight does not " sweep " any complete square that it passes), Castling, and the Pawn's Capture En Passant. These remain to be described.

For the benefit of the reader who approaches Chess from Draughts, it should be repeated that the Chess Pieces do not capture by jumping. With one exception (the Pawn capturing En Passant), they capture by moving on to the square of a hostile occupant and remaining there, the captured Piece being removed from the Board. To this general rule about capturing, the Knight's move is not an exception, because the Knight does not affect any Pieces that it appears to pass. It can only take a Piece on a square which is its destination.

Needless to say, with the apparent exception of the Knight, no Chess Piece can pass one of its own coloured Pieces on its direct line of motion; and no Chess Piece can capture any Piece of its own colour.

For the further benefit of the Draughts player approaching Chess, it should be noted that all the Pieces, except the Pawns, can move either forwards or backwards.

Finally, capturing is optional. There is no huffing at Chess. A capture is only compulsory when it is the only move available to terminate a state of Check, or the only move that does not expose the King to Check.

say the Knight moves one square along the rank, or along the file (backwards or forwards), and then one square along the diagonal away from its point of origin. Alternatively, one square along any diagonal, followed by one square along the rank or file away from the point of origin.

In this path the Knight ignores any Pieces of its own or hostile colour on the squares it appears to pass, and is only concerned with any Piece that may occupy the square of its destination. In other words, the Knight appears to jump, or to

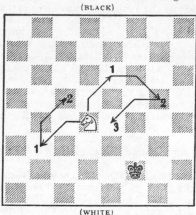

(BLACK)

(WHITE)

The Knight takes 3 moves to arrive at the square adjacent to it on the rank or file, 2 moves to reach an adjacent diagonal square, and 3 moves to check a King 2 diagonal squares away.

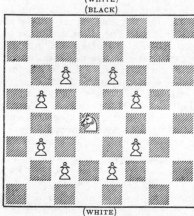

(BLACK)

(WHITE)

Knight cannot move. If, instead, the Pawns were on adjoining squares (all 8 of them), they would not affect the Kt's move.

cross, occupied squares. Pedantically that is not quite correct, because the Knight's path does not sweep out any complete square ; rather it is across the edges of squares. It is as if, on the battlefield which is the Chess Board, the Knight does not move along any special road, but always alights at places which happen to be on the recognised roads.

From any rank or file except the two sets of double ranks and files bordering the Board, the Knight has a field of 8 possible squares ; 8 squares around the edges of a field of 25 squares ; and each move of the Knight creates a new area for it. It is thus an important " middle range " Piece. It has great difficulty in reaching squares adjacent to its point of origin on the rank and file (these require three moves to reach). It takes two moves to reach an adjacent square on the diagonal, four moves to reach the next but one on the diagonal, i.e., 3 moves to Check a King there. Also it takes several moves to cross the Board. On the other hand, as we shall see when we come to compare it with the heavier Pieces, there are many ways in which its powers give the Knight a value as great as that of the Bishop.

THE PAWN (French, Pion ; German, Bauer ; Russian, Peshka : English Notation, P).

The Pawn differs from the other Pieces* in several respects. All the other Pieces can move either forwards or backwards at will. Only the Pawn, the Infantry of the game, is condemned to a perpetual advance. The range of other Pieces is not confined in both extent and direction ; the Pawn resembles the Infantryman in that the extent of its range as well as its direction is limited. The Pawn's normal move is one square forward on the file, with the alternative of a two move advance for each Pawn's first move only. (This right, incidentally, cannot be reserved. If a Pawn moves one square at its first move, it cannot move 2 on its second). Further, other Pieces capture opponents that purport to block their path. The Pawn cannot do so. Anything standing the square ahead of it on the file stops its normal advance. One the other hand, the Pawn captures in a direction which is not that of its normal move, viz., one square ahead

*So far, the word Pieces has been used to include, in its denotation, Pawns. There will be contexts, however, in which the word Piece or Pieces is used in contrast to the word Pawns, e.g., as where a Piece is said to be lost for a Pawn.

This ambiguity is inevitable in Chess literature (not only Anglo-American Chess literature). It is hoped that in every case the context will make the meaning clear.

on either diagonal. Thus a Pawn can change its file, but only with the aid of the hostile Pieces that it captures. Finally, the Pawn has this compensation, that it can be translated to a higher realm. The values of other Pieces become translated according to the position. Only the Pawn changes its nature. This is called *promotion*. When a Pawn reaches the eighth rank it must cease to exist; and there is substituted for it, at the player's will, either a Queen, Rook,

(BLACK)

THE PAWN.

(WHITE)

Bishop or Knight. Something must take its place. The player can choose which Piece he pleases. The normal choice, of course, is the Queen, but, as we shall show, there are instances where a sub-promotion (to Rook, Bishop or Knight) is preferable.

It follows that a player can possess, at some stage of a game, more than one Queen, and/or more than two Rooks, Bishops or Knights. There has, indeed, been a famous win, King and three Knights against King and one Knight. The tactical and strategic value of the Pawn will be considered later. Here suffice it to say that promotability obviously raises it above the ordinary Infantry standard. Because of this it can be said that the Pawns are the only Infantry that the General regards as more than cannon fodder.

THE PAWN'S FIRST MOVE AND THE CAPTURE EN PASSANT

The right of the Pawn to move, at the player's option, two squares forward instead of only one, on the first move, is a modern invention. It does not exist in the Indian game even now*. The option of a double move does not affect the advancing Pawn's power of capture. Thus a Pawn on the second rank cannot capture on the adjoining file on the fourth rank, but only on the third. The option of two squares instead of one applies to an ordinary advance, not to a capture.

On the other hand, the Pawn's double first move has been

(BLACK)

EN PASSANT.
If the Black pawn advances 2 squares in one move, then, on the next move only, the white pawn can behave as if the Black pawn had moved one square.

(WHITE)

offset by the award to opposing Pawns of a special kind of capture. Thus, if a Pawn is standing on its fifth rank, and a hostile Pawn on an adjoining file has not yet moved, then obviously, if that hostile Pawn moves to its third rank (our Pawn's sixth), there can be a capture. If, however, the hostile Pawn moves two squares, apparently there can be no capture. This is where the En Passant rule comes into force. If in those circumstances (where a Pawn stands on the fifth rank) a Pawn on an adjoining file makes a double move (i.e., its first move), then, *on the next move, and the next move only*, the Pawn on its own fifth rank of the adjoining file (the advancing Pawn's fourth rank) can capture the Pawn that has made the double move—exactly as if it had made a single move. Thus, in terms of the notation ; a White Pawn is standing on KB5 A Black Pawn from its KKt2

*Also, the Indian game differs in respect of promotions. There, the Pawn is promoted to a Piece equivalent to that on whose file it gets promoted. On a Rook's file, it becomes a Rook, on a Bishop's file a Bishop, on a Knight's file a Knight ; on the Queen's file or King's file it becomes a Queen.

moves two squares to Kt4 The Pawn on KB5 can capture that Pawn immediately as if it had moved to KKt3. The captured Pawn is removed from KKt4 and the capturing Pawn stands, not on that square (its own Kt5), but on Kt6. This is the only case in Chess of a capture in which the capturing Piece does not occupy the square of the Piece captured.

(BLACK)

(WHITE)

PAWN CAPTURES.
P, on KR file cannot move.
If P on Kt file advances, Black P on R file can capture it or be captured by it.
P on KB file can either capture P on K file, or advance one square without capturing.
P on K file can capture or be captured.
P on Q file if it advances one square can be captured by either flanking pawn.
P on Q file if it advances 2 squares in one move, can, on the next move, be captured by either flanking pawn as if it had moved one square only.

To make the matter clear beyond doubt, let it be repeated that any Capture En Passant must either be done immediately, or else not at all. It is a right that cannot be reserved beyond the immediate occasion of its creation. If the Pawn is not captured En Passant on the opponent's immediately following move, then it cannot be captured En Passant at all.

THE KING (French, Roi ; German, König ; Russian, Korolj ; English Notation K).

Last, by reason of its greatest importance, and in some senses least, of the Pieces, lacking the Knight's distance and the Pawn's promotability, the King yet has a quite considerable power. The King's move is the Queen's move in miniature, one square in any direction ; that is to say, one square either way along the rank, or one square backwards or forwards along the file or diagonal. Thus it has a range, from any square not on the edge of the Board, of eight possible moves. This we shall see to be a not negligible power at any stage of the game. The King is most potent in the Endgame, among Pawns, and it can reach squares closed to either of the Bishops as the case may be*.

Many restrictions hedge in the King, since, as we have seen, in this war game (which continues dynastic, even while the King's power has constitutionally diminished), the King remains the *sine qua non* of the game. If the King is lost, everything is lost.

CASTLING (French, Rochade ; German, Rochade ; Notation, 0–0 ; 0–0–0).

To compensate for the diminution in the King's power in the modern game, there has developed the privilege in which

(BLACK)

(WHITE)

After Castling K side.

the unmoved King participates together with an unmoved Rook. It is, incidentally, a quick method of bringing the Rook nearer to the centre of the Board.

For Castling to take place, the King, and the Rook with which it is proposed to Castle, must stand on their original squares—not having moved—and there must be no Piece in between. Then the King can move two squares to its right or

*There is reason to believe that before the rise of the Vizier (now Queen) the power of the King was greater than now (no one knows how great). Yet the name has not been changed. Even in Republican countries this Piece is still called the King, and nobody has yet suggested G.H.Q., or War Office, or any other name that signifies a military function at once highly important and not too dynamic.

left as the case may be; and the Rook towards which it moves jumps over it, and lands on the square between the original King's square and the square to which the King has moved. Thus, in Castling King's side, the King moves to the King's Knight's square and the King's Rook moves to the King's Bishop's square. In Castling Queen's side, the King moves to the Queen's Bishop's square and the Queen's Rook moves to the Queen's square*.

(BLACK)

After Castling Q side

(WHITE)

A number of conditions govern Castling, which, incidentally, is the only instance in Chess of two Pieces of the same colour simultaneously altering their positions. For Castling to take place:

1. Obviously the King and Rook concerned must be on their original squares with no Pieces intervening.
2. Neither the King nor the Rook concerned may have made a previous move. If the King has moved there can be no Castling at all for the player whose King it is. (It follows that one cannot Castle twice.) If only the Rook has moved there can be no Castling with that particular Rook, though there can still be Castling with the other Rook if that has not yet moved. Obviously

*It is normal, in Castling to move the King first because that particular King's move necessarily implies that you are Castling, whereas if you move the Rook first your opponent may think that you have made a complete move. As the rule in serious Chess is that a Piece touched must be moved, the policy of moving the King first in Castling avoids technical objections of a pedantic nature.

there can be no Castling with a " promoted Pawn " Rook.

3. The King must not be in Check. It is not true to say, as many bad players think, that once the King has been in Check there can be no Castling. That is just incorrect; but at the moment of Check the King cannot get out of Check by Castling. That is very important.

4. The square to which the King must move, and the square which the King must pass in order to Castle, must not be under attack by a hostile Piece. Thus, in Castling King's side, not only must you not be in Check, but your King's Bishop's square and your King's Knight's square must not be immediately reachable by a hostile Piece. On the other hand the fact that the Rook is attacked does not matter at all. In Castling Queen's side, the Queen's square and the Queen's Bishop's square must not be immediately reachable by a hostile Piece. The Queen's Knight's square and the Queen's Rook's square do not matter.

(BLACK)

(WHITE)

CASTLING.
White cannot Castle either side, and if the Kt be placed one square right or left, White cannot Castle for a different reason (i.e., being in Check).

Since Castling can be quite an advantage—it usually is—an opponent will prevent Castling if he can. The ways of doing this follow from the rules given above. To cause the King to move, or to cause to move that Rook with which the King is likely to Castle, or to cause both Rooks to move, is a good method but not an easy one. A more usual method, and very effective if the situation can be maintained, is to have Pieces stationed so as to control the squares that the King has to pass or arrive at in order to Castle. To achieve this without loss is usually to achieve superiority.

On the other hand, it must be pointed out that Castling is not always good. Sometimes the King is best placed in the middle of the Board (e.g., when the Endgame is approaching.) It is also true that Castling can, on occasion, incur a quick loss because the opponent's attack may be, in the circumstances, more easily directed to the wing than to the centre. Typical is what is sometimes called the " Greek Gift Sacrifice." It is a warning that in Chess there is no room for automatism. (See next Chapter.)

CONSEQUENCES OF THE SPECIAL IMPORTANCE OF THE KING

The treatment of the King was purposely left until after the other Pieces had been considered, because, whereas other Pieces are only limited by their geometric scope, the King, whose geometric move is tactically and strategically important, is also limited by the fact that it alone of all the Pieces dare not be lost. Other values can be transvalued, but not the importance of the King.

(BLACK)

(WHITE)

CHECK.
White King in Check. This Check can be terminated.
  (a) by K move.
  (b) by capture of B.
  (c) by interposition of KT.

The reader has already been introduced to the ideas of Check and Mate. It is now proposed to consider them in detail. *Check* differs qualitatively from all other attacks, because it is obligatory upon the player checked to terminate the Check. Other Pieces can be allowed to be lost—can be left, or placed, En Prise.* Obviously, since the purpose of the game is the capture of the King, it may come about that you can allow your opponent to capture any of your Pieces, because the loss will leave you in a position, immediately or ultimately, to effect the downfall of your opponent's King. Then the Piece concerned is said to have been sacrificed. A sacrifice is one instance of what has been called above "trans-valuation," where the formal values of the Pieces are subordinated to the functions of all the Pieces operating in the game. By virtue of that reasoning, the King can never be allowed to sacrifice itself.

Again, other Pieces may be lost unsacrificially, but their loss, whether in exchange for something or not, does not necessarily put an end to the game. But the King, be it repeated, must not be lost if the game is to be continued.

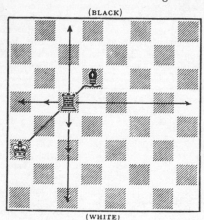

(BLACK)

(WHITE)

DISCOVERED CHECK.

DOUBLE CHECK.

If the R moves away, White is in Check (Discovered Check). If the R moves 2 squares to the White side of the Board or 2 squares to White's left the Check is Double Check.

It follows that a state of Check must be terminated. A simple Check (by one Piece) can be terminated either by the capture of the checking Piece, or by the interposition of a Piece between the King and the attacking Piece (evidently this cannot be done when the attacking Piece is a Knight or a Pawn, or a Piece on an adjacent square to the King); thirdly, by moving the King. This can coincide with the

*En Prise is a useful term to express the capturability of a Piece—especially capturability for insufficient exchange. The term is never abbreviated to e.p., which is the shorthand for en passant.

first method when the checking Piece is adjacent to the King and unguarded (i.e., its square is not covered by another Piece of the same colour).

These three methods apply also when the Check is a discovered Check. A discovered Check arises when a Piece, which does not itself give Check, moves out of the path of a long-range Piece opening a battery on the King. A diagram illustrates this. The distinction between discovered Check and simple Check is only psychologically important; discovered Check gives alarm to weak players.

(BLACK)

(WHITE)

CROSS-CHECK.

If the Black Rook moves, say, one square, White can Cross-check by moving the King or interposing the Kt. If the Black Rook gives Double-check, a King move gives a Cross-check. In the case of a Cross-check by interposed piece, the fact that the checking piece is pinned is immaterial. (The first King to fall loses.)

More difficult to deal with is double Check. That is a discovered Check with the addition that the Piece unmasking the battery itself gives Check. Then there are two Pieces checking the King; a Rook or a Queen on the rank or file, and a Knight, Bishop or Pawn also checking; alternatively, a Queen or Bishop checking from long range on the diagonal and a Knight or Rook checking independently. Double Check is an extremely useful weapon because it forces the King to move. Sometimes it can be followed up with very great advantage.*

To complete the account of Check, a player can extricate himself from Check, in the same move giving Check, e.g., he can interpose a Piece in answer to a simple Check, which Piece, moving to the square required, either itself gives Check, or discovers Check; alternatively, the King, by moving, can open a battery on the opponent's King. On the other

*It stands to reason that there cannot be a treble Check.

hand, the King's move can never give double Check, because the King itself cannot give Check. On similar reasoning, the reply to a Check cannot be the capture of the opponent's King, because that would imply that the opponent, in giving Check, has either exposed his own King to Check—which he must not do—or has failed to terminate the condition of Check in which his own King stood at the moment of moving.

It remains only to be added that the value of Check varies with the position. Check can be a bad move, if the position after the Check has been replied to is more favourable to the player who has been checked than it was before. The only Check which is bound to be good is Mate. On the other hand, the player who said, " Never miss a Check, it might be Mate," was contributing to the humour of the game, not to its serious study.

MATE AND LOSS

If, unhappily, a player is in Check, and has at his disposal no move that can terminate the Check, then he is Check Mate, or, as it is more usually called, Mate. Mate is the state of

(BLACK)

(WHITE)

This is Mate.

the game when your opponent's next move will be the capture of your King, whatever move you make in the meantime. Since the object of the game is the capture of the King, it follows that to be mated is to lose.

Mate can happen after few moves or after many moves— but it is always the end of the game.

Conversely, the game is not lost, strictly speaking, until Mate. But in most games it happens that the player who realises that Mate of his King later has become inevitable, in the light of the position, and on the assumption of his opponent's capacity to bring it about, anticipates the Mate by resigning. So for practical purposes, it may be said that the game is lost —and resignation justified—when Mate is either immediately

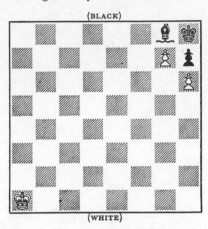

This is Mate.

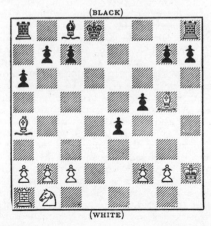

This is also Mate. It arises from the following play:

1. P to K4 ; P to K4
2. Kt to KB3 ; Kt to QB3
3. B to Kt5 ; P to QR3
(Ruy Lopez)
4. B to R4 ; Kt to B3
5. O—O ; Kt × P
6. P to Q4 ; P × P
7. R to K1 ; P to Q4
(Riga Defence)
8. Kt × P ; B to Q3
9. Kt × Kt ; B × Pch
10. K to R1 ; Q to R5
11. R × Ktch ; P × R
12. Q to Q8ch ; Q × Q
13. Kt × Qch ; K × Kt8
14. K × B, P to KB4 ?
15. B to KKt5 Mate.

impending, or certain though not immediate. Mate, or the reasonable certainty of Mate, is, then, the condition of loss. The reasonable certainty of Mate may exist in an infinite variety of circumstances, but the main characteristic of most positions that are resigned is a decisive preponderance

(BLACK)

(WHITE)

LOSS.
This is a typical instance of loss. White will soon be a Queen to the good and will force Mate.

of force. This may vary from a Queen, or more than a Queen, to the good, down to the preponderance of a single Pawn in a position where sooner or later it can be promoted. Those are instances of material advantage, which, other things being equal, give one side the conditions of victory. But let the reader notice that the expression used above was preponderance of force. That is not the same thing as excess of material. Excess of material only wins, other things being equal. Now Chess is one mode of activity where other things are very rarely equal. In Chess it can quite often be said that the many have been delivered into the hands of the few. A player may sacrifice much of his material in order to bring about a Mating attack, and may finally achieve Mate when materially he is several Pieces to the bad. Or it may be the case that a player is material to the bad, but his Pieces are so well placed that he controls the Board and can win his opponent's material at his leisure. Then what he has is a preponderance of force. But where neither player is in a position to control the Board or to force a decisive series of moves, then, and then only, material counts ; because in those circumstances material can be turned into effective force, and a sufficient excess of material will guarantee victory.

Thus it may be said that there are two main types of victory in Chess—victory by Mate, or victory, of a more sedate kind, by the accumulation of an overpowering advantage in the form of force, which may be positional dominance, or excess of material not offset by positional disadvantage. Most games of Chess are struggles to achieve this kind of accumulation—the mediate victory rather than the immediate Mate. But it must be borne in mind that at all stages of the game Mate is a factor. The threat of immediate Mate may be part of a forcing process by which you compel your opponent to yield ground and/or material. Thus it may happen that an attack against an opponent's King results, not in Mate, but in a considerable gain in material; it may also happen that, in the struggle for material, the player that succeeds in gaining or saving material finds himself the victim of a Mating attack. It follows that in a well contested game there is always a dovetailing and an integration of purposes; and the game must always be looked at as a whole.

It remains only to be added that, although the loss of the King is the loss of the game, in practice the game never ends that way. If a player exposes his own King to attack, or fails to terminate a state of Check, he must correct the move. That is the only move which, in ordinary Chess, is allowed to be retracted. Games are lost, either by Mate, or by resignation in anticipation of immediate or eventual Mate.

STALEMATE AND OTHER TYPES OF DRAW

There is one special situation, which is so important that it affects the whole nature of Chess, where a preponderance of force—and that of a striking character—produces not a win, but a draw. That is when one of the players is not in Check but is in such a position that he cannot make any move at all without exposing his King to immediate capture. This position is called *Stalemate*. It must not be confused with what we describe in the Continental term Zugzwang, where the player whose turn it is to move incurs disadvantage through having to move. In Stalemate the important fact is that any move allows the capture of the King on the move, though the King as it stands at the moment of moving is not attacked. Roughly, it is Mate without a Check. This position can come about when there are quite a number of both coloured Pieces on the boards. That, however, is rare. More usually it comes about in an Endgame where the forces are small. Then the player with the passive—usually, but not necessarily, the lesser—material can find himself with his Pawns, for example, blocked, other Piece or Pieces pinned (i.e., in such a position that they stand between the King and an attacking Piece and cannot move without allowing Check), and the King itself without an available square. One of the most important situations, however, is where one player has an excess of force just

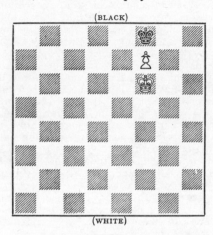

STALEMATE.
If it is Black's turn to move.

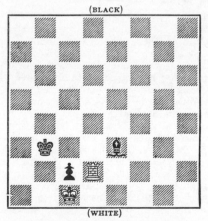

STALEMATE.
If White has to move.

insufficient to bring about Checkmate. Thus, as we shall see, a King and Bishop alone, or a King and Knight alone, cannot bring about the Mate of a lone King ; but they can bring about Stalemate. A King and two Knights can Mate a lone King, but they cannot force Mate. The most that they can force is Stalemate. Again, a King and Pawn can defeat a King if the Pawn can be brought to promotion; but if the defending King is properly placed relatively to the other, and no mistakes are made, again all that can happen is Stalemate. The foregoing are the circumstances where Stalemate is most frequent; and it is from these circumstances that it derives its importance. For the consequence of the Stalemate rule is that there is a margin of excess of force which is not adequate for victory. There is a margin of Draw, so to speak, on either side of equality. That fact makes Chess a harder game to win even than might be expected. Needless to add, it is almost invariably easy to lose !*

Another type of Draw—theoretically the normal—is where both sides have absolute equality of material and force and neither side has any available process of seeking victory. The extreme case, of course, is King against King. But a draw can be agreed—and usually is agreed among good players—where it is clear that neither side has any preponderance, or any likelihood of achieving preponderance.

*Very rare is the draw that results from the fact that the player whose turn it is to move *physically* cannot move.

(BLACK)

(WHITE)

DRAW.

A ridiculous, but not impossible position. White to move, cannot move

B

This kind of situation can develop even when the Board is crowded with Pieces. It happens when the skirmishing is over and the strategic lines of the game are so set that neither side can attempt any attack without incurring the risk of loss.

(BLACK)

(WHITE)

AGREED DRAW.

This is a typical situation, fairly early in the game, where a draw can easily be agreed.

In addition there are rules of the game which increase what has been called above the margin of Draw. One of these rules is that *perpetual Check* is a Draw. This can happen early in the game, but it usually happens towards the Endgame, when the side with inferior chances has available a powerful Piece like the Queen, or a couple of Pieces, which can so move as to keep the opposing King in Check move after move without being stopped. In some instances the geometry of the Board is the factor that prevents the Checks from being stopped. In other cases, the Check could only be stopped by heavy loss of material. Both of these types are illustrated later. The rule, shortly stated, is that an unending series of Checks bringing about no change in the position, amounts to a Draw.

Perpetual Check is a draw by way of terminating the interminable. A harder rule relates to the occurrence, 3 times or more, of an identical position in the same game. Then, a claim to a draw may be made, *instead of a move*, (*a*) by the player whose move can cause the recurrence : (*b*) by his opponent, when the recurrence has taken place.

Another rule is that if 50 moves have been played without any change in the material, and with no Pawn having been moved, the game is also a Draw. (See note at end of chapter).

The last rule is relatively rare in its direct operation. But the rule about repetition can operate at any stage where both players refuse to commit themselves to any change of plan.

(BLACK)

(WHITE)

DRAW.
White, at a material disadvantage and in great danger, draws by repeating the Checking moves . . . Q to Kt5 and B6.

In conclusion, let it be said—and this may already have occurred to the reader—that by reason of the margins that exist in Chess, the normal result of a well-contested game should be a Draw. But that does not mean that a winning advantage has got to be a perceptibly big advantage. A winning advantage can be slight and subtle. That slight and subtle advantage will be the thin edge of a wedge. What requires to be pointed out is that all advantages are not winning advantages. There is usually counter-play ; and in the hands of a good opponent the counter-play will usually be dangerous and will suffice at least to prevent the eventual difference that crystallizes from being sufficient for your victory.

NOTATION

The rules governing the English (or Descriptive) notation are as follows :

1. Each file is named after the Piece whose original square is at the base of that file. Thus we have Queen's Rook's (QR) file, QKt file, QB file, Q file, K file, KB file, KKt file, KR file. (Where there is no ambiguity the K or Q in QR, KKt, etc., etc., can be dropped.)

2. Pieces are referred to by their initials ; e.g., K, Q,

QB, KR, etc. (Where there is no ambiguity, the extra letter can be dropped as in the case of the names of the files.) Each Pawn is named, not after its original file, but according to the particular file on which it happens to be at the moment of the move being registered. A Pawn can be QR P, QKt P, etc., etc. (Where there is no ambiguity, one or both of the extra letters can be dropped, leaving, e.g., BP or P.)

3. The destination of any Piece or Pawn is described by the specific square to which it moves on any particular file.

4. To this end the squares along each file are numbered 1 to 8. Thus a move is registered as P to K4, B to Kt5, R to K1, etc., etc.

(BLACK)

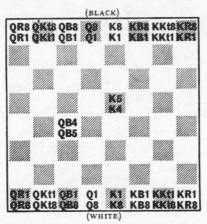

THE NOTATION.

The Black description of each square is below the White description.

(WHITE)

5. Each player numbers the Board, for the purpose of describing his own moves, from his own back rank, counting that as 1, his second rank as 2, and so on to 8. His opponent describes his (the opponent's) move, and he describes his opponent's moves, from his opponent's end. Thus the Board falls into two completely overlapping frames of reference; one for White moves, the other for Black moves.

Thus, White, moving his King's Pawn two squares on the first move, writes P to K4. If Black replies with a similar move, that is registered in Black's column (by both players) as P to K4. Now suppose Black did not make that move, but some other, e.g., P to K3, and White, on his next move, advanced his Pawn one square further, that is registered in the White column as P to K5.

Once it is remembered that the system of description is double—one frame of reference for White's moves, and one frame of reference for Black's moves—there is no difficulty. The method has been described as clumsy, but there is something natural about it.

6. Certain symbols are useful ; viz., × means Captures, e.g., P×P. 0–0 (or 0–0–0) signifies Castles (K side or Q side). Ch. signifies Check. The plus sign is sometimes used for Check, but as this sign also means " with advantage," the former use is relatively rare.

ALGEBRAIC NOTATION

So far the English notation. The continental, or Algebraic, notation will be found described in the next diagram. It only requires to be explained that the files are a, b, c, d, e, f, g, h, *from White's left to White's right, and the numbering of the squares on the files is always from White's side of the Board, whether Black is moving or White is moving*, i.e., there

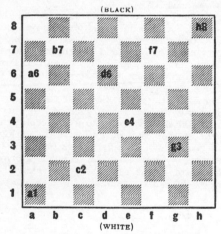

(BLACK)

ALGEBRAIC
NOTATION·

is only one frame of reference. Further, in the continental notation, Pawns, the object of militaristic disregard, are never described by initials ; P to K4 is e2 to e4. Further, " Captures " is described by a semi-colon, and the Piece captured is not mentioned—only the square on which the capture takes place, e.g., B g 8 ; Finally, an obelus signifies Check†. A double obelus, Mate‡.

FORSYTH NOTATION

This is a neat and ingenious method of recording the position without the labour of making a diagram.

Looking at the Board from White's side, one reads off from the top left-hand corner—as in ordinary reading—the number of vacant squares and the names of Pieces present on the back rank, the next rank and so downwards from rank to rank.

White Pieces are described by a Capital initial ; Black Pieces by a small initial. Thus, suppose Black's King is on his King's square and the White King is facing it on the next rank but one (i.e., White's K6), and there is a White Queen on the right of the White King (i.e., White's KB6).

This position, which, incidentally, is a good example of Stalemate, would be described in the Forsyth notation as follows : 4k3 ; 8 ; 4KQ2 ; 40.

Any position can be quite quickly written down by this method, however crowded the Board.

Note on the 50-move rule.

There are some (very few) endgame positions in which the win that is demonstrable occupies more than 50 moves unpunctuated by captures or by Pawn moves.

Instances are : some cases of King and 2 Knights against King and Pawn ; some cases of King, Rook and Bishop against King and Rook, and at least one case of King, Rook and Pawn against King, Bishop and Pawn.

Because of these demonstrations it has become the practice of organizers of Chess events to declare their acknowledgement of certain exceptions to the 50-move rule, and to declare the number of moves, in excess of 50, that they allow in the various exceptional classes of position. (This practice is pursuant to amendments to the Laws of Chess made by F.I.D.E. during the 1950's. The new form of the rule about the Draw by repetition of position (p. 34) derives from the same source.)

CHAPTER II

THE FUNCTIONS AND RELATIVE VALUES
OF THE PIECES :
THE ELEMENTARY ENDGAME.

IN the language of the Persian poet the purpose of the Chess player is to "mate and slay." He judges the value of his Pieces in terms of their capacity to capture other Pieces and to mate the King. At all stages of the game these capacities vary. But this varying is more likely to occur on a crowded Board than on a relatively empty Board. It is on the relatively empty Board that it is easiest to compare the strength of the Pieces. Particularly, their power to co-operate in Mate is a good index to their value ; and the reader would be well advised to master as soon as he can some of the operations of mating that can take place on an open Board. It may appear to him that in doing this he is starting at the end, not at the beginning. In making this criticism he will have grasped an important truth about Chess—that the study of it starts at the end. The final purpose is what matters from the beginning. As we have seen, the game is won by preponderances of force sufficient to carry out an eventual mating operation. A very simple strategic process (too simple to be the whole of strategy, but always an aspect of it) is to aim at acquiring more material than your opponent possesses ; then, by repeated exchange of Pieces, to leave yourself with some striking force in addition to your own King against your opponent's lone King. Now there is no purpose in carrying this out unless, having achieved that final superiority, you can turn it into eventual Mate. Nor indeed will you be able to force the simplification unless you can Mate. Therefore, one must begin the study of the game by learning how to finish the game. In studying this one learns to see the game as a whole ; also one acquires some degree of intimacy with the functions of the Pieces.

MATING BY THE QUEEN

A surprising number of games liquidate themselves eventually into King and Queen against King. King and Queen against King is the logical finish of any closely contested game where the final difference in force is a Pawn that can be

promoted. If, then, resignation does not take place, that
Pawn gets promoted into a Queen, rapidly disposes of anything
that requires to be disposed of, and the King and Queen are
left working together to bring about Mate.

Now the Queen, though extremely powerful, cannot mate
unaided, because, as will already be evident to the reader,
the 27 squares that she controls cannot include the same
squares as the 9 that constitute the hostile King's field (the
square on which the King stands and the 8 squares to which
it has the choice of moving). This follows from the fact that
the Queen cannot occupy the King's square at the moment
of the King's occupancy.

(BLACK)

(WHITE)

The Queen about to
give Mate.
(at e2 or c1)

Moreover, even if the King's scope be reduced to 5 squares
(at the edge of the Board), or to 3 squares (at the corner of
the Board), the Queen unaided cannot Mate. To do so she
would have to include in her capacity the power of making a
Knight's move, which, of course, she does not possess. (That,
incidentally, may be a reply to those would-be reformers who
wish to add to the Queen's power the power of moving like
a Knight).

At the side of the Board (a fortiori at the corner of the
Board) the Queen and the King combined can bring about
Mate. They cannot Mate in the middle of the Board. But
they can so co-operate as always to drive the hostile King to
the side of the Board. Then Mate is easy, though the player
must always be careful to avoid the risk of Stalemate.

The first diagram shows a position just before the end. From this position, in order to Mate, the Queen must arrive either at a square immediately in front of the hostile King on the file and guarded by her own King ; or else must be able to check on the rank when her own King is so placed as to prevent the checked King from escaping from the back rank. If one gives the Board a quarter turn, the same effect can be

K and Q *v.* K.

Most favourable position for Black.

White wins as follows.

1. Q to Kt4 ; K to B4
2. K to B2 ; K to K4
3. K to B3 ; K to Q4
4. K to K3 ; K to K4
5. Q to Kt5 Check.

and the process is repeated until the Black K is on the back rank.

STALEMATE

B*

seen on the file edge of the Board. It may be observed that the King is a particularly useful co-operator with the Queen. Together they can give a bigger range of Mates than could the Queen and Bishop together or the Queen and Knight together.

The diagram on page 40 shows the mating process being completed. But the reader must learn how to bring this final stage about. The next diagram shows the Pieces separated from each other, with the hostile King in the centre.

The series of moves beside the second diagram shows the method of bringing about the kind of position that we saw in the first diagram. The third diagram shows a possible mishap. In approximating with the Queen and King, White has contrived to give not Mate but Stalemate. His last move should have been not K (from K2) to B1, but Q to Kt4—a more patient move.

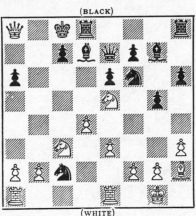

(BLACK)

(WHITE)

A possible Mate.

The Queen's power as a mating Piece will be better realised when mating processes by other Pieces have been considered. Meanwhile, in case there is any misunderstanding, let it be made clear that the Queen can appear at her maximum strength on a full Board as well as on an empty Board. On a full Board, for example, it can happen that the Queen delivers Mate single-handed. That is when the hostile King is hemmed in by its own Pieces. Here are two examples. One early Mate (in which the Queen's full powers are not seen, but which the reader should learn) consists in the so-called

Fool's Mate. This is the quickest Mate in Chess—on the second move. It can only be done by Black—and that when White plays extremely badly.

White plays P to KKt4, a weak move which does very little development and puts a Pawn on a square where it is not useful yet. Black replies P to K4, a reasonable move developing some Pieces and occupying a good square. White then plays a perfectly horrible move P to KB3 and Black replies Q to R5; and, if you look at that, you will see that the Queen is delivering a Check to which there is no answer.

The diagram on p. 42 (also illustrative of the Queen's power) shows a position that can come about more rationally. Black has Castled Queen's side. White's Bishop has taken a Pawn on his QR6, Black has recaptured with a Pawn from Black's Kt2, and White's Queen, moving down the diagonal from KB3, arrives at QR8 and Black is mated, because the King is hemmed in in all directions that the Queen's range does not cover.

More usually the Queen mates in co-operation with at least one other Piece. Here, e.g., is the Scholar's Mate—in four moves—

White	Black
1. P to K4.	P to K4.
2. B to B4.	B to B4.
3. Q to R5. Not really a good move, because there is a good answer to it; but it threatens two things, including the capture of the Pawn on White's K5.	P to Q3. Guarding the Pawn on his K4, but overlooking another threat. Necessary was Q to B3 or K2. Less good than that would be P to KKt3, allowing Q × KP Check, followed by capture of the Rook.
4. Q × BP Mate.	

The above are occurrences that do not often take place. Nobody invites the Fool's Mate; and nobody tries to do the Scholar's Mate, because Q to R5 is not a good move if Black makes the correct reply. As will be seen later, it is not wise to parade the Queen round the Board except for very good reason.

The following few moves constitute one instance of a vigorous Queen move early in the game. This same example shows the importance of Mate as a tactical threat. The Mate is not achieved but material is won.

White	Black
1. P to K4.	P to K4.
2. Kt to KB3 apparently attacking a Pawn.	Kt to QB3 defending the Pawn.
3. B to B4	B to K2. Not bad, but not vigorous. Better is B to B4.

White	Black
4. P to Q4. A vigorous develop-ing move.	P × P. Not a good capture: Kt × P is not so bad, but P to Q3 is better.
5. P to QB3. The sacrifice of a Pawn: if, e.g., 5 . . . P × P 6. Kt × P. White will have lost 2 Pawns for one. The capture, however, is a pitfall.	P × P. A mistake. P to Q3 (or Kt to B3) is necessary.
6. Q to Q5. And now Mate on KB7 is threatened. Black is now forced to play . . .	Kt to KR3. Losing a Piece but stop-ping the Mate. He could not play P to Q3 because of 7. Q × BP Ch. K to Q2 8. B to K6. Mate.

White will now capture this Knight with his Queen's Bishop; Black will not have time to recapture, but will be obliged to Castle (in order to stop the Mate) and the Bishop will return home, having won a Piece for the Gambit Pawn. Incidentally, White's task will still not be easy; because his own development is now imperfect—as often after a successful skirmish.

As well as a good mating Piece, the Queen is also, and obviously, a good capturing Piece. On a Board where the Pieces are in any degree spreadeagled, the Queen's power to attack in several directions simultaneously can be devastating. The next diagram shows a simple instance of this.

(BLACK)

(WHITE)

The Queen attacking three unguarded Pieces.

And even earlier in the game, on a crowded Board, a Queen's move can force the win of material quite soon in the game. Typical is the following variation :—

White	Black
1. P to K4.	P to K4.
2. Kt to KB3.	P to Q3. Defending the Pawn.
3. B to B4.	B to K2.
4. P to Q4.	P × P.
5. P to QB3. A sacrifice similar to that in the previous example.	B to Kt5. With the idea of preventing the King's Knight from moving. This is called "Pinning" the Knight. At this early stage it is a mistake. P × P would also be dangerous, because of 6 Q to Q5 B to K3. 7 Q × KtP. The best answer is 5 ... Kt to KB3.
6. Q to Kt3. With a double threat. The Queen is attacking the Knight's Pawn; and the Bishop, supported by the Queen, is attacking the King's Bishop's Pawn.	

It is impossible for Black to parry both threats.

This type of manœuvre is very frequent; but it should be added, as a warning, that if both sides are equally well-developed (as they are not in the example given), the capture of the Queen's Knight's Pawn can be dangerous to the capturer because it loses a lot of time, and may involve the Queen in remaining badly mobilized; and that consideration may be well worth a Pawn to the opposition. (An example of this is given in the Chapter on Strategy.)

LIMITS OF THE QUEEN'S POWER

On a crowded Board the Queen can be far from omnipotent. Indeed a Master, expert in the use of all the Pieces, can give the odds of a Queen to players of mediocre skill and can win.

On a crowded Board, the Pieces are usually not loose or spreadeagled unless they are being very badly handled. Most of the Pieces will be guarded; that is to say, if they are captured, another Piece (Pawns are particularly useful here) will be standing ready to recapture. In that kind of situation —which is the normal one—the Queen's power is limited by her own value; and that value can only be ignored if a process is in operation which justifies some loss of value for its fulfilment. Failing this, a wandering Queen can amount to a helpless target, prevented by her value from engaging in combat and exchanges with lesser Pieces.

Here are some examples to illustrate the vulnerability of the Queen and her liability to capture by a combination of weaker Pieces. Two at least of these examples, incidentally, should be useful to the reader as illustrations of the aggressive power of the Knight.

The first is a short game played about 1923 by the author :—

White (The Author)

1. P to K4.

Black (W. R. Thomas)

P to Q4. The Centre Counter Opening, now a little out of favour, but quite playable. It solves some problems of development quite early, but loses a tempo.

2. P × P.

Q × P.

3. Kt to QB3. Attacking Queen and gaining a move. The minor Piece comes out without the opponent being able to develop a corresponding minor Piece immediately.

Q to R4.

4. P to Q4. Opening the game up and controlling the centre.

Kt to QB3. An experimental move invented by Mieses. The idea is to lure White into too quick an attack with P to Q5. Better than the text, and usual, is P to QB3, guarding the centre and affording the Queen a retreat.

5. B to Q2. Creating a masked battery against the Queen. The danger is not immediate however.

Kt to KB3. A plausible move, but not the best. Had Black realised what White's Pieces could do in the next two moves, he would have played B to Q2 with the idea of Castling on the following move. It should be added, however, that White's threat, though short, was hard to see among the many possible lines of play that Black had to consider.

6. B to QKt5. Pinning the Knight. One threat is P to Q5. The other will be seen next move. Actually P to Q5 is not a threat unless the other is a threat as well. But in practical Chess it is very easy to see some possibilities without seeing the full implications.

P to K3. A move with some positional merits, but revealing that Black has not seen what is going on. At this stage his only safe moves are awkward ones, like K to Q1 or Q to Kt5, the latter with the idea of replying to P to Q5 with P to QR3, etc., driving the Bishop away or bringing about exchanges.

7. Kt to Q5. Winning the Queen. Thus, if Q × KB, Kt × P Check, forking the King and Queen—a good example of the Knight's "fork." If, instead, B to QKt5, intervening between the Queen and the Bishop that is attacking it, then simply B × B, and the situation is unaltered because the Knight is pinned—a good example of the effect of a pin.

Resigns. For the reasons given opposite. The best Black can do is to play Q × QB Check followed by the capture of the Knight at Q5. Then he will have given a Queen for two minor Pieces—which, at this early stage, is insufficient, especially in view of the fact that White's development is very good.

There have, in fact, been games when one player has given a Queen for two minor Pieces, and by that sacrifice has been enabled to win. An historic position from the Match between McDonnell (a North Irish Master of the 1840's) and La Bourdonnais (one of the last known really great French Chess Masters) is shown in the accompanying diagram.

(BLACK)

(WHITE)

From the 50th game between La Bourdonnais and McDonnell. Black plays Kt × Kt!

McDonnell played

White	Black
13. . . .	Kt × Kt.
14. B × Q.	Kt to K6 Ch.
15. K to K1.	K × B.

And Black has an overwhelming attack unless White resacrifices. La Bourdonnais was too opinionated to do so.

The above two examples took place on the full Board. Here,* now, is a composition by Adamson (an English Composer who specializes in the construction of elegant Endgame positions) in which the Queen is rendered helpless on the relatively open Board. With a very big range, she is so situated in relation to the King that she cannot escape capture.

1. B to B6. And now the Queen is in difficulties, e.g. she cannot go to KKt8 because of the immediate Kt to B3 Ch. — This " fork," as it is called, is impossible, however, to avoid. e.g. 1. . . . Q to R4. 2. BK4! (threatening Kt to B3 Ch. and Kt to B6 Ch. to follow) and the threat cannot be avoided. If, again, 1. . . . Q to R2. 2. Kt to B3 Ch. K to Q6. 3. B to K4 Ch.—and the Queen is lost next move. The advanced student can easily work out other variations.

*Diagram on next page.

This example, together with the others, should be sufficient to show the reader that the values of Chess Pieces are not constants, but variables in the context which is the

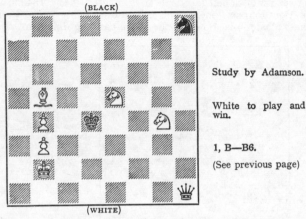

(BLACK)

Study by Adamson.

White to play and win.

1, B—B6.

(See previous page)

(WHITE)

position—i.e. the possibilities of the combined forces at the stage of the game that is being considered.

OTHER RELATIVE VALUES

The last example will have shown the difficulty of assessing the value of the Queen against a combination of two other Pieces. When processes are in operation, involving the possible promotion of Pawns, attacks on King, etc., etc., the valuation must entirely depend on the position. But geometrically, on an empty Board, it may be said that the Queen is definitely better than any two minor Pieces. Her range is evidently greater than the combined range of two Knights, or the combined range of two Bishops (even at their maximum range which they rarely enjoy) ; and it is greater than the range of Rook and Bishop, for these can never control a total of 27 squares unless they are mutually unguarded ; and, in addition, the Queen will always be able to find diagonal moves that the Bishop in question cannot find.

Nevertheless, it does not follow that King and Queen against King and two minor Pieces, or King, Rook and one minor Piece can win. That, too, will depend on the position. Provided the lesser Pieces are well placed and the play is careful, a draw should be the result. In the case of Queen against two Knights, which is the weakest of these oppositions, the processes of winning and drawing respectively have taxed Chess Masters beyond their powers.

TWO ROOKS

Two Rooks are demonstrably superior to the Queen on an empty Board, given that they are mutually defending, and are not forced to abandon mutual defence in order to stop a Mating threat ; but the difference in value is slight, and normally insufficient to win because of the Queen's enormous checking power and pinning power.

But the slight superiority that they have is evident from this consideration : that two Rooks can force Mate without the aid of their own King ; the Queen, as we have seen, cannot do so.

Mate by 2 Rooks.

The diagram shows a Mate by two Rooks. And this is quite easily brought about. The King is checked down the Board by alternating Rooks. Thus, for example, a Rook checks on the fourth rank or file driving the King to the third or fifth. The Rook that has checked stays where it is, and the other Rook checks on the rank or file, as the case may be, to which the King has gone. Thus the King is driven further towards the edge of the Board. Again the Rook that has last checked stays where it is and the other Rook checks the King ; and so on until the edge of the Board is reached— when the Check that is given will be Mate.

If the King, while this is going on, approximates to one of the Rooks, or to a square that a Rook requires to go to, that only delays the process, but does not alter it. The Rook in question simply moves to the other end of the rank or file as the case may be, and the process continues.

Another aspect of the strength of two Rooks as compared with the Queen can be seen when there are Pawns to be attacked or defended. A Queen is insufficient to defend an attacked Pawn (or any attacked Piece, or attacked square) against two Rooks—or indeed against any two Pieces—for the simple reason that the Queen is only one Piece.

It follows that two Rooks and a Pawn represent winning chances against Queen and Pawn, because, assuming that one of the Pawns is defended by Queen and King, the two Rooks can give themselves up for the Pawn and Queen, leaving King and Pawn against King. Everything will then depend on the relative position of the Kings and the remaining Pawn. And, of course, while this situation is developing, much will depend on the Queen's checking power—i.e. the relative position of the King and the various Pieces involved.

(BLACK)

(WHITE)

Q *v.* 2 ROOKS
The Queen, to move, wins.

The accompanying diagrams show the resources of a Queen against two Rooks. In the first diagram a position is shown in which the Queen, by a short series of Checks, captures one of the Rooks. The moves are as follows: Q to Q7 Ch. If the King goes to the back rank, Q to Q8 Ch. wins a Rook: if the King comes its 3rd rank, Q to K6 Ch. wins a Rook.

Then the Queen is left, playing one Rook, and that is a win, though it has to be carefully handled. The process is to bring up one's own King ; squeeze, as it were, the King and Rook ; then, failing Mate, find a series of Checks that leads to the capture of the Rook. The following line of play is illustrative—1. K to Kt6 R to K3 Ch. 2. K to B7 R to K2 Ch. 3. K to Q6 R to KB2. 4. Q to K5 Ch. K to Kt3. 5. K to K6

(BLACK)

White to move, wins (K to Kt6, etc.).
Black to move, draws (R to K4).

(WHITE)

R to KKt2. 6. Q to B4 (not 6. Q to B5 Ch. K to R3. 7. K to B6 R to B2 Ch. draw) and Mate or the capture of the Rook will follow quickly.

The reader is not advised to try and learn this kind of process by heart.

The main task of the beginner is so to grasp the possibilities of the Pieces that he can see any process when required. Chess is a matter of vision, not of memory. All that one can learn is sufficient acquaintance with the possibilities of the Board to be able to recognize them and discover new ones ; i.e. exactly as a Medical man learns to diagnose.

PERPETUAL CHECK

It is when a Queen is alone against two Rooks that one is most likely to find the game ending in the special type of draw which is Perpetual Check. (Other Pieces, of course, can be the instruments of Perpetual Check, but the Queen is the most likely Piece to bring it about.)

In the next diagram the Black Rooks are safely placed,

guarding each other on QKt2 and KKt2. The King is at QKt1. Now Black is safe but cannot win, wherever the White King is, if it is White's move. The Queen can Check at her Q8 (Black's Q1); the King must go to R2. Then the Queen checks at R5, King goes back to Kt1, Queen checks at Q8 and so on for ever. That is a Draw.

(BLACK)

(WHITE)

QUEEN against
2 ROOKS
Perpetual Check.

Now alter the position in this diagram by putting the White King on its KR8 ; put the Black King on its QR1. Add a Black Knight on Black's QKt6 and let the Queen be checking on QB8. Now the King will go to R2 (if the Rook goes in, pinning the Queen, Queen captures with Check, then the King captures the remaining Rook leaving King and Knight against King—which is a Draw). At this point White makes his Perpetual Check by playing Q to QR8 Check. If the King takes it the result is Stalemate ; if the King goes to Kt2 then the Queen goes to QR6 Check again, and so on in-definitely. That is the kind of trick that the Queen is capable of performing.

The Queen is, indeed, so resourceful that she has been known to force a Draw against Queen and Rook. This can happen when the Pieces are grouped in the corner. Thus place the Black King on White's QR8, the Black Queen on White's QKt8, and the Black Rook on White's QKt7 (let the White King be on King's square). Now, if the White Queen can manage to check on QR5, there is a perpetual Check in being ; because whichever Piece intervenes the

Queen will have either Q5 or Q8 to check on ; after that she will have QR5 or Q5 or Q8 to check on as the case may be ; and so on for ever.

Finally, illustrative of the Queen's power in combination with other forces, here is a position that occurred in a game played in 1907 by the late Emmanuel Lasker.*

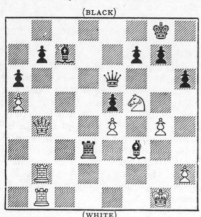

(BLACK)

(WHITE)

A finish by Lasker (Black).

At the end of a brilliant middle game, in which Lasker, as Black, has obtained the advantage by the creation of subtle threats, White seems to be on the point of equalizing.

	White	*Black*
35.	R to QB1. Threatening (after the Bishop's move) to take the Knight's Pawn with the Queen and bring the Rook up to QB6 with an attack.	B × KtP ! A sacrifice that White had not anticipated.
36.	R × B.	B × Kt.
37.	P × B.	R to Q8 Ch.
38.	K to Kt2.	Q to Q4 Ch.
39.	K to B2.	Q to R8 !
40.	Q × P. One of many possible moves ; but there is none to save the game.	Q to B8 Ch.
41.	K to K3.	R to Q6 Ch.
42.	K to K4.	Q to B6 Ch.
43.	K × P.	Q to K6 Ch.
44.	Q to K4.	P to B3 Ch., followed by Mate.

* Emmanuel Lasker. Distinguished Mathematical Philosopher who was one of the greatest Chess players in the history of the game. Held the World Championship a generation (1894–1921), and after that, until his death in 1954, remained in the very forefront of Chess Masters.

ONE ROOK

From any of the foregoing examples it will be clear to the reader that the Queen is much more powerful than one Rook.

King and one Rook lose against a Queen. King and one Rook with something else, even a Pawn, may draw if the position is favourable, may even win in exceptional positions. But King and Rook alone can only save the game if, at the moment the position crystallizes, the Rook can capture the Queen by a pin or a fork or a thrust. (Diagram on page 51 with Black to move.) Failing that, it is only a question of time. The process was shown above.

Nevertheless, the Rook is a powerful Piece. The Rook does not exceed the Bishop or the Knight to the extent to which the Queen exceeds the Rook, because the win by Rook against Bishop or against Knight is exceptional—the win by Queen against Rook almost invariable. But the Rook has this in common with the Queen ; that the Rook and the Queen are the only Pieces which, alone save for a King, can force Mate. Also, the Rook is the only Piece, apart from the Queen, which in one move can put itself within reach of any given square on the Board. The King and the Knight can reach any square given time ; the Bishop only operates on one half of the Board (squares of a specific colour).

If a Rook is lost, or given, for a Bishop, or for a Knight, the player giving up the Rook is said to be losing, or sacrificing *The Exchange*—and, of course, the other player is winning The Exchange. Some players use the phrase Major Exchange, to signify the difference between the Queen and the Rook. The description is not very accurate, because, as we have seen, the difference is disproportionately bigger; but the expression is quite often used. Again, some players describe the gain of a Bishop in exchange for a Knight as a gain of the Minor Exchange. But this, too, can be misleading because the superiority of Bishop to Knight is entirely a function of position ; and it can happen, quite easily, that a Knight is more valuable than a Bishop. This will be discussed later in the Chapter. Suffice it here to say that for practical purposes the Bishop and Knight can be regarded as roughly equal. Vis-à-vis the Rook, they are both inferior (hence the expression " loss " of the Exchange when a Rook is lost for either), and the degree of inferiority is similar. On an empty Board the Bishop (against the Rook) is a little more likely to hold its own than the Knight. For the rest, Bishop and Knight together are definitely a stronger force than a rook ; so, in a sense, are two Knights—a fortiori two Bishops. But their joint superiority, though definite, is slight. Roughly, it may be said that a Rook and Pawn are almost equivalent to two *minor Pieces* (the term applied to Bishop and Knight) ; Rook and two Pawns are slightly better.

MATING BY KING AND ROOK

The main superiority of the Rook to a minor Piece consists in its capacity to Mate in conjunction with the King alone. The process is not easy, and depends on the principle of Zugzwang, i.e. at a critical stage the lone King will be short of moves and will have to move to its detriment.

(BLACK)

(WHITE)

Mate by K and R.

The above diagram shows a King and Rook having Mated. It will be observed that this reproduces one of the possible Mates available to the Queen; but the Queen has others, e.g., on Q2 in this diagram—or, with the Black K on White's K1 or QB1: at K2 or KKt1 in the one case, at QB2 or QR1 in the other.

Now how to get this position. The next diagram shows the King not directly opposite the King. A finesse is now required. The Rook wastes a move, R to B3 or 5,6,7,8, not conceding any space, but leaving the King to go back to the square opposite the King. Then it Mates.

Now by a similar method, starting from anywhere, the King can be forced down the Board. From time to time it will be necessary to use that little finesse to make the King lose ground. This is well illustrated in the following series of moves. The White King is at its K3, R on KB2. Black King at its Q4 ; and the moves are somewhat as follows—1. R to QB2 K to K4, 2. R to B5 Ch. K to Q3, 3. K to Q4 K to K3, 4. K to K4 K to Q3, 5. R to QB4 K to K3, 6. R to B6 Ch. and so on.

The reader will appreciate that the Zugzwang here depends on the emptiness of the Board. But it can happen that the Rook is so placed as to be able to " squeeze " a King and

White forces Mate by —e.g., R to B3.

ENDGAME BY PLATOFF.
White to play and win.

Bishop or King and Knight. Here is an ending by Platoff.

White wins by 1. K to B3 K to Kt8. 2. K to Kt3 B to R2 (best to avoid double threats) 3. R to QR6 B to B4 (best) 4. R to R6. If now 4. . . . . B to Kt8 5. RR1 wins If 4. . . . K to B8 R to QB6 wins. If 4. . . . . B to K6 5. R to R1 Ch. B to B8 6. R moves on rank and wins. If at move 1 Black plays B to K6, 2. K to B2 wins, and there are other variations in which White can threaten mate and attack the Bishop alternately until both threats arrive together.

THE EFFECT OF THE " EXCHANGE "

The Platoff ending shows the superiority of Rook to Bishop on an empty Board. There are similar chances (also rare) of a squeeze by K and R against K and Kt. These, be it repeated, are rarities. But the Rook has other superiority. Thus, a King and Rook can usually draw against King, Rook and Pawn ; King and Bishop, or King and Knight, generally speaking, cannot do so. Among other things the Rook can cut the hostile King off from the part of the Board where King and Pawns are operating against the Bishop or the Knight.

Again, when it comes to destructive work among Pawns, the Rook is evidently superior.

(BLACK)

(WHITE)

White, with the Exchange down, does not lose.

On the other hand, a Bishop with aggressively placed Pawns can defeat a Rook with Pawns. Thus a Rook on its Rook's square, can find itself hemmed in by a Bishop at its Kt8 and a Pawn at R7, while, elsewhere on the Board, the Bishop's

King establishes a winning advantage among the remaining Pawns. Again, a well-placed Bishop or Knight with the aid of the King may prevent a Rook from penetrating among the Pawns. Exceptionally a Bishop can hold its own against Rook and Pawn—a Knight, more rarely.*

As we go back earlier into the game, we find that the more

Bishop draws against Rook and Pawn. The Bishop keeps the King away. If P to B7, of course K to Kt2.

Sacrifice of Rook.
If 1 ... B × R
2. Q × Kt P. R—B1
3. B—Kt5 wins.
If 1 ... K—B1.
2. B—R3 Ch.
   K—Kt1
3. R—Kt1 B—Kt2.
4. R—Kt3 B—R4.
5. Q × Kt P Ch.
   K × Q
6. R—Kt 3 Ch.
   K—R3
7. B—B1 Ch. K—R4
8. B—K2 Ch. K—R5
9. R—R 3 mate

*A locus classicus is the following position defended by Emanuel Lasker against Edward Lasker (New York 1924).
32: Kt K3 k2, 1p 4r1, 16: Drawn because White King can be kept away.

crowded the Board is the less likely the Exchange is to matter. A Rook is slow of development on the crowded Board. Until it is fully mobilized it is worth less than its nominal value. Aggressive players would as soon give odds of a Rook as of a Minor Piece.* Nevertheless, in the absence of good reason (defence or attack), the loss of the Exchange should be resolutely avoided. Other things being equal, the loss of the Exchange is at least as serious as the loss, without compensation, of a Pawn.

The last diagram shows an instance of the total sacrifice of the Rook at an early stage in the game. A mobilized Minor Piece is removed from the defence, while the attack only loses an unmobilized Rook.

It follows that the sacrifice of the Exchange can be tactically advantageous when the Piece removed is important to the defence.

THE MINOR PIECES

The Rook is a major Piece ; the Bishop and Knight are minor Pieces—though not infantile.

The relative valuation of the Bishop and the Knight forms one of the most difficult features of Chess.

At first sight it would seem that a Bishop, with a maximum range of 13 squares, is better than a Knight with a maximum range of 8 squares. Yet no good Chess player regards himself at a disadvantage merely because he has given a Bishop for a Knight. In very many openings this exchange is normal. Everything will depend on the utility of the Knight one is left with. If it is well placed, e.g. established (supported and unassailable by Pawns) on a central square, such as K5, its power can be considerable.

There is more to be said for the superiority of two Bishops to two Knights than for the superiority of one Bishop to one Knight. Here is an extreme case : White K on K6, Bishops on K4, Q4 ; Black K at K1, Kt on KR5, QR5 : clearly Black loses. Two Bishops fully mobilized control 26 squares, 10 more than 2 mobilized Knights. Again, this may be an illusory advantage if the Knights have plenty of work to do—e.g. attacking Pawns, etc., while the Bishops are merely covering empty space.

It may be conceded that on a relatively empty Board two Bishops with a Rook, or with Pawns, are likely to win against

* When odds of a Rook are given the player can still Castle, making the King's move only, unless the square of the Rook in question has been occupied by a hostile Piece.

two Knights with a Rook, or with Pawns, as the case may be. But to value these Pieces from that point of view is to over-simplify. Nor is it advisable to dwell on the fact that two Bishops can force Mate whereas two Knights cannot force Mate. These endings are rare.

In practice, as the game comes towards its climax, Minor Pieces tend to be exchanged for an infinite variety of reasons. And if a player tries so to conduct his game as to avoid the loss of Bishop for Knight, he will find his scope restricted, and will find himself losing tempo—which, incidentally, may be much more important than any slight difference in formal value. A good example of that slight error is seen in the diagram below.

(BLACK) AUTHOR

(WHITE) MENCHIK

White to move—
Best is B × P.

Here B×P, allowing exchange of Kt for B, is better than Kt×P which after Kt exchanges and P to B4 for Black (with gain of tempo) leaves Black well placed. And there are numerous other examples.

To sum up : although, formally, the Bishop appears to be stronger than the Knight, and although, strategically, it would seem desirable to keep Bishops against one's opponent's Knights, in practice the vicissitudes of the game do not allow players to attach importance to what differences there are. Theoretically a Bishop can immobilize a Knight. If, e.g. the hostile Knight is on your Q1, your Bishop on Q4 deprives it of all its scope. If one could maintain a position like that, the advantage would be clear. But in a fairly level game the probability is that the Bishop would not be allowed to stay there, or could only be maintained by, e.g., a King which would thereby be prevented from proceeding with its work among the Pawns.

Also a Bishop can guard Pawns, and attack Pawns, from longer range than a Knight—which is an advantage. On the other hand, Pawns can be so grouped that a Bishop cannot touch them while a Knight may be able to work havoc among them. Moreover, they cannot avoid the pursuit of the Knight by changing the colour of their squares, as they would avoid the attack of a Bishop. Indeed an endgame can quite easily crystallize in which the Pawns are so placed that the player with the Knight will win against the player with the Bishop.

(BLACK)

(WHITE)

KNIGHT AMONG PAWNS.

Typical Endgame in which Knight is superior to Bishop.

Further, although a King can do more damage to Pawns guarded by a Knight than to Pawns guarded by a Bishop (especially if the Knight is in front of the Pawns), it can happen that a Knight and Pawn can win where a Bishop and Pawn cannot win ; that is, when the Pawn is a Rook's Pawn whose Queening square is of a different colour from the squares controlled by the Bishop.

To show the difficulty of assessment, it may be added that there is one position in a King and Rook's Pawn ending where a Knight is inferior to a Bishop, because of the Knight's inability to lose a move !

Finally, although a Bishop can do so much more in one

move than a Knight, in two moves or three moves the difference diminishes.

For the rest, the powers of the two Pieces are so different, and their scope varies so much from position to position, that no valuation is reliable which attempts to establish the superiority of one Minor Piece to the other. It comes down to a question of taste and style. The late J. R. Capablanca* who

B and RP v. K.

Once the King is in the corner, the Bishop is powerless to evict it.

DRAW.

The Knight can never drive the hostile King away, because it cannot approach without Check and cannot lose a move. If this Kt were at K6 or K4 with Black to move, White would win.

*J. R. Capablanca. A Cuban Chess prodigy. World Champion 1921-192?

aimed at subtle simplifications, preferred the Bishop. The late Alexander Alekhine*, a player whose style lent itself to combinations on the crowded Board, seemed to prefer the Knight. Typical of Capablanca's style is his play from the following position—play which incidentally shows how strong Bishops can be when the diagonals are available to them.

(BLACK)

(WHITE)

Capablanca *v.* N.N.

After a badly played Stone-wall Defence, Black made a try for freedom with 11. . . . P to K4. Capablanca now proceeds to take excellent advantage.

White	*Black*
12. P × KP.	Kt × P.
13. P × QP.	P × P. Kt × B Ch. loses a P.
14. Kt to B4 ! Pretty and forcing.	P × Kt. Slightly better was KKt to B2, but even that yields White an overwhelming attack.
15. B × P Check.	KKt to B2. Best.
16. R × B.	Q × R.
17. Kt × Kt.	B to K3. At move 14 Black (if he saw so far) had probably relied on this and the next for salvation.
18. R to Q1.	Q to K2. The only alternative was Q to Kt3, which would be met by 19 Kt to Q7 !

* Alexander Alekhine. A great Russian player, who won the world Championship from Capablanca in 1927—and held it, with a gap of two years (1935–7), until his death in 1946.

	White	*Black*
19.	R to Q7.	B × R.
20.	Kt × B.	KR to QB1 (If Q × Kt . 21 Q to B3).
21.	Q to B3.	R × B.
22.	P × R.	Resigns. The best that Black can hope for is an ending with Rook against Bishop, Knight and Pawn, and those so well placed as to give him no drawing chance.

The above is an excellent example of the power of Bishops, and carries many strategic lessons.

(BLACK)

(WHITE)

Alekhine
v. Bogoljubow
(5th game of the first Match.)

In contrast the diagram position from a game in a Match between Alekhine and Bogoljubow is an interesting example of the Knight's powers. In the moves leading up to the diagrammed position, it is probable that Bogoljubow failed to anticipate the finesse consisting in the threat of a Knight's fork after the capture of a Pawn—which threat deprived him of the tempo required for equalization.

The moves played were as follows—

	White	*Black*
23.	. . .	QR to Kt1.
24.	Kt to Kt5.	Kt × Kt.
25.	R × R.	R × R.
26.	Kt × P.	R to Kt1.
27.	Kt to B5.	K to K2.
28.	P × Kt.	and White has gained a Pawn.

THE KNIGHT'S FORK

The Knight's fork, which is seen threatened in the last example, is different from the normal attack by any Piece on two other Pieces simultaneously, because the Knight is usually attacking two Pieces which cannot react along the line of attack, because they are not Knights. The Knight, which, incidentally, is very difficult to deprive of moves,

THE KNIGHT'S FORK.

THE KNIGHT'S FORK.

Black is threatening Kt × Q: also Kt to B6 Ch.
If (1) Q to K4 Q × Q (2) B × Q, Kt K7 Ch. wins a piece.
But White can meet the immediate danger with B to K4.

C

can execute a long series of changing threats; these are difficult to prevent, and, psychologically, difficult to follow. The eight squares of its range are on the edges of quite a large rectangle, and every move made brings into its range a different area. The vast number of possible courses that the Knight can trace in any two or three moves makes it the commando of the Chess Board.

PIN.
The Knight is pinned by the Bishop. The KP is pinned by the Rook. Therefore, White can play Kt × QP.

PIN.
White wins by P to B6, because if R × P, B to B7 pins and wins the Rook. Of course, if 1 ... R to QR2 2. B × P Ch.

THE PIN

A tactical device that the Bishop and the Major Pieces can carry out, though the Knight cannot do it, is the Pin. That is the holding down, on a rank or file (in the case of a Rook), on the rank, file or diagonal (in the case of a Queen), on the diagonal (in the case of a Bishop), of some Piece which cannot move without exposing to capture either the King, or some-

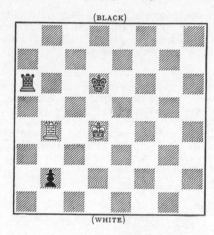

BLACK WINS.
A pretty pin 1... R to R5 enables the Black Pawn to be promoted.

A KNIFE-THRUST
(see p. 68)
"Accipe hoc."
B to Kt7 Ch. wins the Queen

thing else of value, which it covers by its presence. Pins can be important or unimportant. Their effect may be temporary or permanent. They may bring about the loss of an Exchange, or even of a Queen. Applied to a Rook, the Bishop's Pin is particularly effective, because it gives the player with the Bishop the option of winning the Exchange.

Some examples of the Pin are shown in the diagrams on pages 66 and 67.

Good examples of the Bishop's Pin will also be found in later chapters, e.g., in Morphy v. Isouard, and in Alekhine against Böok, in which the great Master of Knight manœuvres is seen handling Bishops to superb advantage.

OTHER TACTICAL POWERS

Different from the Pin is another power that the Knight lacks, a power, as it were, to stab in the back. One example of it (p. 67) shows the Bishop able to check the King along a diagonal where there is another opposing Piece on the other side of the King, and winning that Piece in consequence. In contrast to the Knight's fork this might be called " the Bishop's Knife." That, however, is not the technical term—nor is there a term to describe this type of thrust. (" Skewer " is used.)

(BLACK)

(WHITE)

A DELAYED THRUST.
1. White Queens; if 1 . . . Black Queens, then Q to R8Ch. wins. But Black can draw by 1 . . . K to Kt7.*

Looking at it more generally, one sees that this power is not peculiar to the Bishop, but is possessed by any long range

* But not if the White King were one square further left (e.g., on e2). In that case white manœuvres so that the Queen arrives at c3 with check. Then follows K—Kt8 for Black; and White, with K—Q2 creates a threat of mate, forcing Black to promote Pawn to Knight (and lose).

Piece. The Rook has it on the rank or file; the Queen has it on the rank, file and diagonal.

This can be an extremely important tactical feature, especially when it takes the form of a resource at the end of a line of play; e.g., 2 Pawns (one Black, one White) are racing for promotion; one Queens: the other Queens immediately after; but the first promoted Pawn, now a Queen, may be able to give a Check along a file, rank or diagonal which will involve the loss of his opponent's newly-made Queen. The diagram opposite illustrates such a situation.

Obviously the Knight can do nothing like this, though it can come away from a sub-promotion giving a damaging fork. But the reader has already been sufficiently warned not to infer on that account that the Knight can now be written off as inferior. As we have seen, there are things that only the Knight can do. Among them is a special kind of Smothered Mate.

SMOTHERED MATE

We have seen that the King can be Mated with the aid of its own Pieces, in that their presence deprives the King of flight squares. When this happens the King may be said to be smothered in some degree. But the expression Smothered Mate is normally applied to a Mate which can only be carried out by the Knight. One of the simplest forms of this results from the position in the next Diagram.

(BLACK)

(WHITE)

PHILIDOR'S LEGACY.

1. ... K to R1.
2. Kt to B7 Ch; K to Kt1.
3. Kt to R6 Dble. Ch.; K to R1.
4. Q to Kt8 Ch.; R × Q.
5. Kt to B7 Mate.

The moves which follow have been called Philidor's Legacy on the assumption that the method was discovered by the great French Master of the eighteenth century. But there is reason to believe that the idea is older. Here are the moves :

Black, being in Check, plays K to R1. White plays Kt to B7, Check. Black can now give up the Rook for the Knight, but, not seeing the danger, or because there may be a Mate on the back rank if the Rook moves off it, finds himself unable to do so. He therefore plays K to Kt1. Then comes Kt R6 Double Check. The King is forced to R1. There follows a thunder bolt, Q to Kt8 Check, sacrificing the Queen. (A player who thinks in terms of the formal values of the Pieces would never anticipate this move, which is only possible to a player who thinks in terms of the functions of the Pieces.) Black must take this Queen with the Rook. Then White plays Kt to B7 Mate.

The above is the best known Smothered Mate ; but it is not the only kind. Much less familiar is that which occurs in the position shown in the second diagram.

(BLACK)

A FINISH BY
NAJDORF.

(WHITE)

The position in the diagram was reached by Najdorf, the Polish Master, on one of his Boards in a simultaneous blindfold display. He announced Mate in four. It may be remarked that the Mate in four would not be apparent to the majority of really strong players playing with sight of the Board and not simultaneously. It is a fine example of vision in Chess.

The moves are as follows :

White	*Black*

Q to R5. This threatens Q × BP Mate.

B × QP. Stopping the Mate. Had Black played P to Kt3, then Q × RP would have been Mate. Q × R. Forced, and apparently winning the Exchange.

R × B. Removing the defender. This is a sacrifice of the Exchange.

Q × BP Check. Sacrificing the Queen, a beautiful surprise. Its real value, to a Chess player, consists in the fact that the Master making the move saw it before he announced his Mate in four—perhaps a good deal earlier.

Q × Q. Forced ; apparently winning the Queen, but in reality doing exactly what the Rook did in the previous example.

Kt–Q7 Mate. A very fine example of Smothered Mate.

To conclude this survey of the Minor Pieces, let the reader realize that these are the Pieces to be mobilized first in any game—and they, with one or two Pawns, bear the brunt of the opening. Also they have endgame functions.

How to Mate with two Bishops and with Bishop and Knight. See diagrams.

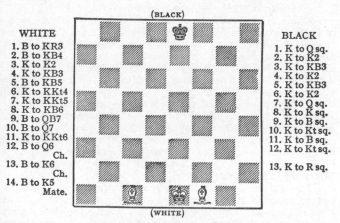

WHITE

1. B to KR3
2. B to KB4
3. K to K2
4. K to KB3
5. K to KB5
6. K to KKt4
7. K to KKt5
8. K to KB6
9. B to QB7
10. B to Q7
11. K to KKt6
12. B to Q6 Ch.
13. B to K6 Ch.
14. B to K5 Mate.

BLACK

1. K to Q sq.
2. K to K2
3. K to KB3
4. K to K2
5. K to KB3
6. K to K2
7. K to Q sq.
8. K to K sq.
9. K to B sq.
10. K to Kt sq.
11. K to B sq.
12. K to Kt sq.
13. K to R sq.

K, B, B *v.* K.

In order to reach the end position, the Bishops quickly limit the King's field, making an " edge " to the field of play.

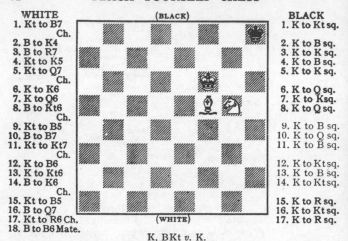

WHITE	(BLACK)	BLACK
1. Kt to B7 Ch.		1. K to Kt sq.
2. B to K4		2. K to B sq.
3. B to R7		3. K to K sq.
4. Kt to K5		4. K to B sq.
5. Kt to Q7 Ch.		5. K to K sq.
6. K to K6		6. K to Q sq.
7. K to Q6		7. K to Ksq.
8. B to Kt6 Ch.		8. K to Q sq.
9. Kt to B5		9. K to B sq.
10. B to B7		10. K to Q sq.
11. Kt to Kt7 Ch.		11. K to B sq.
12. K to B6		12. K to Kt sq.
13. K to Kt6		13. K to B sq.
14. B to K6 Ch.		14. K to Kt sq.
15. Kt to B5		15. K to R sq.
16. B to Q7		16. K to Kt sq.
17. Kt to R6 Ch.	(WHITE)	17. K to R sq.
18. B to B6 Mate.		

K, B Kt v. K.

In order to reach this position, it is fairly easy to force the King to the side, since B, Kt and King can create a directive pressure. If, above, 4. K–Q1, 5. B–K4, with Kt–B4, prevents escape to a black corner.

THE CHANGING VALUE OF THE PAWN

We have seen, already, that a factor inhibiting the movement of those Pieces that seem to control a good deal of the Board consists in the normal undesirability of their being taken in exchange for Pieces of lesser value. Since, formally, the Pawn is the least of the Pieces (because its move is so limited), it acquires tremendous tactical importance as an inhibitor of all other Pieces. If a Pawn is guarding something, then what it is guarding is well guarded—particularly against attack by anything larger than the Piece attacked. Pawns guarding Pawns can, consequently, form a barrier that can only be broken either by Pawns or else by the sacrifice of value. Moreover, the Pawn as an instrument of attack is a force not to be under-estimated. In a crowded centre of the Board a feature of the play is always likely to be the power of a Pawn to fork two Pieces such as a Bishop and Knight, or else to advance, dislocating a minor or major Piece from a good square, and, to that extent, disrupting the defence of, e.g., the castled King. From this point of view, the centre Pawns tend to be more important than the Pawns on the wings. The nearer they are to the centre, the more likely they are to be participating in the attack, given that the game is reasonably open. We shall see that, in the ordinary way, Pawns are stronger when they are not doubled and when they are not isolated. In the centre their isolation, or their doubling, can be a source of strength as well as an element of weakness.

Because of the fact that the tactical value of the Pawn is functional rather than formal, depending entirely on what the Pawn is doing or likely to be doing in the immediate future, it comes about that, during tactical operations, players are apt to treat the loss or gain of a Pawn as relatively unimportant—as a difference which is transitory, as a cheap sacrifice. This is particularly true of the attitude adopted to idle Pawns on the wings, or Pawns that are being used to cause the vacation of important squares. But, as the strategic lines of the game become set, the Pawn is likely to gain in importance. If the strategy is along the simple lines of " saving up and exchanging down," it may well be that the extra Pawn will mean victory. No hard and fast rules can be laid down. One Pawn may be so placed as to be worth two or even three Pawns. But, other things being equal, it is safe to say that as the Endgame approaches, or in so far as one is playing with a view to the Endgame rather than the middle game attack, the importance of the Pawn increases. On a relatively empty Board a Pawn progressively acquires the status of a Piece. No transvaluation in Chess is more important than the promotion of the Pawn. Therefore, in most games, some Pawns at least will not be regarded, or disregarded, as cannon fodder. Indeed, as we have already seen, at the end of the game the possession of a Bishop or a Knight with a lone King is inadequate for victory. The possession of a Pawn, on the other hand, can bring about victory.

If, then, a Pawn is to be lost, it is only well lost if the loser of the Pawn is gaining sufficient in tempo, or mobility, or general control of the Board, etc., etc., to make him confident that his game as a whole is superior to his opponent's, and that at the worst, he will be able, sooner or later, to regain at least the material that he has lost. On the other hand, a player will think twice about deploying his forces, however temporarily, in order to win a Pawn. In a well integrated game, where everything depends on the availability of counter moves to many possibilities, any excursion away from the main scene of operations, even by one square, may be fatal. The consequences may be immediately demonstrable, or they may be more mediate—possibly strategic rather than tactical ;

C*

in either case they are likely to be of more importance than the Pawn concerned. In a word, then, the gain of a Pawn can win a game ; it can also lose a game. Once again, everything depends on the position.

GAMBITS

At the very outset of the game some Pawns in their original positions need to be moved, so as to give the major Pieces access to the open Board. Also it is usually thought desirable to move them in such a way that they will exert pressure on the centre, thereby creating a maximum of manœuvring space for the other Pieces. For those reasons it very often happens that, as early as the second move, Pawns are moved where they can be taken without immediate compensation. Such moves are called Gambits. Thus, after the moves 1. P to K4, P to K4, a very popular move used to be 2. P to KB4—the King's Gambit. This opening is less frequent now than it was. Nevertheless, it is still formidable and introduces play of great interest and difficulty to both sides. On the other wing one of the most frequent openings in Modern Chess consists in the moves P to Q4, P to Q4. 2. P to QB4. This is the Queen's Gambit, which introduces a slower but more lasting development, less likely than the King's Gambit to result in a too early skirmish, from which it may be difficult to ensure the retention of a permanent advantage.

Both of these Gambits can either be accepted, by the immediate, or slightly postponed, capture of the Gambit Pawn: or they may be declined. The Queen's Gambit is more frequently declined than accepted ; the King's Gambit is more usually accepted than declined. If a Gambit is accepted, it usually happens that the player who has won the Pawn allows his opponent to regain a Pawn at a later stage, when the continued holding of the Gambit Pawn involves either the loss of tempo in development, or the undertaking of a difficult line of play in which the player does not wish to become involved. In this way a Gambit differs from a sacrifice. In a Gambit the Pawn is rather lent than given. However, there are Gambits, such as the Wing Gambit (P to K4, P to QB4. 2. P to QKt4), in which the Gambiteer may lose interest in the offered Pawn and go for long without attempting to recover it.

A clear example of the difference between a Pawn sacrifice and a Gambit may be seen in one of the normal variations of the Queen's Gambit declined.

White	*Black*
1. P to Q4.	P to Q4.
2. P to QB4.	P to K3.
3. Kt to QB3.	Kt to KB3.
4. B to Kt5. A move made popular by the American Master, Pillsbury. It is a developing move which pins the Knight, not with any serious threat, but by way of creating a slight pressure.	QKt to Q2. A good developing move, offering the sacrifice of a Pawn. Apparently, since the King's Knight is pinned, the Queen's Pawn, twice attacked and only once guarded, can be won by White. This, however, is an illusion.
5. P × P.	P × P.
6. Kt × P, falling into a trap.	Kt × Kt. Black is not sacrificing the Pawn after all. What he is sacrificing is his Queen.
7. B × Q.	B to Kt5 Ch.
8. Q to Q2, the only move.	B × Q Ch.
9. K × B.	K × B. And Black is a Piece to the good.

Because of the existence of this pitfall, White on the fifth move usually plays P to K3 or Kt to KB3. Then the threat is on ; because Black's checking resource will no longer win the White Queen. Therefore, in answer to P to K3 or Kt to KB3, Black usually plays some such move as B to K2 (unpinning the Knight) or P to QB3 (giving additional support to the Pawn at Q4).

Incidentally, the point of declining the Queen's Gambit (which will be considered more fully later on) is to prevent White from establishing a Pawn on K4, from which point it can make a dangerous thrust forward ; also the Queen's Pawn can become dangerous ; and, generally, the Black Pieces will find less space in which to operate than is available to White.

The acceptance of the Gambit involves a different strategy. Black allows White the occupancy of the centre, crystallizes it so as to allow squares like KB4, QB4, etc. to the Black Pieces, and later undermines the centre, or attacks it from a distance along the diagonal. These methods have become very popular in modern times, owing to the example of players like Niemzovitch, Alekhine, Tartakower, and the Modern School generally.

When, however, a player achieves (from any opening) a good development of the centre Pawns as well as of the minor Pieces, then, if his opponent is behind-hand in development, the Pawns can be instrumental in bringing about a devastating attack. (See Illustrative Games ; e.g., by Bird).

ISOLATED, DOUBLED, AND PASSED PAWNS

Pawns are at their strongest if they are on adjoining files, preferably on the same rank, but also if one is guarding the next. If a Pawn has no allied Pawn on either flank, then it is said to be an *Isolated Pawn*. Because it can only be guarded by Pieces, it is more vulnerable to attack by Pieces than if it could be guarded by a Pawn. This matters at all stages of the game. It is only unimportant when the Pawn in question is a factor in the attack. Then many things may happen. It may change its file through a capture. It may advance until a hostile Pawn is exchanged for it. It may be captured on terms that the possessor of it wins some other Pawn, or even a Piece. But if the game settles down into relative stability the isolated Pawn is usually a permanent target for the enemy. In a King and Pawn Endgame its strength or weakness will depend on the position of the Kings.

(BLACK)

(WHITE)

The White Pawns on QKt file are *doubled and isolated*.
The Black Pawns on KB file are *doubled* but not isolated.
The White RP is isolated. It is also a Passed Pawn.

When two Pawns stand on the same file they are said to be *Doubled*. *Doubled Pawns*, formally regarded, are evidently less than two Pawns on different files, because one inhibits the other. In conjunction with adjoining Pawns, doubled Pawns can be very useful, creating a special kind of Pawn chain. Doubled-Isolated Pawns are, however, very weak, unless they are playing a tactical role (e.g. controlling central squares in the middle game).

From the standpoint of the ending, one of the things that matters about Pawns is their ability, or inability, to proceed without interference from hostile Pawns. If a Pawn has a clear run forward with no hostile Pawns on either of the flanking files, then it is a *Passed Pawn*. Left to itself a Passed Pawn is easily promoted. Therefore it amounts to a danger. An Isolated Passed Pawn, and doubled isolated Passed Pawns,

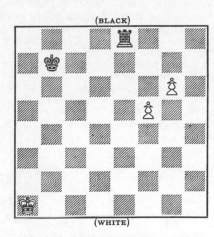

(BLACK)

(WHITE)

POWER OF PAWNS.

White to move wins by advancing either Pawn. Obviously if both White Pawns were on the 6th it would be a win even with Black to move. As it is, Black to move, wins.
1. ... R to K8 Ch.
2. K to Kt2, R to KKt8.
3. K to B3, R to Kt4, etc.

(BLACK)

(WHITE)

POWER OF PAWN.

White to move, draws. If the Rook were at Kt8, checking, it would still be a draw.

are, of course, relatively easy to stop. United Passed Pawns are extremely difficult to cope with.

On the assumption that the hostile King is out of striking distance, two united Passed Pawns on the sixth rank can cope with and defeat a Rook or a Knight or a Bishop, unless the Piece in question can capture one of them immediately. Making the same assumption, it follows that two united Passed Pawns, one on the fifth, one on the sixth, can defeat a Rook, Knight or Bishop if it is the turn to move of the player who has the Pawns, and if he can advance from the fifth to the sixth without either of the Pawns being immediately capturable (see Diagram on p.77).

One advanced Pawn, accompanied by the King, can force a hostile Rook, Bishop or Knight to sacrifice itself for the Pawn, provided the hostile King is far enough away (see Diag on p.77).

Moreover, a Passed Pawn on the seventh rank of the Bishop's file or the seventh rank of the Rook's file can, if its King is correctly placed, enable a player to draw with minimal force against King and Queen.

(BLACK)

(WHITE)

A DRAW.
Black to move, can only draw. The pawn is uncapturable. White to move, will play K to Kt8.

The reason for this is the Stalemate resource available to the King when the Pawn is on one of those squares and the King is at R8. If the Pawn is on Kt7, Q7 or K7, the draw is not available because the player with the Queen can gain a tempo every few moves so as to bring his King to join in the attack opposite. The Process is shown beside the next diagram Also a proximate hostile King can upset the drawing plan wherever the Pawn is.

(BLACK)

(WHITE)

BLACK WINS.

1. K to Q8, K to K5
2. K to K7, Q to B2
3. K to K8, Q to K4 Ch.
4. K to B7, Q to Q3.
5. K to K8, Q to K3 Ch.
6. K to Q8 and the Black King can move again.

PAWNS FACING EACH OTHER

Equal numbers of Pawns facing each other are effective, of course, to hold each other off. An interesting exception to this rule exists in the following position. Pawns at, e.g., QR5, QKt5, and QB5, are facing Pawns at R2, Kt2, B2. White to move plays P to Kt6. If RP×P, White replies P to B6, and the Rook's Pawn (or Bishop's Pawn) will Queen. If, on the other hand, BP×P, White plays P to R6, and now the Bishop's Pawn (or Rook's Pawn) will Queen. Had the Black Pawns stood at QR3, QKt2, QB3, White to move could do nothing. This is an exception to the rule that Pawns are at their best horizontally adjacent to each other.

SUB-PROMOTION.

The next diagram affords an interesting example of the struggle that can take place when a Pawn is nearing promotion and the opposition consists of a powerful Piece which is just not in a Position to stop it. The play also illustrates the point that the promotion to a Queen is not always the best promotion. Finally, the example shows the mental act in Chess—the act of seeing further than the obvious, and then seeing further than that.

Thus in the accompanying position, which was reached in a game between two English amateurs of the last century, Fenton and Potter, the Rook cannot stop the Pawn, but the Rook's Checks involve a resource. If the King goes alongside the Pawn, the Rook pins the Pawn and next move sacrifices itself for the Pawn. If, on the other hand, the King comes quickly onto the B file, the Rook comes down to the back rank and when the Pawn Queens, wins the Queening Pawn immediately by Check (the thrust mentioned above). Therefore the King must pursue a path which brings it on to the B file low enough down the Board for the Rook's thrust not to be possible. But at that point the player with the Rook finds a neat resource. He places his Rook where, when the

(BLACK)

(WHITE)

FENTON v.
POTTER.
WHITE WINS.
1. K to Kt5, R to Q4
   Ch.
2. K to Kt4, R to Q5
   Ch.
3. K to Kt3, R to Q6
   Ch.
4. K to B2, R to Q5.
(Now, if White
Queens, R to B5 Ch.
effects Stalemate,
therefore) . . .
5. P = R threatening
Mate. 5 . . . R to R5.
6. K to Kt3 wins.

Pawn Queens, it can sacrifice itself giving Stalemate. Again, very clever. But the player with the Pawn double crosses him. He makes a Rook. Now it would appear that the game is level ; but it so happens that owing to the position of the Kings, Black is in a mating net and loses a very pretty ending.

THE KING

Normally, the Piece that is called upon most frequently to cope with Pawns is the King. More will be said on this topic when we deal further with the end game. Here, suffice it to show one or two features of the King's power against and with Pawns.

The accompanying diagram shows what is called the Square. If you want to know whether the King can stop a Pawn, an easy way of reckoning it, according to some people, is to draw an imaginary line making a square based on the number of squares the Pawn has to travel in order to become a Queen. Now, if the King is within that square when the Pawn moves it can stop the Pawn. Allowance must be made for the Pawn's first move, so that if the Pawn is on the second rank, the square must be drawn as if it were on the third rank because of the Pawn's double first move. Some players,

(BLACK)

(WHITE)

THE SQUARE.
White to move wins, because the King cannot overtake the Pawn.
Black to move, draws.

(BLACK)

(WHITE)

Endgame by Reti.

White to play, draws!

(Solution overleaf).

including the author, find it easier to work out the King's moves without the aid of this device.

It can happen that the King, if it has on its side another Pawn, even of apparently innocuous character, will gain moves sufficient to get itself into the square. A famous Reti ending is an exceedingly pretty example of this. The play is as follows :

1. K to Kt7.   P to R5.
2. K to B6.   P to R6.
3. K to K7   forces his own Pawn forward.

Therefore on move 2 Black must play K to Kt3. Then follows 3. K to K5 threatening K to Q6—If then 3 . . . K×P, 4. K to B4 and White catches the Pawn.

If the hostile King is otherwise engaged, a King within reach can hold off two Pawns, though, paradoxically, it is as strong against two united Pawns as against two separated Pawns. The diagram shows this. Also, there can be a position where a King holds off three united Pawns, though it may have to let them through if and when it has to move.

(BLACK)

(WHITE)

DRAW.
White can play K to B3, but cannot capture a Pawn. Black cannot capture either and must play carefully. Thus:
1. K to B3, K to B2.
2. K to Kt2, K to B3 for if 2 . . . K to Kt1, P to B6 and the Black K is squeezed.

THE OPPOSITION

The basis of all End game play is King and Pawn against King. In the diagram the player with the Pawn, having the move, can only force Stalemate. But let it be Black's move or (which is the same thing) put the Black King opposite the Pawn, with White to move, then the Pawn can be forced

Draw, if White to move.
1. P to K7 Ch., K to K1.
2. K to K6 Stalemate.
If (1) K to B5, K to K2 ; (2) K to K5, K to K1.
Then if —
(3) K to B6, K to B1.
If (3) KB5, KK2, etc.

THE OPPOSITION.

White to move, loses. Black to move, draws, by K to B2 or K to Q2, but *not* by K to K2, which loses (to White's K to K5).

through. The difference may be described by saying that in one case Black has the *Opposition ;* in the other case White has the *Opposition.* This, incidentally, is only one instance of a relationship which is dealt with more fully in the chapter on End Games. Here, let it be said that the Opposition is a relationship between the Kings such that when it comes to a King's move, the player who has to move out of Opposition is at a disadvantage. It is a sort of Zugzwang, and is particularly important when Kings are facing each other, each preventing the other from access to the hostile Pawns. According to the position of the Pawns, the Opposition may amount to victory, or it may fall short of that. Normally it is a great advantage. In the last diagram White to move loses, because he has to concede a square on which Black can attack and capture one of his Pawns. Black to move, however, does not lose provided that he does not make the error of K to K2, when White could play K to K5, and Black to move would lose. On his first move therefore, Black must play K to Q2 or K to B2. If then White plays K to K5, K to K2 regains the Opposition temporarily. Then White has to be careful and must play K to Q4, so as to be able, in answer to K to K3, to play K to K4.

The Opposition can sometimes be an effective drawing factor (even a winning factor) when the Pawns are not equal in number, and the side with the Opposition has fewer Pawns. Normally, however, the Opposition matters when there is equality. Then, as the diagram position has shown, it can be aggressively decisive or defensively adequate.

It follows that one of the most important factors in the end game is the position of the King. And this is true irrespectively of Opposition theory. As the middle game turns into end game, the King should be as favourably placed as possible for co-operation with its own Pawns, or for dealing with hostile Pawns, whichever is the more important. As the Board clears, the King must be mobilized. To make the King a fighting Piece is always good policy, so long as the danger of a mating attack can be controlled. In the transvaluations that take place in Chess it may be said that the King, and with it the Pawns, increase considerably in value as the end game approaches. " The King is a fighting piece." (*Steinitz*). In Master Chess, at even an early stage of the game, players are careful to have their Kings where they are most useful for the total purpose.

TRANSVALUATION AND REVALUATION.

At this stage the reader may find himself discovering that though he started with a fairly clear idea of the degrees of power of the various Pieces, he is now not at all sure which are strong and which are weak. If that is his experience let him be comforted. What has happened to him is typical of the growth of the mind in Chess, and in most other subjects to which the mind applies itself. Eventually he will arrive at valuations which are subtler because they are more fluid ; at the same time firmer because they are arrived at after criticism and not before criticism.

In other words, the reader is moving from Chess statics to Chess dynamics. He has seen the formal values of the Pieces. Then he has seen their functions, in which the formal values become blurred in the light of the general purpose. As the general purpose becomes clear, and as the reader learns to appreciate the points of any position, the fluid values will steady themselves. Just as, in learning a language, one needs very much more than the bare meanings of words—one needs to know how to use each and every word in different contexts —so the Chess player has to learn more than the simple recognition of the Pieces. As the reader learns to use the Chess Men, the fact that their values vary from time to time will cease to puzzle or disturb him any more than he is puzzled by the easily recognised ambiguities of well known words.

To put the matter of sacrificing simply, once the reader has grasped that in Chess the Pieces co-operate together to carry out processes and to achieve purposes, there should be nothing difficult in the realisation than an individual Piece can fulfil its function in the game by giving itself up in order to make possible some move or series of moves that is decisive. The difference between sacrifice and loss is not difficult. When there is positive total advantage—and not merely the staving off of worse consequences—then the giving up of a Piece is a sacrifice. How to sacrifice or when to sacrifice cannot be taught, just as to see or to do the best move cannot be taught, and just as the neat and effective use of words cannot be taught, because these things imply the recognition by the mind's eye of the point or purpose of some given situation. But, just as through reading and listening one improves one's capacity for using the instrument of language, so the student of Chess may be assisted by having his attention drawn to some examples. Since the essence of Chess is vision, the only way of learning Chess in general is to have features of the game pointed out. By concentrating on these the student does not learn a fixed rule that he can apply universally, but, in some mysterious way, he acquires a capacity for the recognition of possibilities when they are present. Be it added that he will also, as his familiarity with the Board increases, acquire some conception of the impossibilities as well as of the possibilities. He will see, when he appreciates the point of any given sacrifice that such a sacrifice is not always on, and that he need not cramp his style through a constant fear of miracles.

SOME ILLUSTRATIVE SACRIFICES.

Sacrifices are quite impossible to classify. Any kind of position, or any purpose that you are carrying out, may contain the possibility of ignoring the value of any given Piece. To take a very elementary example. While your opponent is attacking your Queen, you threaten Mate with other Pieces. You are sacrificing your Queen. There is nothing very clever in that. What is clever is to see, some moves ahead, that as your purpose develops you need not be side-tracked by the attack on your Queen because you have a threat so strong as to make it impossible for your opponent to capture the Queen. In such a situation, any time he may have relied on gaining by the attack on the Queen may prove not to be gainable. A manoeuvre of this type is shown in the first diagram. There the play is good because Black's move is made in the knowledge that when his Queen is attacked he will be able to proceed with a threat which even at that point is not terribly obvious. The sacrifice is a good sacrifice and all the better if it has been seen a relatively long way ahead.

(WHITE)

(BLACK)

QUEEN
SACRIFICE
(Author—1929)

Black plays Q to R5 allowing P to KKt3, because this is met by Kt to Kt4.

The second diagram shows a position that developed between Euwe and Yanofsky, the young Champion of Canada, in a tournament at Groningen in 1946.

EUWE
YANOFSKY
1. B to B5.
With winning chances.

The ending is a particularly difficult ending for White to win, because when the Bishops are of opposite colour each Bishop controls squares from which the hostile Bishop cannot shut it off. Therefore, each player can make the advance of his opponent's Pawn exceedingly difficult. It follows that clever manoeuvring is necessary if, and when, there is a win to be extracted from such an endgame. Here there were chances; and Euwe's first move from the diagrammed position was B to

ENDGAME
(AFTER
TROITZKI)
White to play and win.
(Solution overleaf)

B5, putting his Bishop *en prise*. That is an instance of a sacrifice for the specific purpose of closing a path to an opponent; alternatively it gains a Pawn.

Adapted from a composed ending we have a subtle example of sacrifice in order to close a line to an opponent's Piece. 1. B to Q4. Then if P×B, K to Q3 blocks the Bishop's line of action. If B×B 2. K to Q3 followed by K to K4 has the same effect. N.B.—Not 1. K to Q3 P to K5, ch. 2. K×P K to K2 and draws.

If the reader will look back through this book he will find that already he has seen examples of sacrifices in positions of a very different type, and different from each other. For example, we have Capablanca's sacrifice of the Knight in order to open the lines for his Bishop. We have Najdorf's sacrifice of the Queen in order to bring about a smothered Mate. In the games cited in later chapters the reader will find more than one sacrifice of material in order to carry through a long and decisive attack. All these are subordinations of the formal value of the Pieces to the purposes of the game.

(BLACK)

(WHITE)

STEINITZ
LASKER

Here is another—and historic—example.

In the diagram is a position, from which Emanuel Lasker rapidly demolished his opponent's defences by the sacrifice of two of his minor Pieces. This is a fine sacrificial attack because it had to be determined so accurately that the opponent had no intervening moves to upset Lasker's plan. Lasker

played 15 . . . Kt×P.   16. K×Kt B×P Ch.   17. K to B2:
(If K×B, some Queen Checks are followed by R to K5, etc.)
17 . . . P to KB3, followed by P to KKt4 and with logical play
Lasker overwhelms his opponent.

COMBINATION

Play of the type illustrated above is sometimes called
combinative play.   Strictly speaking all Chess is combinative
in that a player aims at co-operation and combination among
his Pieces so as to achieve a decisive advantage.   But in
practice there is a distinction between logical processes and
imaginative undertakings, between relatively safe play,
making good developing moves, logical moves, sound strategic
moves, and, on the other hand, the play which introduces
big changes into the position through moves in apparent
disregard of the value of the Pieces.   Players of Chess of
the latter type, combative, sacrificial, surprising and convincing, have come to be called combinative players ;   the less
imaginative tend to be called positional players.   The great
players are of course well equipped for combinative as well as
for positional play.   At that level the difference is one of
degree only—a difference of style.

At an earlier period of the game (during the 19th century
in particular) the outstanding players, Morphy, Anderssen,
Zukertort and others won their best games with the aid of
fine and spectacular sacrifices.   The plethora of sacrificial
combination during this, the Romantic, period of Chess is
due in part to the fact that the great Masters were playing
against players not only deficient (relatively to them) in
Chess genius, but ill-equipped in the strategy which enables
relatively weak players to-day to preserve themselves against
the greater violences.   Steinitz and his successors have
equipped the ordinary player with a strategy and technique
which reduce the scope for the unexpected.   Consequently
the great combinative players of the 20th century, players
like Alekhine, have only been able to produce their sacrifices
after some subtleties of strategic manœuvring.   They occur
then as variations, lines of possible play in a struggle to
restore the balance of position.   The modern sacrifices include
many of great beauty, and with a value enhanced by the fact
that they rest on finer differences and have to be calculated
more closely and further ahead.   For the rest, spectacular
sacrifices of the traditional type imply, if not a considerable
difference in the playing strength of the players, then a considerable deficiency in the position of one of them.   The difference

of level is, as it were, re-capitulated in the progress of players as they pass through a stage where they are annihilated by sacrifices, before they reach (if ever) a stage at which they can only be annihilated by the thunderbolts of outstanding genius. Such a thunderbolt can, however, still strike in this century—witness the famous endgame Capablanca—Bernstein (diagram). Forty years later, it may be added, we find Bernstein avenging his own memory with a

A THUNDERBOLT

Black (Capablanca) has allowed a Pawn on c3 to fall (after exchanges) and now plays Q to Kt7, winning outright.

BERNSTEIN—
KOTOV (1946)

White wins.
1. R to R8 Ch., K to Kt3.
2. P to B5 Ch., P × P.
3. Q × RP Ch., P × Q.
4. QR—KKt8 Mate.

thunderbolt against a Russian aspirant to the Capablanca succession.

The spectacular classical (or some would say Romantic) attacks are wonderfully illustrative of the way in which well co-ordinated forces can destroy larger, less well-organized, arrays of pieces. Typical is the attack with which Morphy disposed of that quite considerable player Paulsen. In the

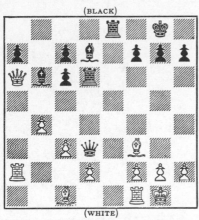

(BLACK)

(WHITE)

PAULSEN—
MORPHY

diagram it is noticeable that Paulsen's position is not at all integrated.

The Pawns and Pieces are spreadeagled, i.e., not well co-ordinated. Paulsen has relied on his last move Q to R6 to free himself. Morphy who has played, not only with greater insight, but along lines of more reasonable development, is now able to demolish Paulsen's position with a few powerful moves, including a Queen sacrifice. 1. ... Q×B 2. P×Q R to Kt3 Ch. 3. K to R1 B to R6 4. R to Q1 (forced: if R to Kt1 4. ... B to Kt7 Ch., and 5. ... R to K8 Ch., with mate next move) 4. ... B to Kt7 Ch. 5. K to Kt1 QB×P Dis. Ch. 6. K to B1 B to Kt7 Ch. 7. K to Kt1 B to R6 Ch. 8. K to R1 B×P 9. Q to B1 (forced) 9. ... B×Q 10. R×B R to K7 11. R to R1 R to R3 12. B to B1 B to K6 and mate follows after a few moves.

Even more meritorious is the finish to the Evergreen Game achieved by Anderssen against Dufresne. The whole game deserves reproduction.

THE EVERGREEN GAME

White	Black
ANDERSSEN	DUFRESNE
1. P to K4.	1. P to K4.
2. Kt to KB3.	2. Kt to QB3.
3. B to B4.	3. B to B4.
4. P to QKt4. **The Evans Gambit.**	4. B × KtP.
5. P to B3.	5. B to R4.
6. P to Q4.	6. P × P.
7. 0—0.	7. P to Q6.
8. Q to Kt3.	8. Q to B3.
9. P to K5.	9. Q to Kt3.
10. R to K1.	10. KKt to K2.
11. B to R3.	11. P to Kt4.
12. Q × P.	12. R to QKt sq.
13. Q to R4.	13. B to Kt3.
14. QKt to Q2.	14. B to Kt2.
15. Kt to K4.	15. Q to B4.
16. B × QP.	16. Q to R4.
17. Kt to B6 Ch.	17. P × Kt.
18. P × P.	18. R to Kt sq.
19. QR to Q sq. (See diagram.)	19. Q × Kt.
20. R × Kt Ch.	20. Kt × R.
21. Q × QP Ch.	21. K × Q.
22. B to KB5 Double Ch.	22. K to K1.
23. B to Q7 Ch and Mate follows.	

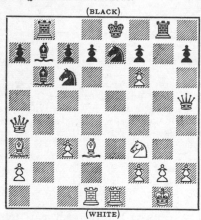

(BLACK)

(WHITE)

ANDERSSEN—
DUFRESNE

Black plays 19 . . .
Q × Kt.
Then follows :
20. R × Kt Ch., Kt × R.
21. Q × QP Ch., K × Q.
22. B to B5 Dble. Ch., K to K1.
23. B to Q7 Ch. and Mate next move.

The position in the diagram, which is the consequence of strategically inferior play by Dufresne (who started a counter attack before he had dealt with his opponent's more dangerous looking offensive) is yet a very close affair. Black also has chances ; and moves like 19. . . . Kt to K4, or 19. . . .

R×KtP Ch. only just fail. Dr. Lasker has gone so far as to suggest that 19. . . . R to KKt5 would give White great difficulty ; and Lasker suggests that White would have done better at move 19 to play a quiet move like B to K4 instead of the brilliant QR to Q1. Nevertheless it is generally held that Anderssen's move was sound as well as brilliant (if what is called brilliance does not imply soundness) and the whole undertaking is of the greater beauty because White had to see a large number of variations clearly; the slightest oversight would have turned his advantage into a loss. That ability to see conclusive sequences through many variations is the essence of fine Chess.

Many sacrifices occur in positions where the unbalance is so obvious, or the possibilities so clear, that no great merit attaches to them. In point is the frequent sacrifice of the Bishop at KR7, or B or Kt at KB7. Sometimes this is easy to follow mentally, sometimes hard—and the merit varies directly with the difficulty. The Diagram on page 94 shows the penalty being exacted for the cramping of Black's game. Sacrifices are the normal consequences of this kind of cramp.

But what good Chess players regard as the best sacrifices are those lines of play which, in an apparently level game, with resources available to both, determine the game in favour of one player. Examples of such sacrifices are seen in later chapters.

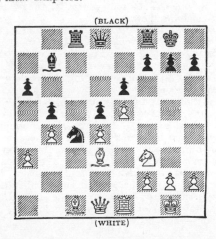

(BLACK)

(WHITE)

"THE GREEK GIFT."
B × RP Ch. K × B.
Kt to Kt5 Ch.
If 2. . . . K to Kt1.
   3. Q to R5.
If 2. . . . K to Kt3.
   3. Q to Kt4, et seq.

(BLACK)

(WHITE)

Sacrifice against
Cramped Position

White wins by :
B × P Ch., K × B.
Kt to K6 ! K × Kt.
Q to B4 Ch., etc.

In conclusion, the last few examples amount to excellent proof that what matters on the Chess Board is not the aggregation of material but the dynamic of efficient force. In Chess, as in War, the many can be delivered into the hands of the effective few. What was shown repeatedly in recent world history is not a novelty to the Chess player. In Chess as in War, the operator can ignore quite large arrays of force because they are not mobile. They only matter if the attack does not decisively conclude the campaign. At all stages, therefore, the player must look through and beyond the value of the Pieces—all the Pieces other than the King. In appreciating any possibility of disregarding the obvious the learner is taking an important step towards competence in a game where the obvious is always becoming doubtful and the not obvious always becoming clear.

That is not to say that the obvious must be ignored. It must be included and transcended. In an elementary position the formal values of the Pieces are a safe enough guide. But the player who is learning can never be sure—and must never let himself feel sure without reflection—that the position is elementary. Later he will appreciate the stresses and tensions that make a position promising for sacrifices. At the present stage every position has difficulties and latent problems that are likely to make it into a task. If a player is not conscious of what is going on—or what can be going on—then he is not in control, and his opponent may well produce something unexpected, something surprising, a departure, so to speak, from the conventions. He will suddenly put a Piece where it can be captured ; he will ignore your attack on one of his Pieces ; he will take a small Piece in exchange for a big Piece. In a word, he will depart from the logic that is based on a formal valuation. Then, probably, you will have the melancholy alternative of allowing him to retain the advantage that he has unconventionally acquired, or else of accepting his sacrifice and finding yourself involved in some forcing sequence which will culminate in your discomfiture.

Let it be emphasised that in most cases the sacrificer is not doing anything remarkable. The player who allows the sacrifice is playing badly. A sacrifice is just a move, necessary for the achievement of some object, which happens to allow material to be captured. A sacrifice only becomes praiseworthy when it is at once unexpected and part of a long plan. A sacrifice seen in the distance is valuable. (Capablanca's sacrifice against Bernstein was such a one). So is an immediate sacrifice whose consequences are distant or difficult (see the game, Zukertort-Blackburn in a later Chapter). But there are many other moves besides sacrifices that are meritorious—quiet moves that bring about a control of the Board, gain time subtly, etc., etc. Sacrifices are most likely to surprise the novice only because the formal values of the Pieces are dominant in his mind. At a later stage he may find quiet moves harder to see than sacrifices. But the general factor is that one has to see beyond the immediate ; beyond the apparent valuation ; and, more widely, beyond the present situation. Seeing through the values of the Pieces is one instance of seeing ahead. Seeing ahead is the essence of Chess. In every tactical situation—that is to say in every Chess position—what matters is not only what exists but what is going to happen. The reader who has learnt the moves, and some of the functions of the Pieces, has to learn to interpret situations in which these values and these functions are the elements and the total significance. So far the reader has learnt the meanings of some words, some rules of accidence, some principles of syntax. What he has to acquire, however, is the art of understanding what he reads. Eventually he will want to construct sentences, paragraphs, arguments of his own.

PART II

TACTICS AND STRATEGY.

CHAPTER III

THE MIDDLE GAME AND INTRODUCTION TO TACTICS.

PHASES OF CHESS

Chess is conventionally divided into three phases, Opening, Middle Game and End Game. The distinction is convenient because it corresponds to a difference of scope. The endgame, which is not always reached—because the game can be lost to a middle-game, or even opening, attack—comes into being when the game is reduced to relatively small forces, and (usually) Pawns, with their capacity for promotion, become rather more important individually than they were in the early stages. The endgame calls for exactitude, subtlety, and that blend of skill and experience of the general pattern which is called technique.

The Opening on the other hand, is more crowded with Pieces and possibilities. In the opening, a certain amount of book learning can be useful, though its importance must not be exaggerated. But the normal phase of Chess, and therefore, that part to which the student should quickly be introduced, is the Middle-game. Indeed, from one standpoint, Chess is all Middle-game, because if you do not know book variations in the openings, and if you do not know the standard types of position that constitute the endgame, you can still do well by using, if you have attained it, that capacity for seeing variations which is the essence of Chess, and which is the main equipment required for the Middle-game.

At the outset then, it is advisable to treat Chess as if it were all Middle-game, to imagine yourself faced at any particular moment with a critical position in which you are called upon to find the best move. To see the best move means to see a number of possible moves, the answers to those moves, the answers to the answers, working out each series separately and deciding which move is going to produce the relatively best position that you can achieve. What you have to work out, for the most part, is tactical. That is to say you are concerned with moves, which, if they are constructive, endeavour to bring something into being—something perceptible and completely advantageous Both you and your opponent are initiating processes which, if uninterfered with, will bring about a definite result. For the most part the pursuit of these processes, and the conflict of processes, is analogous to close fighting and skirmishing in warfare. In Chess the forces are generally so inter-locked that clever fighting is always necessary and usually going on.

The game is largely tactical. But tactics do not exhaust the game. The student will eventually discover that there is such a thing as choosing the terrain, avoiding conflicts on occasion, preparing for one type of attack rather than another, so playing as to induce an attack, or to prevent it, according to choice, etc., etc. These are features of strategy. They are different from tactics but inseparable. At the outset, however, it is more important to be able to fight than to try and arrange the battlefield. Consequently the first lessons in Chess must be lessons in tactics. In any event tactics are the bulk of the game. A Chess player is always playing tactics as a person is always talking prose. Just as it is im-portant to be conscious of what is going on when one is talking prose, so the student may be assisted by considering what kind of mental operation he is undertaking when he plunges into the tactical complexities of the Middle-game, i.e., whenever he plays Chess.

MENTAL APPROACH

When Edgar Allan Poe said that in Chess one calculated, he was demonstrating to Chess players his complete innocence of their mental processes. In Chess there is very little of the deductive, very little of the arithmetical; and there is hardly anything in the way of formula that can help a man of limited vision to work out—or calculate—what he should do. The reader will, indeed, eventually encounter and acquire certain abstract principles, such as the unlikelihood of attacking successfully against a superior development. These principles, though useful, are negative, regulative, disciplinary, rather

D

than constructively helpful to the student who wants to learn how to approach the Chess Board. Again, there are certain concepts derived from experience—particularly of the endgame —which enable a player to consider his position in the light of the ultimate Pawn structure, etc. These help to the formation of one's strategic equipment. But they, too, are not useful unless and until the player possesses the faculty for seeing what is going on among the Chess Pieces in any given position. If he cannot see the specific possibilities—and impossibilities— of any concrete situation, then he is lost in the skirmishes ; he is incapable of tactical effort, or the control of the tactical situation—which is any situation on the Chess Board. From tactical operations strategy is inseparable ; in abstraction from them it is meaningless.

Very good examples of how the Chess mind works have been given on occasion by the leading Masters in their explanations of their own play.

Here is a position from the match between Lasker and Marshall, in which Lasker has explained his reasoning. Lasker was Black.

(BLACK)

(WHITE)

MARSHALL
LASKER
Black plays P to KB3

Black has to consider his twelfth move. Now there are quite a number of safe moves to consider, but what Lasker selects is a choice of two aggressive moves. Strategically, Black is no longer at the disadvantage of tempo that he normally has to struggle against in the opening. Now it is his turn to take the initiative ; he does not wish to give his opponent a chance for further development. The two most aggressive moves available are 12. . . . P to KB4 and 12. . . . P to KB3 ; both of these moves being attempts to give effective attacking value to Black's King's Rook.

Now consider 12. . . . P to KB4. If the Pawn captures *e.p.* the Rook is already in action ; if the Pawn does not capture there is a threat of P to KB5.

Now suppose White, faced with this threat, counter-attacks :

White	Black
12. . . .	P to KB4.
13. P to KB3.	P to B5.
14. P × Kt.	P × B, and now there is a serious threat of Q to B7 Ch. followed by the clever P to K7. White cannot avoid this by Q to K2, nor by R × P, without heavy loss.
	If he plays R to KB1 he loses a Pawn at least ; and after Kt to QB3 he remains under severe pressure.

But all this is short-circuited by the consideration that in answer to 12. . . . P to KB4 White can reply with P to KB4 ; and the result is not so convincing : thus :—

White	Black
12. . . .	P to KB4.
13. P to KB4.	P to KKt4. Now White can defend with Q to B1, or more boldly—
14. P to KKt3.	Kt × P (the most vigorous).
15. P × Kt.	Q × P Ch.
16. K to R1.	And Black, although he has perpetual Check (since the White King dare not go to B1), has no way of bringing additional material into the attack in time to prevent White from mobilizing his Queen's Rook and Knight to the defence. Thus Black cannot play P × P while his Queen is at Kt6 because of R to Kt1 ; he cannot mobilize the Bishop along the diagonal Kt2 to KR8 because White can block that diagonal by playing B to B5. Also the Black Rook can only penetrate the game slowly via squares B2 and Kt2. Against this, White has time for QKt to Q2 and either Q to KB3 or Kt to KB1.

Black therefore considers a different line of play, to which White's only vigorous reaction must be a counter attack.

White	*Black*
12. . . .	P to KB3.
13. P to KB3.	P × P.
14. P × Kt.	P to Q5.

And Lasker judged that, at this point, if the Bishop surrendered itself Black would have a winning endgame with Bishop against Knight and better placed Pawns, and at least one open file; whereas if White plays to keep the Bishop with 15 B to Q2, Black's attack, with B to Kt5 and R to B7 would be too good to need analysing. (The threat would be a Mating attack involving the possibility of R × P Ch.)

In the result Marshall played in answer to 12. P to KB3, 13. P to KB3 (there was nothing better) and play proceeded.

White	*Black*
12. . . .	P × P.
14. P × Kt.	P to Q5.
15. P to KKt3.	Q to B3.
16. B × P.	P × B.
17. R to KB1.	Q × R Ch.
18. Q × Q.	R × Q Ch.
19. K × R.	R to Kt1.
20. P to Kt3.	R to Kt4.
21. P to B4. To stop eventual R to B6.	R to KR4.
22. K to Kt1.	P to B4.
23. Kt to Q2.	K to B2.
24. R to KB1. Ch.	K to K2.
25. P to QR3.	R to KR3.
26. P to KR4.	R to QR3 with a winning endgame.

The mental processes involved in that piece of Chess are most interesting. It will be seen that Lasker mainly used direct vision of move and counter move. At one or two points that vision included the perception of surprises, unexpected moves, threats that would not readily be anticipated. This means that Lasker was using that degree of vision which is imagination. On the other hand in some phases of the game he was not endeavouring to see exhaustively, but was seeing general characters of the position, and the general scope, i.e., he was using judgment, and applying his grasp of strategy.

Another position, fairly easy to understand, is taken from the first match game between Zukertort and Steinitz, and illustrates a failure to think clearly or judge adequately.

(BLACK)

(WHITE)

ZUKERTORT—
STEINITZ

In this position, which arises after an opening in which Black has played strategically more wisely than White, there is a threat impending of a profitable sacrifice by Black on K6. This is typical of what requires to be seen. A bad player would miss it. There is hardly room to doubt that Zukertort saw it—and saw that tactically his game would be much improved if he played Kt to Kt3 giving his King a flight square. Zukertort probably thought that that would make his Queen's side attack too slow, and took a risk. He may have judged that Steinitz's attack would prove unsound, and/or sufficiently failed to analyse the sequences that would follow the sacrifice.

There followed 14. P to Kt5, KtR5. 15. P to Kt3, Kt Kt7 Ch. 16. K to B1, Kt×KP Ch. 17. P×Kt, KB×KtP. 18. K to Kt2, B to B2 and White cannot prevent a winning attack from developing. The moral of this story is that one cannot afford, in complexities, not to work out the sequences in analytic detail.

Alternatively it is possible that Zukertort got out of his own depth and relied on possibilities that later proved unfounded.

From the standpoint of practical Chess the average good

player in that position would regard the situation as relatively easy, and take it for granted that he needed to take the precaution of Kt to Kt3 in order to provide his King with a flight square.

There are many positions in Chess comparable to this : in that they can be regarded as easy if one wishes to avoid risks, and are extremely difficult if insecurity is contemplated.

THE TACTICAL COMPLEX

The Chess position is never isolated, never static. It is a phase in an argument. If one is obsessed with the difficulty of spelling out and translating the words, the argument cannot be followed. But once the elements can be interpreted, one is able to perceive the sort of argument that is going on— the consideration of possible changes in the given position, and the consequences of those changes. Each move considered is a step in an argument, and is effective, or interesting, according to the answers that are available, and the way in which the moves can be followed up. There may be many answers or few ; and each answer may have many answers or few ; each of these in turn has its few or many answers. What the Chess player requires to do is to follow as many possible lines as he can, each separately, and each as far as he can. His vision, therefore, must be wide and deep—and above all, clear.

The essence, let it be repeated, is clear vision. That, be it emphasized, is something that does not follow automatically from knowing the moves, or from knowing the maximum of which each Piece is capable, or from knowing particular devices. Always you have to see the reality of a changing situation, and see it as a whole.

Vision, as we have seen, varies from something like ready wit to the higher degree which is imagination ; just as the capacity for argument varies with the capacity to give adequate answers varying from the obvious to the ingenious, original or profound.

For the rest, vision is not the only mental activity that goes on in Chess, as we have seen, or, indeed, in any intellectual undertaking ; but it is fundamental. The important thing about vision, as distinct from items of information, and from technique, etc., is that it is the least capable of mental operations of being taught. We all enjoy it in some degree. We can all, somehow, learn to see ; but nobody can be taught to see. One is reminded of Dr. Johnson's observation that he could convey reason but not understanding. In Chess a player can be shown examples of what people have apprehended. He can be presented with situations in which he himself has to find the truth of the matter. If he has some faculty of vision, he will find himself acquiring, quite mysteriously, from his studies, the capacity to apprehend different possibilities in totally different positions. And then he will be quite amazed that he could not see before what is now so obvious. The puzzle picture should not have been puzzling! That is how the mind grows. But let no one attempt to achieve this by learning examples by heart; that way staleness lies. Be it repeated, there is no direct teaching of how to apprehend, just as there is no teaching that will make the obtuse acute.

What, however, can be done—and that is the purpose of these pages—is to direct the reader's mind to essentials. A study of examples, and illustrative games, should make the reader more ready to recognize what is important, i.e. what he requires to concentrate on in most positions. The examples already given have served to show that he is no longer concerned with isolated Pieces; that he is concerned with a tactical complex made up of all the powers of all the Pieces. The second stage is the recognition that not all the powers of all the Pieces matter equally all the time. On every Chess Board something is important and something relatively unimportant; something is relevant to the argument, something is irrelevant.

RELEVANCE

Before passing to examples, this general truth may usefully be re-stated. The good Chess player, like the good arguer, concentrates on the relevant. Once the reader has passed the stage at which the Board is a polychromatic mystery, he will appreciate that, in the mass of possibilities that exist in any given Chess position, a great many possibilities are likely to be unimportant. One does not approach one's move on the assumption that the choice is between all the available moves of all the available Pieces. There will be some moves that are clearly not to be thought about Just as in any argument a great deal of one's vocabulary, and masses of knowledge, are not in point, so on the Chess Board there is always the distinction between what is in issue and what is not in issue. Having passed the stage of general confusion, the Chess player manages to focus his vision on the relevant. He must recognize it. There is no way of showing anybody how to pick out the relevant. That is an act of vision, which, as we have seen, is unteachable. But if in looking at the Chess Board the reader sees something going on, sees, for example, that a Piece is attacked, defended, can be again attacked, and again defended, then he is already isolating some relevant point ; and, in some degree, he is playing Chess. At first his field of relevance will be narrow. Concentration makes it so. As vision improves, and concentration becomes more dynamic, the field of relevance widens and/or lengthens. A Pawn that one player disregards may be very important to another player, who is planning a long series of moves and has to consider, for example, a check upon, or an escape to, a square guarded by that Pawn. Even at that advanced stage the good player will not be laboriously working out the consequences of every possible move by every possible Piece. His vision, trained, by practice, in seeing the essentials in that kind of material, is grasping a sort of pattern—a group of possibilities arranging themselves into purposes. Much of what he is considering would never occur to the weaker player ; on the other hand he will have seen his way through, and be excluding from consideration, much that obsesses the novice, and will be paying no more attention to it than the artist who chips away the material round the figure that he has seen in the marble.

How, then, to set about finding the relevant, and improving one's grasp of possibilities ? First, *concentrate*, consider one line at a time and do not let the attention be diffused on to other thoughts. Take particular care of the absence from the Board of Pieces that will have been removed. After you have concentrated, then the mind will expand to let in outside ideas that will prove relevant. Second, a good idea is suggested by the military metaphor with which this book opened. Chess has something in it of combat. A good approach, therefore, is to think in terms of a quasi-military type. Think bellicosely. Think of threats and manifestations of force. These will not exhaust the possibilities that are latent in your position. But they will give you some kind of guide through the sequence of moves. Eventually what you thought was a threat may prove not to have been a threat. What you thought forced may prove not to have been forced, and you may have failed to see what was necessary for you to do. But in so far as you have thought in terms of these necessities, you have been playing constructively. Eventually you will find yourself seeing wider plans, and you will make no move without a sufficient reason.

THREATS AND FORCING MOVES

From the very beginning there is something going on on the Chess Board—one or other of the infinite variety of processes that are called tactics. These are the things that require to be seen, the possibilities of winning Pawns, embarrassing minor and major Pieces, threatening to Mate the King, etc., etc. Some players start their careers by evading this task of seeing. They endeavour to learn long opening sequences by heart. This is an idle undertaking. The strain on the memory is likely to be greater than the strain on the mind's eye that exists in direct vision. Also, what the learner will have learnt by heart amounts to nothing more than a number of tactical operations that good players have undertaken because they saw what to do; and they did that by looking at the position and not by reference to memory; and they would have made equally good moves in other positions, and in answer to other lines of play, which is precisely what the player who approaches Chess mnemonically will not be able to do. For the rest, the effort to learn Chess by heart pre-supposes enormous difficulties at all stages in a game of which a great many aspects and processes are really quite easy.

To show the logic of the game, and to illustrate the idea of threats and forcing moves, let us examine some elementary opening play. White plays: 1. P to K4. Already he is playing constructively. This move allows two Pieces access to the Board—the Queen and the Bishop, the latter being the more important because it is less effective on its original square than in the centre of the Board. Also P to K4 gives a certain control over the centre squares, and in some degree inhibits the opponent.

Black now replies P to K4, with the same kind of end in view, and challenging White's control of the centre.

Now White plays Kt to KB3. This move has several advantages including the fact that it makes a Piece that was very much out of the game participate actively in it. But the main feature of this move is that now Black's Pawn is attacked. If nothing else were to happen White could capture it.

This threat is, in fact, not immediately so serious as it looks. If White were to capture the Pawn, probably there would be counter-attack by Q to K2 etc. which would re-capture it. But it is generally considered advisable either to defend the King's Pawn, or else to counter-attack immediately with Kt to KB3. These are, incidentally, good moves of development. Of Defence, the most usual moves in this position are for Black 2. . . .Kt to QB3 or (slightly less popular) P to Q3, the defect of the latter being that it gives Black's KB less scope than is possessed by White's KB.

Let us, however, consider a plausible move for Black. 2. . . .P to KB3. At first sight this move looks rational, because it defends a Pawn with the aid of a Pawn, which, as has been pointed out, is a good guard since it is a cheap one. Black has, of course, taken a square away from his King's Knight, but if he is only worried about the Pawn that fact will not concern him unduly.

But let us concentrate first on the question whether the Pawn is guarded. This is the concentration on the relevant that is the first essential of Chess ; and one does not stop concentrating on a relevant line of Chess argument simply because something looks obvious. Is Black correct in supposing that P to KB3 makes Kt×P impossible for White ?

Look, then, at 3. Kt×P. What happens? The logic of P to KB3 suggests 3. . . . P×Kt. But if White has looked at this he will have seen that after P×Kt, White has 4. Q to R5 Ch. In answer to this Black has a limited choice ; and we are encountering, thus early in the game, a good specimen of forcing play ; moves that threaten, and replies that are forced. If Black plays 4. . . . K to K2, then he is in trouble. White plays 5. Q×P Ch. Black is forced to play 5. . . . K to B2 ; and there follows a most destructive attack commencing with 6. B to B4 Ch. The Black King (after the QP has desperately sacrificed itself) is driven on to a most awkward square, and White has many ways of winning Therefore, on the fourth move Black must play P to Kt3. In the ordinary Chess sense this is forced, a move being forced when it is the best available and others involve worse consequences.

After 4. . . . P to Kt3 White plays 5. Q×KP Ch., capturing the Rook on the next move. He will then have gained two Pawns and the Exchange.

At this point the reader may be quite convinced that 2. . . . P to KB3 is a bad move. And that may now seem obvious. But the good Chess player does not stop at that. He is always looking beyond the obvious. If a complete analysis is required, there is still quite a lot to think about before P to KB3 is abandoned.

First, it may occur to the player that after 5. Q×KP Ch., then, if the Black Queen intervenes at K2 and White plays 6.

Q×R, Black's 6th move Kt to KB3 will put the White Queen out of play and into danger of encirclement.

To cut a long story short, the answer is that it takes Black a number of moves to encircle the Queen. He will have to get in P to Q4, then K to B2 (which the former move enables) ; then a QKt or QB move, so that there is no loose Piece on the back line ; then B to Kt2 attacking the Queen. While this is being done White can organize an excellent rescue with P to Q3, Kt to Q2, Kt to KB3 ; and at the proper moment Kt to Kt5, which, if correctly timed, may even be Mate.

Another line of thought is as to what happens if, in reply to Q×R, Black plays Q×P Ch. The answer is that very little happens that Black can be pleased about. White moves King to Q1, threatening soon to operate on the open King's file with the Rook. In the result Black is short of material and the Black Queen is badly placed.

At this stage the analyst is more than ever satisfied that P to KB3 is a bad move. But he still has one feature to look at. What if, after 3. Kt×P, Black replies not 3. . . . P×Kt, but Q to K2 ? Then 4. Q to R5 Ch. may seem good for White, but is bad, because, if Q to R5 Ch., Black plays 4. . . . P to Kt3. Now, if the Knight takes that Pawn, the Pawn cannot recapture, because the Queen will capture the Rook. So it looks good. But Black can reply to Kt×KtP with Q×KP Ch. Then, if the Queen retreats to stop the Check, there will be exchange of Queens and the Pawn will take the Knight ; if anything else, if e.g. B to K2 is played, the Queen can take the Knight. Black will then have to be careful not to lose his Queen by a Bishop pin : but if he sees that, he will be in no danger of loss. It follows, therefore, that after 3. . . .. Q to K2 the White Knight must retreat and the Black Queen will recapture the Pawn with Q×P Ch. But, then, after 5. B to K2, what has happened is that two White Pieces have developed, the Black Queen is wandering loose around the Board, where it will be attacked in a moment by the developing Queen's Knight or Queen's Pawn ; and the square that should be occupied by the Black King's Knight is occupied by a Black Pawn doing nothing. At the end of all this analysis Black is justified in deciding that 2. P to KB3 is a bad move.

The above example shows not only the occurrence of necessary continuations—forcing lines and demonstrations that certain moves are impossible—at a very early stage in the game ; it also shows how, at an early stage, there can be several variations, some short and some in which long range vision, verging on the speculative, may be called for. Indeed, there is no stage of the game where it is impossible to find oneself plunged into the depths of remote continuations.

This vision of lines of play is the essence and the quintessence of Chess. But in the course of playing many games most players acquire, or manifest, a certain ability to economize mental effort. The average Chess player would reject 2. . . . P to KB3, in the variation shown, by an act of judgment. Without going into the various continuations in detail he would have a general notion of the shape that the game would take ; and he would also reject the move because of its relative lack of immediate utility; it develops nothing and it creates tension. This judgment, which operates at all stages of the game, is a great labour saver ; but when the line has to be clearly seen, then vision, not judgment, is invoked. In practice, and in the ordinary mind, these functions are not separable in the simple way that this analysis might suggest. In Chess, as in other activities, the mind uses many methods ; but vision is the moving edge of the Chess mind. That is the important fact that the player has to act upon.

To illustrate the perpetual necessity for vision and vigilance, and to show incidentally the importance of thinking about moves like P to KB3, here is a famous opening in which many masters for long assumed that P to KB3 was unplayable :—

White	Black
1. P to Q4.	P to Q4.
2. P to QB4.	P to QB3. The Slav Defence.
3. Kt to QB3.	Kt to KB3.
4. Kt to KB3.	P × P.
5. P to QR4, in order to put pressure on the Pawn that may defend the Black Pawn on White's QB4.	
5. . . .	B to B4.
6. Kt to K5.	P to K3.
7. P to KB3.	

This was long thought to be a preparation for something unsound and was avoided even in world Championship games. Nevertheless it is good, because if now

White	Black
7. . . .	B to QKt5.
8. P to K4.	B × P.
9. P × B.	Kt × P.
10. B to Q2.	Q to R5 Ch.
11. P to Kt3.	Kt × P.
12. P × Kt.	Q × R.
13. Q to Kt4 with a splendid game.	

If, instead,

	White	Black
10.	. . .	Q × QP.
11.	Kt × Kt.	Q × Kt Ch.
12.	Q to K2.	B × B Ch.
13.	K × B.	Q to Q5 Ch.
14.	K to B2.	White has more material than is compensated for by Black's attack.

Thus, again, we see speculative possibilities cropping up early in the game. Some of them require a long analysis before they are adopted or dismissed.

The important thing is to see the forcing line. That does not necessarily mean that it is to be adopted. Here is a study in a quite early forcing line which is useful because it shows that the forcing line does not necessarily achieve advantage.

	White	Black
1.	P to K4.	P to K4.
2.	Kt to KB3.	Kt to QB3.
3.	B to B4.	Kt to KB3. The Two Knights Defence.
4.	Kt to Kt5. This is a forcing move because it makes a serious threat which the defender cannot afford to ignore.	P to Q4. Forced: i.e., the only way of preventing White from winning the KBP. But Black's move, though compelled, is good on its own merits.
5.	P × P.	Kt to R4. Black starts forcing now.
6.	P to Q3.	P to KR3.
7.	Kt to KB3.	P to K5.
8.	Q to K2.	Kt × B.

And Black has a good deal of freedom in exchange for his Pawn. It is only fair to add that no less an authority than Lasker prefers White ; but that is a matter of taste. It should be noted, incidentally that on move 6, White can play B to Kt5 Ch., which can lead to highly speculative play after P to QB3, 7. P×P, P×P, 8. Q to B3, etc.

An even better refutation of a vigorous line is due to the Russian Master, Rabinovitch.

	White	Black
1.	P to K4.	P to K4.
2.	Kt to KB3.	Kt to QB3.
3.	B to Kt5.	P to QR3.
4.	B to R4.	Kt to B3.
5.	0–0.	P to QKt4. Not the best, but playable, as the continuation shows.
6.	B to Kt3.	P to Q3.

And now if White plays the apparently good 7. Kt to Kt5, forcing P to Q4, then he is a victim of Fata Morgana, because if 8. P×P, Black develops a highly interesting counter-attack with 8. . . . Kt to Q5. 9. P to QB3, Kt×B. 10. Q×Kt, Q×P, with good play for Black—and there are other, more speculative variations.

It follows that while the forcing process is an important feature of Chess, it is not to be considered good merely by virtue of its vigour. If the forcing move can be met by play which yields the opponent an advantage, then it must not be pursued.

The player who sees a possible forcing line, and a convincing answer to it, and therefore abandons it in favour of something else, is improving as a Chess player. He is playing the board —not the man—playing against all possibilities. He is now seeing battles as part of the war ; seeing the whole as an interplay of forces, in which the various campaigns are variations to be analysed. But, be it understood, the process which forces something positive to your advantage must be adopted, because it is desirable that the player shall control the game so as to make as much as possible of it follow of necessity. This control cannot always be achieved ; and there is such a thing as losing through trying to force the pace. But if you can proceed vigorously without causing your opponent's game to become better integrated, if you can keep him cramped by threats while you develop, evidently it is good play to do so ; and given the choice between static play and dynamic play, the dynamic line should be chosen. Lasker's game against Marshall, with which this chapter opened, is an excellent demonstration of the proof that in Chess there is no room for Micawbers. If you wait for it, it won't turn up.

EXAMPLES OF FORCING PROCESS

If the reader will turn back to the Lasker position, he will see that even when Lasker had gained some advantage, he still chose forcing moves wherever he could find them. On move 19 he played R to Kt1, forcing P to Kt3 and incidentally depriving White's Knight of that square. Then he brought the Rook to Kt4, threatening R to B4 and eventual R to B6 ; so that White was forced to move the QBP, leaving his game hollower than ever.

The next diagram shows a neat and pointed forcing series. White is threatening a process of Pawn promotion on the King's wing, with the aid of a Knight's sacrifice, but it appears as if Black can hold the threatened attack with the aid of the King and the two Pieces, so that 1. Kt × RP will fail after K × Kt. 2. R to R8 Ch., K to Kt2. 3. R to R7 Ch. K to Kt1, etc.

White therefore plays 1. R to QKt8, threatening to win a Pawn and to break up the Q side. 1. . . . P to B3 is no defence because of R to QB8. Black therefore plays 1. . . . B to Kt3. Now an important change has been made in the position. White can now play 2. Kt × RP, K × Kt. 3. R to R8 Ch., K to Kt2. 4. R to R7 Ch., K to B1 (forced because the Bishop no longer guards the Rook). 5. P to R6 wins, because after R × R, P × R the King cannot stop the Pawn.

(BLACK)

(WHITE)

White to move.

It is worth noticing that if on move 1 Black plays R to Q2, aiming at counter play, the sacrifice is also on, for a similar reason ; and if the Rook checks a couple of times, it gets hopelessly entangled : but the sacrifice is perhaps no longer necessary ; the game can be won without it by R × P and R to Q5 if required. Incidentally, the reader must not suppose that one achieves a piece of play like this by thinking in terms of " purpose " (" the Bishop is a nuisance—let me displace it "). These things are seen as a whole—or not at all.

There is no need for an accumulation of examples of forcing processes because the reader will discover, in every game he plays, or plays through, that a certain amount of compulsion characterises the play at some stages, whereas in other stages there is relative freedom. What is important is to see, if possible, the obscure possibility that makes something necessary to the player who sees it, or makes his opponent able to achieve something if the defender does not see it.

The diagram shows an ingenuity by Alekhine. Playing against Tartakower at San Remo, in a position which was slightly advantageous, but which looked as if it might have been tenable by the defender along logical lines, Alekhine introduced the finesse which brought about a decisive result quickly. After 32. ... Kt to K1, giving the diagram position, Black was sure that White could not get any advantage from Kt × P, B × Kt; B × B Ch., K × B; R to K3 Ch., K × P, etc. What he failed to appreciate was a change of order. 33. B × P Ch., B × B. 34. P to Kt4 Ch. and now if 34. ... K to B5. 35. Kt to K6 is Mate. Therefore Black must play 34. K to B3 leaving White to capture the Bishop with full control of the game.

(BLACK) TARTAKOWER

White to move.

(WHITE) ALEKHINE

An interesting feature of this position is that another point of order makes White's manoeuvre harder to see. To play P to Kt4 Ch. before B × P does not give the same result as the line played, because after K to B5, B × P could be met by R × Kt, leaving an endgame of tremendous difficulty.

For the rest, do not confuse forcing moves with "loud" moves. The threat need not be of an immediate capture.

In the next diagram position the "loud" move is 1. ... R to Q6, hitting something, and if Q to K2 of course White is in trouble, e.g., 1. ... R to Q6. 2. Q to K2, KR to Q1. 3. 0–0, B × Kt, etc. If 3. Kt to Q4, B × Kt. 4. P × B, KR × P. 5. 0–0, R to KKt6! wins.

However, White is not obliged to play Q to K2. 2. Q to

B4 is playable—and Black cannot comfortably double Rooks, although his game is still good. If he doubles Rooks—each player wins a Bishop, and after exchanges Black has a slightly superior endgame.

But if Black plays 1. . . . R to Q3—less loud, but still threatening, White is relatively helpless. If 2. Q to K2, B to Kt4. If instead, 2. Q to B4 2.... B to R3 is playable, and B × Kt and KR to Q1 are threatened. If 3. Q to B5 Ch., R to K3 Ch. 4. B to K3, R × P. 5. Q × BP, R × B Ch. wins.

(BLACK)

(WHITE)

Black to move.

WHAT ARE TACTICS : SOME HINTS

By this time the reader, whom it is the aim of these pages to teach to think like a Chess player, may have noticed, or been disappointed to find, that in a Chapter relating to tactics he has not been given any rules. If he is already thinking like a Chess player, he will have the answer ; that tactics do not lend themselves to rules. Tactics consist in dealing with a situation according to the forces available and the nature of the situation. Knowledge of tactics is simply the awareness of the powers of the Pieces and the geometry of the Board, plus the ability to control (i.e. plan in the light of) those factors. There is no rule about dealing with them effectively. The materials that one is using are the functions of the Pieces described in the second chapter. When the player has mastered the functions of the Pieces to the extent of being able to use them in his plans, then he is a tactician.

Most of tactics consists in the straightforward use of the Pieces in the light of common sense. Common sense is not quite an accurate description, because the ability to think in terms of the Chess moves already places the reader beyond ordinary common sense. But it is common sense relatively to the more imaginative degrees of vision. Bringing to bear as much force as possible in attack or defence of any given point; capturing the greater with the lesser; making squares of escape for Pieces that are hemmed in, etc., etc., these are tactics. The tactical efficiency of a player increases in the measure to which the powers of the Pieces and their idiosyncracies have become part of his equipment.

Important factors in tactical operations include several that the reader has already been made aware of.

The pinning of Pieces and Pawns by the Pieces that can pin (Bishop, Rook and Queen) is one important feature of the tactical complex. To know this is not enough, because the pinning operation may in the total situation be unimportant. That is something that can only be assessed by the player who has learned to concentrate and to seek for answers to all his threats. Imagine for example that your opponent has moved his Queen's Pawn, so that you can, with your Queen, pin his Knight at QB3 by placing your Queen at QR4 or QKt5. That may be a very good undertaking if it is part of a general pressure and creates threats in addition to the temporary immobilization of the Knight.

For example it may be coupled with an attack on the Queen's Knight's Pawn or Queen's Rook's Pawn, which it may or may not be safe to capture. Or it may be coupled with a threat of P to Q5 and the possibility of winning the Knight. On the other hand your move may in the long run be useless as the opponent's Bishop may be able to place itself at Q2. It may be that you want to compel it to go there. On the other hand B to Q2 may embarrass you, not your opponent. He threatens to " unmask a battery " by a Knight move. If nothing else, this may cause you to lose tempo.

The unmasking of batteries is quite an important feature of tactics. The principle is that of discovered check. It can quite easily come about that even a light pinning Piece can be lost, even when it is pinning against a heavy Piece. Thus, your Queen is on K1, your Knight on QB3, your opponent's Bishop is on his QKt5, his Queen on K2, and he has castled King's side. Your move Kt to Q5 may win a Piece, because if he takes your Queen, you take his Queen with Check, and capture the Bishop next move. The efficacy of this depends on whether the Knight can later extricate itself. Probably, if the worst comes to the worst, it can sell itself for a Pawn. That, too, suggests a feature of tactics. In Chess as in other undertakings it is wise to play with the bookmaker's money. The so far unrecaptured Piece, the "hanging Piece," so to speak, is a tactical weapon; it can sell itself for what it likes and whatever return it obtains is profit.

But let the reader not endeavour to learn Chess by making a list of notions like unmasking batteries, hanging Pieces, etc. If the student is getting familiar with the powers of the Pieces these manoeuvres will be perceptible by him even if he does not know the name of each manoeuvre. Knowing the name is an advantage only because it may heighten awareness. But the awareness must come first.

To revert to pins, there are many ways of relieving a pin. One of the most familiar is the relief of the pin of the Queen's Knight by P to QR3 and P to QKt4. That is particularly effective against a Queen : it may also upset a Bishop. In the Noah's Ark Trap (later in this Chapter) it helps to win a Piece. On the other hand, while this may be good counterplay (and incidentally a method of developing the QB) it may also create a weakness on the QB file.

On the King's wing the manoeuvre P to KR3, P to KKt4 has a similar effect but may be more dangerous to the defender, because it often happens that the attacker can sacrifice a Knight for the KtP, recapture with the Bishop and have a permanent pin.

A permanent, unrelievable pin is a very good thing if it is not purchased at too high a price. It is sometimes worth while to sacrifice in order to hold a Rook permanently (or even for a move or two) pinned on KB7 while forces can be brought up to attack it. The so called Dilworth Defence to the Ruy Lopez illustrates this principle (see chapter on openings).

Another instance of permanent pin can happen when a Rook checks on the back rank, and a Bishop is forced to interpose itself, and the defender finds it impossible, or laborious, to get his King off the back rank without at the same time losing the Bishop. If he can move his Pawns, he can escape, but the Pawn moves may be dangerous because they may open new lines of attack.

Obviously your opponent's King and Queen are good pieces to have behind the Piece you are pinning; they make the pin more serious.

A few lines of opening play are understandable when one

considers that they turn on the fact that, if a minor Piece captures a Pawn on the King's or Queen's file, that Piece may be pinned against the King or Queen by a Rook, while a Pawn comes up to attack it. It may well be that there is tactical counterplay as in the diagram position below. Once again the total situation has to be taken into account, but the pinning possibility is always to be borne in mind. Again, the Queen is not a very good Piece to pin with unless it is clear that there is no effective counter such as a masked battery. Queens that pin at Kt5 are usually attacking at the same time a Knight's Pawn. But tactically the capture of the Knight's Pawn may be dangerous.

(BLACK)

(WHITE)

TACTICAL COMPLEX

Black to move :
1. ... Kt × P.
2. Kt × Kt, Q × Kt.
3. R to K1, Kt to K5 with counter-play.

Suppose you are attacking a Knight's Pawn and your opponent Castles on the other wing ; the capture may put your Queen into difficulties. These difficulties constitute a feature of the tactical complex.

White	*Black*
1. P to Q4.	P to Q4.
2. Kt to KB3.	B to B4.
3. P to QB4.	P to K3.
4. Q to Kt3 taking advantage of the weakness of the QKtP.	Kt to QB3. A clever reply.
5. Q × P.	Kt to Kt5. And the Queen is in difficulties. There is a threat at least to draw by the repetition R to Kt1, R to R1, etc.

Here is another example—a position reached by the author, in which Black has played Q to Kt3 attacking a Bishop and putting pressure on the centre, but White replies Kt to QB3, threatening Kt to R4 ; and if Q×B, that same Kt to R4 actually wins the Queen.

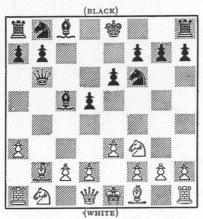

(BLACK)

(WHITE)

TACTICAL POINT

White to play :
1. Kt to QB3.

In this last example the Knight's powers are well illustrated as part of a Chess situation. The reader has already seen examples of the Knight's fork—another instrument of tactical operations. The reader has also seen the Smothered Mate. It may also be mentioned that a Knight can find itself hemmed at the edge of the board. Thus, place it on QR4 ; give the opponent a Pawn on Q5, a B on K2, a P on QR2, and if you have a Pawn on QKt2, then your opponent's P to QKt4 may win the Knight ; and examples could be multiplied.

All the Pieces have their peculiarities, some of which are harder to appreciate than others ; and the harder ones are worth mentioning. Thus in the next diagram, the advantage of Black's last move P to QR4 is that now it takes White four moves to get his Pawn to QKt4. 1. P to QKt3 (not P to QR3 which is answered by P to QR5) 2. P to QR3 3. B to Kt2 (this is necessary to guard the Rook) and finally P to QKt4. Very often, therefore, a player who wishes to establish a Kt on B4 precedes this move with P to QR4.

This diagram, incidentally, shows a kind of pin in being— the Rook's prevention of 3. P to Kt4:P×P 4. P×P R×R.

This rather differs from the Rook's pin on the King's file, e.g. when a capture of a Pawn is under consideration.

The Pawn, incidentally, is quite a hard Piece to master. In the centre of the Board it has latent threats. Thus given a Bishop on QB4, your opponent may be able to play Kt × KP, and in answer to Kt × Kt, P to Q4. Or again this may be quite ineffective because either the Knight or the Bishop may be able to move away with a threat or a check, gaining a tempo to save the second piece—another instance of the hanging Piece.

(BLACK)

(WHITE)

TECHNICAL
POINT
Effect of Pawn on R4.

Here is a harder example. Your opponent has a Rook on his QR4, a B on QB4, a Knight on Q5. You have a Kt on Q1, Pawns on QKt2 and QB2 ; P to Kt4 wins a Piece ; because if B × P, P to QB3 forks Kt and B.

This last example illustrates the difficulty and the inutility of attempting to make a list of tactical factors. They are too empirical, too numerous, too inconstant. The functions of the Pieces are always functions varying with the positional setting.

Some Masters have claimed to be able to teach Chess, including the art of sacrificing, on rational mathematical lines. They speak of bearing in mind the maximum moves of each Piece : or thinking of the most " restrictive " moves. That is an error due to the analysis of some combinations into mathematical statements. The Rook, e.g. which sacrificed itself in some particular position made its maximum move, finally putting itself *en prise*. On the other hand, some Rooks sacrifice themselves without going so far. Again, going too near the enemy, restrictively, may not be the best (see Diagram on page 113). If you try to think of all the powers of all the Pieces you will be considering a great many irrelevancies; you will be doing the opposite of what is required above all else in Chess, concentration on the relevant. The relevant is intuited, not worked out mathematically. If you have absorbed the functions of the Pieces your capacity for the perception of the relevant is better; that is all that can be said.

Acccording to your grasp of the Board, you will be less liable to surprise. The element of surprise is always present in Chess. Even good players can be surprised. There is

(BLACK)

(WHITE)

ALEKHINE
NIMZOWITCH

A STUDY IN
PINNING.

White wins:
16. KR to K1, B to K5.
17. B to R5, Kt × B.
18. R to Q8 Ch., K to B2.
19. Q × Kt. Resigns.

Note the achievement of a permanent pin.

always something beyond any player's field of vision. The reader has already seen several examples of surprise; and he will see many more; the putting of Pieces *en prise*, in order to gain a square, to effect a pin for a critical moment, to inveigle a Major Piece into a difficult situation, etc., etc. All these require to be seen rather than deduced.

That very good players can be surprised by manœuvres not many moves deep, but yet having an element of unexpectedness in them, is illustrated by the play in the above and two following positions. These were three of a great number of triumphs that Alekhine achieved at Bled in the days of his supremacy. They were scored against Nimzowitch and Flohr, at that time two of the very greatest players in the world.

Each of these positions is describable, after play, in terms of some geometry—open lines, closed lines and the like. But good players proceed with the manoeuvres they wish to execute, even when they do not like all the geometrical features, because it is very rare to have the kind of position in which one likes all the geometrical characteristics. Besides, and more important, the existence of open lines, masked

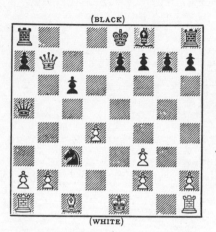

NIMZOWITCH
ALEKHINE
COMPROMISING
THE QUEEN.
12. ... Kt to Q4 Ch.
13. B to Q2, Q to Kt3.
14. Q × R Ch. K to Q2 and White's Queen is in difficulties.
There followed :
15. O–O Kt to B2.
16. B to R5, Kt × Q.
17. B × Q, Kt × B, etc.

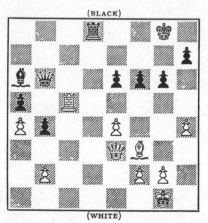

ALEKHINE
FLOHR
Unusual effect of a " battery."
28. P to K5. P to B4.
29. R to B8. Wins.

batteries, possibilities of pins, etc., are insufficient to constitute a decisive process. They condition the process—not bring it about. If the good player cannot see his opponent's exploitation, it may be because the opponent cannot do anything decisive. But a particularly clever opponent sometimes finds ingenuities and resources in a position that the other has missed; (equally, the best of players might fail to extract anything from an apparently more favourable setting). That is how good players fall victim to surprise. They engage in hard combat; and the enemy finds somewhere a source of strength, effects a neat hold, which, in close combat, is quite easy for the victim not to anticipate.

The student of Chess may learn from these examples that the very best players fail to deduce dangers that exist, and fail to see them. It follows that the student cannot hope to work out a Chess geometry, or a set of mechanics which will keep him safe. The only safe structure for the Chess Pieces is the box in which they are contained. On the other hand better players, relying on their vision and their judgment, enter into compromised positions which the student should avoid—at least approach cautiously. The Master, whose position is compromised, has that position because he is endeavouring to gain something or to hold something, or to defy the consequences of something which he thinks, to use a colloquialism, that he can get away with. The student, if he is experienced enough to grasp that a position is strained, or subject to stress—compromised in some way, will proceed more cautiously ; and he will avoid the kind of situation in which he has to leave in being masked batteries, dangerous pins, etc. He will not, without great thought, leave a Piece to be recaptured for any length of time. That is the kind of situation to be careful of, because the opponent may be able to use that Piece sacrificially. Your Piece that the opponent has in hand is a Desperado. (That term is also applied, for no good reason, to either player's Piece which is apparently blocking his line of attack and which can be sacrificed in order to gain a tempo.) More fundamentally, it is important not to play a line in which you will have to spend a number of moves restoring safety, restoring the equilibrium, while your opponent proceeds with his game.

To put the matter shortly, it is wise to avoid any tactical compromise, unless your opponent is worse compromised. Avoid looseness in a position ; also avoid tensions and stresses. Avoid loss of time. Some of the tactical possibilities described above are the features that constitute strain and stress.

But more important than any rules enabling one to judge whether one's position is safe or dangerous, is the general principle laid down above that the Chess player must endeavour to see the consequences of what he does. The Chess player must keep within his depth. If Chess is a cold bath for the mind (as a distinguished amateur has described it), then it also has analogies to swimming. In Chess, as in swimming, it is important to keep within one's depth; it is also hard to know what that depth is. What the reader can see from examples is the kind of whirlpool to avoid. Experience will make him conscious of the dangerous waters and the relatively safe shallows. It will also teach him to keep swimming.

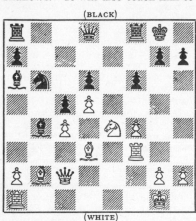

(BLACK)

(WHITE)

DESPERADO PIECE.

The Knight gives itself away to clear two lines.

1. Kt to Kt5, P × Kt.
2. B × P Ch., K to R1.
3. B × KtP Ch., K × B.
4. Q to Kt6 Ch., K to R1.
5. R to R3, Q to Q2.
6. B to Kt8 Ch., Q × R.
7. P × Q wins.

Once again, let it be stated, one cannot play Chess under guarantees of security. You have to move forward. If you are swimming correctly, there is no reason to suppose that the waves will easily overwhelm you. Chess is a dangerous game, not a safe game. If your position is reasonably well developed you should not be afraid of becoming involved in a struggle. Indeed you must seek it, as Lasker did against Marshall. When Marshall's play lacked incisiveness, Lasker attacked and won. To adopt the metaphor of combat, in Chess your forces are joined with your opponent's as in a duel or wrestling bout, and you cannot escape him by doing nothing, nor can you easily disentangle yourself. In Chess as in war the maxim is " engage the enemy." If he is developing you too must develop, and at the same time limit his development. If he is not developing, move aggressively against him. When you are doing that you may be embarking on an undertaking of which you cannot see all the consequences. What is important is to see that, in the position which you can see ahead, your affairs seem to be in good order. If you cannot see that, then do not start the operation.

To recapitulate, the essence of tactics is finding effective moves, undertaking effective operations. Those things have to be seen. Awareness of the possibilities of the Pieces will make you better at seeing the possibilities with some degree of completeness. In addition some elementary arithmetic and common sense will always help your thinking. One of the great features of Chess is the need for doing as much as can be done with what force is available. Therefore, be economical of material and of time. But above all of time. Do not do in two moves what you can do in one. If you can alter the order of your moves so as to bring about a certain situation in three moves rather than four, then play it that way. It is nearly as bad in Chess to lose a tempo as to lose a Pawn. To lose two tempi against a good player is to invite destruction. In the relative developments, when forces are involving themselves with each other, the speed is a function of the total energy that is being exerted. If therefore, you can save a move, or cause your opponent to lose a move, you have, as it were, advanced a step further, thrown forward a little more weight than your opponent. If you think about it you will realize that many of the advantages that are involved in batteries, forks, etc., consist in gains of time. You are doing more than your opponent can cope with in the time at his disposal. It is reasonable to play on the assumption that if you keep pace with your opponent you will not incur disadvantage. Therefore, conserve tempo. It does not, of course, pay to gain a tempo at the cost of dislocating your position. The reader will see examples of the doubtfulness of some gains of tempo in the chapter on Openings. Again, when a position has crystallized, it may be that time matters less; the processes are clear, and extra precautions can be taken, preparations made, without detriment. The decision in such circumstances is a strategic one. But in general it is safe to say that the player who gains time gains an advantage.

How Far Chess Players See

The consideration of some practical processes brings us to a question frequently heard among beginners, rarely heard among good players ; how far does a good player see ? Good players know this question to be unanswerable in terms of number of moves. Everything depends on the position. Some positions are, so to speak, opaque ; the short range is hard to see. Typical of this is any situation in the openings where Pawns can capture each other and there are great varieties of recapture. Or it may be desired to advance a Pawn to K4 or Q4, and there are so many possible lines, most of them short range, that the effort of exhausting them is considerable ; and there may be one variation which has to be followed a long way. Other positions are more translucent. The possibilities are fewer or more logical, are visible further ahead and are not hard to follow. Many Chess positions have aspects of both translucence and opacity. Most of the variations are easy ; one is hard. That makes the whole position hard. Again we have seen that any position can be characterised by the possibility of a cleverness which, ex hypothesi, is hard to see.

(BLACK)

(WHITE)

White to move.
Advisable is:
1. R to QKt1.
1. P to Q7 is wrong,
   because of 1 . . .
   R x P.
(1. K to B6 is not
   bad.)

Of the phases of the game, it may be said that in the end game one sees a greater number of moves ahead than earlier in the game, because much of it is the counting of Pawn moves and King moves. On the other hand endgames may be extremely difficult, because clevernesses on an empty board are harder than on a crowded Board, if only because one expects them less. Here is a not very hard point of order. The player who has relied on forcing his opponent to give Rook for Pawn is surprised to find that he has done it at the wrong moment.

In the endgame, and in the transition to the endgame, what one is looking for may be a method rather than an immediate line of play: what Pawn structure is being aimed at ; how that Pawn structure can be exploited. The execution of the process—a break-through by Pawns—may be long delayed ; but it need not be difficult to grasp.

Also at this stage of the game one encounters short specific problems that are not hard, though they involve accuracy.

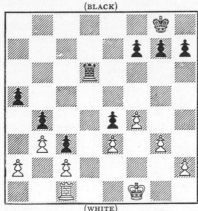

(BLACK)

(WHITE)

White to move.

For example in the diagram position your opponent's Rook is threatening to play havoc among your Pawns. If you panic and start throwing your Pawns forward your opponent will win. But you have a neat resource, you simply move your King to K1. Now if your opponent's Rook comes to Q7, you can play R to Q1 forcing exchanges, because if he takes your Pawn you can mate him. That is not hard to see. What, however, may be hard to see is this same move when you are looking at it from the beginning of a long middle-game process, in which Pieces are to be exchanged and the whole game simplified. And it often happens that a Master wins a game by a reduction of all the forces and an entry into the endgame with the power to gain an important tempo, or seize an important point, with the aid of some cleverness or other ; after which the win follows by careful exploitation of what has become a permanent advantage.

In the middle-game what the good player requires to see is not so much a number of moves as a number of stages. He sees quite a long variation up to a position where some other operation may be starting ; and that other operation has to be followed ; and that operation may work itself out into a situation where something else starts. What makes these analyses difficult, apart from following clearly all the exchanges and removals of pieces, is the intrusion of the unexpected— a manoeuvre which gives a different twist to the game. A good example is the position in the following diagram, reached between Euwe and Lasker at Zurich in 1934. Euwe had seen quite a long way, but had failed to appreciate the effect of Lasker's Queen sacrifice—or had taken it for granted that the loss of the Queen could not be tolerated by his opponent.

(BLACK)

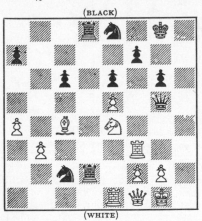

(WHITE)

EUWE—LASKER
A QUEEN
SACRIFICE
White has played
35. Kt to K4.
Black replies :
35. ... Q × P.
36. Kt to B6 Ch., Q × Kt.
37. R × Q, Kt × R (f6).
38. R to QB1, Kt to K5 with advantage.

Typical of the short range are the following positions from a game in an English Masters' Tournament (1947). In the first position White has just made the mistake of playing QR to QB1, allowing Black to play 14. ... Q to K3. Now 15. B to B3 for White failed to save a Pawn because of Kt × P 16. Kt × Kt P to Q4. Black is well co-ordinated enough to leave a Piece in his opponent's possession for a moment, in the certainty of winning it back with profit. Actually Black went further than this. There followed ; 17. B to Q4 P × Kt, 18. B × B P × B (sacrificing for the attack) 19. B × R Q to K6 Ch., 20. K to R1 P × P Ch. 21. K × P Kt to Q6, and we have a typical middle-game situation in which, opening complications, threat and counter threat, enriched by one or two ideas, have given Black an attack sufficiently good to justify him in leaving at least one Piece " in the air." The threat of R to Q1 is sufficient to give White no time to attempt to save the Bishop. The game proceeded as follows—22. R to B4 (not R to B3 because after Kt×P Ch. R×Kt Q×R the Bishop still cannot escape by B×P because of Q to K5 Ch; Black is already beginning the transition to an endgame with Pawns to the good). 22. . . . R×B, with ample compensation in middle-

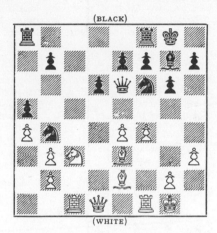

YANOFSKY
—AITKEN.

White to move.
Black is on the point of winning a Pawn.
1. B to B3, Kt × P.
2. Kt × Kt, P to Q4
(If 1. B to B4, P to Q4 is good for Black.)

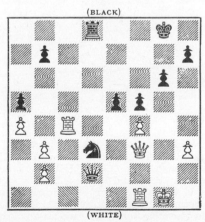

YANOFSKY
—AITKEN.
(contd.)

Strength of a Knight at the 6th.
If R to Q1, Kt to K8, etc.
If P × P, Kt × KP etc.

game and endgame advantages, for the Exchange. There followed 23. Q to Kt4 P to B4, 24. Q to Kt3 Q to Q7 Ch., 25. K to Kt1 R to Q1, 26. Q to B3 P to K4, giving another interesting position, which illustrates, among other things, the immense tactical advantage of a Knight established on a square like Q6 or K6. Note that White cannot free himself with R to Q1, because of the neat Kt to K8. This is the kind of cleverness that is apt to turn up in a promising position. The finding of it near to hand is Resource, or Ingenuity, as distinct from the vision which takes place when it is seen a long way ahead.

White played 27. P×P (the advance of the Pawn being too serious to contemplate) 27. . . . Kt×KP 28. Q to B4 Kt×R 29. Q×Kt Ch. Black has now won the Exchange back; and were he to play 29. . . . K to Kt 2, should win very easily because of his considerable endgame advantage, to say nothing of his control of a great many open lines. However, the diagram shows one of the curious little features of the

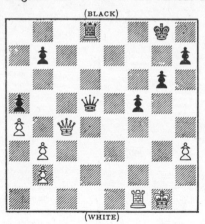

YANOFSKY
—AITKEN.
(concluded)
A PIT-FALL
(Crosspin)
R to Q1 wins for White.

geometry of the Chess Board, which even a very good Chess player (under fatigue) is apt to miss. Black played 29. . . . Q to Q4, giving the diagram position; and White with 30. R to Q1 wins. The point is that after Q×Q R×R Ch. gains a tempo, allowing subsequent P×Q and White is a Rook to the good. This cross-pin is highly amusing as a resource, and illustrates one of the very many difficulties that stand in the way of the player who is endeavouring to turn an advantage into a win. Not the least difficult of Chess operations is the winning of won games.

SOME VARIETIES OF ERROR

The fortunate winner of the game above described (Yanofsky, his opponent being Aitken, the Scottish Master) was the beneficiary of an equally amusing error some years earlier. In the diagram position from the Canadian Championship,

(BLACK)

(WHITE)

ALMGREN—
YANOFSKY

White to play.
1. P to QKt4, P ×
   P c.p.
2. K × P, R to Q5
   Ch., wins.

White (Almgren) can probably draw comfortably with Kt×P— and there are other moves. He played however, P to QKt4 ; and this is quite a good tactical idea. If P×P *e.p.*, then the idea is to capture the QP, and when the Knight's Pawn advances to stop it with the King and the Knight. This is a quite reasonable way of breaking up dangerous Pawns. However, Black plays P×P *e.p.*, White replies K×P, and is astonished when Black plays R to Q5 Ch. winning, because, after K×R P to Kt7 forces promotion.

From the other side of the world, here is a classic. In the next diagram position White (Rabinovitch) is clearly dominant, and can improve his position with an advance of the KRP.

Evidently Black's strategy has been defective. He plays, now, Kt to K5, in order to dislodge the White Queen. White allows himself to be dislodged into Q to R6, forcing mate. The idea, which the reader has already seen, is pretty but not difficult, and was probably entertained as a possibility by the

E

Russian Master before he allowed his Queen to occupy so exposed a square as Kt5.

(BLACK)

(WHITE)

RABINOVITCH
—GOGLIDZE.

Black played :
1. . . . Kt to K5,
and White replied :
Q to R6, winning.

Sometimes the oversight is actually a failure to see a quick win. One of the classics is the game Marco-Popiel. In the diagram position Marco, with Black, appears to be in great difficulties ; in fact he seems to be on the point of losing a Piece. For that reason he resigns. He had however a

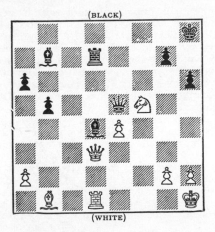

(BLACK)

(WHITE)

POPIEL—MARCO.

Black to play, re-
signed, but could win
by 1 . . . B to Kt8.

better move, viz : B to Kt8 winning. By failing to see this
Marco achieved the wrong kind of immortality.

Enough examples have now been shown to illustrate how easy
it is to overlook the unexpected over a very short range.
Over the longer range what happens is that play and counterplay produce positions which were terribly difficult to assess in
the distance. That follows from the fact that they are quite
difficult when one comes right up to them. Here is an example.
The diagram shows the kind of situation that can develop

(BLACK)

(WHITE)

White to move.

in a closely fought middle-game. Black has evidently sacrificed the Exchange in order to hold on to his strong though
isolated, centre Pawn, and in exchange for some open lines.
White has to move, and evidently has to think hard about
Black's threat of B to B3 Ch. White can play 1. B to K4 ;
but that is met by B to R5—a quite hard move to see even
at one move distance.

White cannot take the Bishop without landing into serious
trouble by Q × B Ch. followed by Q to K7. Failing that
capture, White must lose material. It follows that B to K4
cannot be played on the first move. The only other moves
to be considered are KR to K1 and QR to K1. The answer to
KR to K1 is relatively easy ; 1. . . . .   B to B3 Ch. 2. B to K4
B × B Ch. 3. Q × B Q × Q Ch. 4. R × Q Kt to B7 Ch. wins a Piece.
Therefore White must play 1. QR to K1, and that is met by, and
involves, some clever play thus, 1. QR to K1 B to B3 Ch.
2. B to K4 P to Q6. If now White captures the Queen, he

loses by 3. . . . P×Q 4. QR to K1 B×B Ch. 5. R×B Kt to B7 Ch. winning a Piece, because the Rook cannot leave the back rank.

If, then, on move 3 White tries, as he must, to guard the Bishop, he also has difficulty. Thus, 3. Q to B4 (an awkward move), Kt to B7 Ch. 4. K to Kt1, which looks safe because the Queen is still attacked; however, 4. . . . B×B wins, because if 4. Q×B Black wins a Piece, and if instead 4. R×Q Kt to R6 is mate.

On move 3, then, White has only one move Q to KKt2; and there follows 3. . . . B×B 4. Q×B Kt to B7 Ch. 5. R×Kt Q×R (on B7) and, remarkably, Black has an endgame win. This is quite hard to establish; but the point is that White is not going to be able to capture the dangerous QP. Thus if 6. Q to K3 Q to B7 7. R to QB1 P to Q7; and there are many other variations. Only a remarkable player, seeing, in middle-game complications, that he was likely to arrive after a few moves, at the diagram position just analysed, could be sure that White was incurring a loss.

Even without the intrusion of clever ideas a series of moves can be very hard to see through; particularly a series involving many exchanges.

Here is an example from the openings—

	White	*Black*
1.	P to K4.	P to K4.
2.	Kt to KB3.	Kt to QB3.
3.	B to B4.	P to Q3.
4.	P to B3.	B to Kt5.
5.	Q to Kt3.	Q to Q2.

Here White might be tempted to play for the win of material as follows:

	White	*Black*
6.	B×P Ch.	Q×B.
7.	Q×P.	K to Q2.
8.	Q×R.	B×Kt.
9.	P×B.	Q×P.
10.	R to B1 or Kt1.	Q×KP Ch.
11.	K to Q1.	Q to B6 Ch.

And now the game has burnt itself out into a draw, because if White tries to escape the perpetual check by K to B2, Kt to Kt5 Ch. wins the Queen; and that is something that could hardly be seen by the player meditating 6. B×P Ch. at a stage long before a diagonal, that was then full, had cleared itself of obstructive material.

Celebrated is the quick win of Reti over Tartakower, in

which the former took unexpected advantage of some experimental play by his very strong opponent.

	White	Black
1.	P to K4.	P to QB3. The Caro-Kahn, not nearly so bad as it looks.
2.	P. to Q4.	P to Q4.
3.	Kt to QB3.	P × P.
4.	Kt × P.	Kt to KB3. More usual is B to B4, the real object of the opening being to obtain mobility for the QB.
5.	Q to Q3.	P to K4. This is very enterprising and looks good ; of course, B to B4 had become impossible because of Kt × Kt Ch.
6.	P × P.	Q to R4 Ch. In order to win the Pawn back.
7.	B to Q2.	Q × P. With a dangerous looking pin. White, who could have prevented this by the retreat of the Knight on move 7, has evidently seen the remarkable sequel.
8.	0-0-0.	Kt × Kt. Probably assuming that White is relying on R to K1 to recapture the Knight. It is quite probable that Black has spent all his thought on the series of moves that follow R to K1. But he has completely failed to see his opponent's idea.
9.	Q to Q8 Ch. A thunderbolt.	
9.	...	K × Q.
10.	B to Kt5, double Check, with mate next move—a beautiful performance.	

The richest Chess is seen when cleverness follows cleverness ; when during, or after, a fairly logical process, an ingenious idea intrudes, and is met by an ingenious idea, and so on. That means that both players are exploiting the hidden resources of the board. Here is an example of some very nice Chess. After the opening moves 1. P to K4 P to K3, 2. P to Q4 P to Q4, 3. Kt to QB3 Kt to KB3, 4. B to Kt5 P × P, 5. Kt × P B to K2, 6. B × Kt B × B, 7. Kt to KB3 Kt to Q2, 8. B to Q3 P to B4, 9. P × P Kt × P, 10. B to Kt5 Ch. K to K2, 11. Q × Q Ch. R × Q, it seems that White wins a Piece by 12. Kt × Kt. But there is an answer 12. ... R to Q4 winning a Piece in return. Fairly straightforward. But is White now obliged to sit still and lose back his Piece ? He is playing with his opponent's material ! 13. Kt to R6.

Now follow the consequences. If Black captures the B, then Kt to B7 forks the Rooks ; if he captures the Kt, B to

B6. But the resources of Black's science are not exhausted —13. . . . B×KtP ; and if Kt to B7, of course B×R— But how does this bear on the problem ? What if White quietly plays R to Kt1 ? There lies the concealed cleverness.

White	Black
14. R to QKt1.	R×B.
15. Kt to B7.	B to B6 Ch.

and one of the Rooks that are forked gets away giving a tempo to the other in which to escape.

Very neat, but not conclusive ; because there is an answer that is equally neat—

White	Black
14. R to Kt1.	R×B.
15. Kt to B7.	B to B6 Ch.
16. K to K2.	R×R.
17. R×R.	R to Kt1.
18. Kt to R6. Forces a draw by repetition of moves.	

The player who saw all that, back on move 10, was only seeing eight moves. But he was seeing a great deal more than the man who, approaching an elementary Pawn ending, can see about 20 by simple counting of Pawn and King moves in reasonable order.

An opening that the reader has already seen (Ruy Lopez) is rich in examples of the scope for vision and error.

White	Black
1. P to K4.	P to K4.
2. Kt to KB3.	Kt to QB3.
3. B to Kt5.	P to Q3. (The Steinitz Defence.)
4. P to Q4.	B to Q2.

At this point the variation to be seen is 5. B×Kt B×B, 6. P×P P×P, 7. Q×Q Ch. R×Q, 8, Kt×P B×P— showing that the defensive move B to Q2 amounted to a counter-attack on the King's Pawn. In a small way, the logic of taking and retaking has been departed from and an idea introduced. To continue :

White	Black
5. Kt to QB3.	K1 to KB3. White has defended his own King's Pawn, and Black has attacked it again. White can pin this Knight of Black's, but if Black defends with 6 . . . B to K2 then when B×KKt there will be an additional Piece defending Black's King's Pawn. White therefore develops.
6. 0–0.	B to K2.
7. R to K1.	

Here we are presented with an object lesson on the need for vision in Chess. Black wants to Castle; and he feels safe in castling. His judgment tells him that castling is a logical developing move. But what about the attack on the Pawn? White's King's Pawn is twice guarded. Therefore if White wins Black's King's Pawn, Black cannot immediately regain it. But Black, not being entirely without vision, may have seen something. He may have seen that after the Exchanges 8. B×Kt B×B, 9. P×P P×P, 10. Q×Q R×Q, 11. Kt×KP, Black's B can take the White KP because the White Rook is tied to the back row. That is quite a perception; and the judgment that we have spoken of may support it, because it looks as if Black is at least as well developed as White.

However, to cut a long story short, the move 7. . . . Castles on the part of Black loses material. There follows 8. B×Kt B×B, 9. P×P P×P, 10. Q×Q QR×Q, 11. Kt×P, B×P (best, because the answer to Kt×P would be Kt×B and the possibility of the Check gains a tempo for the recapture of the Knight). And now 12. Kt×B Kt×Kt, 13. Kt to Q3 terminates Black's mating possibility; and leaves the White Rook attacking the Knight and pinning it against the unguarded Bishop.

But there is still a stage further to go—and this illustrates the process previously described. Black plays 13. . . . P to B4. This is answered by 14. P to KB3. Black plays 14. . . . B to B4 Ch.; there is nothing better; and obviously it creates a problem for White, because if he plays K to B1, then after Black retreats the Bishop to Kt3, White cannot safely capture the Knight. However, White has 15. Kt×B Kt×Kt, 16. B to KKt5; and now White wins the Exchange thus; 16. . . . R to Q4, 17. B to K7 R to K1, 18. P to QB4, and in order to save the Knight Black has to lose the Exchange.

At the end of it all Black has lost material. He is a victim of what is called, inaccurately, the Tarrasch Trap, because the Master Marco succumbed to this play against the great Tarrasch. What Marco was really a victim of was the intrusion into the game of ideas that he had not seen.

The so-called Tarrasch Trap is one of the most difficult pieces of Chess to see through unaided; and is one of the few variations whose existence justifies a player in learning some lines by heart. For the rest the line has other aspects of great interest. First it proves that on move 7 Black was forced to play P×P. That is a new conception of the word forced.

It was necessary, not through an immediate compulsion, but in a long perspective. In that sense the best-move (where there is a single best move) is always forced. Finally the line shows the strain that can be put on vision, even when the general principles of the game do not indicate the presence of stresses and strains.

TRAPS.

When an opponent makes a move that seems to lose a Piece, and you accept it and find yourself involved in a forcing sequence that leads to great loss, you may hear yourself said to have fallen into a trap. That is not a very accurate way of describing it. A good player rarely makes moves on the assumption that his opponent will make a mistake. He makes the objectively best move ; one variation arising from which may be unobvious because it involves a disregard of conventional values. You, who have not anticipated this, now find that your opponent had a strong move that you thought was not available, if indeed you thought about it at all. The move need not necessarily be sacrificial, but in so called traps it usually is. If, on looking at it, you find that you can refuse your opponent's sacrifice and have a very good game, then his move probably only amounted to a trap ; and he was playing bad Chess, because he was playing the man not the Board. Needless to say, if your opponent's sacrifice can be accepted to your advantage, then he has simply made an unsound sacrifice. Perhaps his position was bad and he was trying to bluff. Perhaps on the other hand, he was just playing badly.

A good example of the kind of play that is conventionally, and inaccurately, called a trap, is known to Chess players as " The Sea-Cadet " because in the operetta which bears that name these moves were executed by living Chess men.

	White	*Black*
1.	P to K4.	P to K4.
2.	Kt to KB3.	P to Q3.
3.	B to B4. More vigorous is 3. P to Q4, met by 3. . . . Kt to Q2. 4. P × P P × P in White's favour.	P to KR3. A very bad move. Moves of the Rook's Pawn for the purpose that animated this move (to prevent Kt to Kt5) are known as " provincial moves." Kt to Kt5 might, indeed, be the answer to Kt to KB3. But B to K2, followed by Kt to KB3 is good developing play.

White	*Black*
4. Kt to B3.	B to Kt5. A move which at this early stage is aimless—apart from the fact that the player of it missed the reply which this move allows. He intended to tie down White's Knight and is very surprised to discover that this very attempt enables the White Knight to move profitably.
5. Kt × P. A move made possible by Black's last, in conjunction with Black's inferior development. If the Pawn captures the Knight, White has Q × B, showing a profit of a Pawn. The capture of the Queen is bad because of what follows in the main line.	B × Q.
6. B × P Ch.	K to K2
7. Kt to Q5 Mate.	

Now a good commentary on the above play is afforded by the following lines where the same idea is available for White but is not so good—in fact the move loses.

White	*Black*
1. P to K4.	P to K4.
2. Kt to KB3.	P to Q3.
3. B to B4.	Kt to QB3. Obviously better than the provincial move.
4. 0—0. Not the most vigorous.	B to Kt5. Better than in the previous game. While not the best move, this pressure on the Knight is more useful now that White has Castled than it would be otherwise.
5. P to Q3. Quite good.	Kt to KB3.
6. Kt to QB3. Not the best. Better would be B to K3, allowing the Queen's Knight the option of Q2 in order to guard the King's Knight.	Kt to Q5. A good move, made possible by White's last, but not fatal. It creates some inconvenience for White on the King's side. White now requires to play very carefully in order to prevent a disadvantage from becoming a loss.
7. B to KKt5. Not the best. It is only reasonable on the assumption that here, and on the next move, White is expecting his opponent to play bad moves. This may be because White does not see the alternatives clearly ; or it may be that he is playing the man—setting a trap. Correct was 7. B to K3.	P to KR3. Good, but not the best—if this move were not reasonably good in itself it might be said to be setting a trap for the trapper. It is, however, a fairly good move, because, if the White Bishop retreats, Black has gained a tempo for a Pawn move which in this type of position may be useful. If White takes the

E*

White	Black
	Knight with the Bishop the Black Queen recaptures, with a winning attack on White's King's side. (Mate, or the gain of the Queen is threatened in the next few moves.) The text gives Black the advantage. Best, however, was B × Kt,
8. Kt × KP. The Sea-Cadet out of his depth. If Black takes the Queen, there follows, of course, B × P Ch., K to K2, Kt to Q5 Mate. Very pretty, but in Chess prettiness is not enough. White has overlooked or ignored a simple answer in his preparation of this move.	followed by Q to Q2. P × Kt. With advantage. Evidently White can do nothing. If Q × B, Kt × Q, B × Q, R × B and Black is a Piece to the good. If, instead, B × Kt, B × Q, B × Q, R × B, R × B, Kt × BP and Black holds considerable positional advantage.

The above example shows at once the possibilities that exist in Chess for disregarding the obvious formal values of the Pieces, and it also shows that that in turn is insufficient. What is necessary is clear vision of all the sequences, including moves which would be unexpected to conventional players; also moves which can be unexpected to unconventionally-minded players.

Here is a well-known opening variation with a move that may be described as a trap rather than an objectively good move.

White	Black
1. P to K4.	P to K4.
2. Kt to KB3.	Kt to QB3.
3. B to B4.	Kt to Q5. Clever, but not good. The correct answer to it is probably P to QB3 with gain of tempo. But Black has given White a scope for error.
4. Kt × P. A mistake.	Q to Kt4. Unexpected, because it ignores a threat, and illustrative of the Queen's power to make two divergent attacks.
5. Kt × BP. A desperate effort to win some material. B × P Ch. is no better because after K to Q1, White simply has another piece misplaced. Possibly 5. Kt to Kt4 allowing Black to play P to Q4 is the best of many evils. White may emerge with 2 Pawns for a Piece.	Q × KtP.
6. R to B1. Forced.	
7. B to K2.	Q × KP Ch. Kt to B6. Mate. Another interesting example of Smothered Mate.

Now, in that line of play, we saw that Kt to Q5, though clever, was not really good because P to QB3 deprives it of all point and gains time for the opponent. There is, however, one opening variation where this move Kt to Q5 is a good move.

White	Black
1. P to K4.	P to K4.
2. Kt to KB3.	Kt to QB3.
3. B to B4.	B to B4.
4. P to QKt4. The Evans Gambit, a famous opening of British invention, which allows a Pawn to be captured in exchange for gain of tempo. Many brilliancies emerged from this opening in the 19th century. It gives a hard and interesting game to both sides.	B to QKt3. Declining the Gambit. Although there is much to be said for accepting the Gambit and fighting to retain the Pawn, the text, favoured by Dr. Lasker, is undoubtedly a safe line.
5. P to Kt5. Apparently forcing the gain of a Pawn (KP).	Kt to Q5.

Now, if White plays Kt × KP, he falls victim to the disaster that starts with Q to Kt4.

The difference between Kt to Q5 in this variation and Kt to Q5 in the previous example is that here Kt to Q5 is an eminently reasonable move to save the Knight, and possibly to exchange Knights without loss of tempo, because White has used two tempi to get his Queen's Knight's Pawn up to Knight's fifth, where it is not very useful.

It may be mentioned, also, that whereas a player will think twice about taking the Pawn that is offered to him in the variation that we call the trap, he will find the danger harder to see when the move Kt to Q5 has some obvious other reason such as escaping from capture. Psychologically, the point of a sacrifice is hard to see when the player to whom it is offered thinks that his opponent is being compelled to give up the Pawn or Piece as the case may be. This fact does not amount to an encouragement to disguise one's traps, but as a warning to look for concealed dangers in lines that appear to be nothing more than logical. It is easy to be misled by the obvious "reason" for a move. What matters about a move is its consequence. The player who can see the unexpected consequence in the midst of logical processes may be said to have imagination.

Traps, in general, do not need learning. Most of them amount to short clear variations.

E.g. In the Lopez it requires little skill not to fall into the Noah's Ark Trap.

White	Black
After—	
P to K4.	P to K4.
Kt to KB3.	Kt to QB3.
B to Kt5.	P to QR3.
B to R4.	P to Q3. Steinitz Deferred.
5. P to Q4 is only playable as a Gambit, because after—	
5. ...	P to QKt4.
6. B to Kt3.	Kt × P.
7. Kt × Kt.	P × Kt.
8. Q × P. Loses a Piece.	
viz:	
8. ...	P to QB4.
9. Q to Q5.	B to K3.
10. Q to B6 Ch.	B to Q2.
11. Q to Q5.	P to B5.

—a short and easy range of moves.   Or in the Albin Counter Gambit,

White	Black
1. P to Q4.	P to Q4.
2. P to QB4.	P to K4.
3. P × KP.	P to Q5.
4. P to K3 is unwise, because of 4 ...	B to Kt5 Ch.
5. B to Q2.	P × KP.
and then if:	
6. B × B.	P × BP Ch.
7. K to K2.	P × Kt (making a Kt) Ch.

The reader may also be reminded of the variations given in the paragraph on Gambits.   There is nothing in these that normal vision should find opaque.

For the rest, it should be obvious that traps, properly or improperly so called, are not peculiar to the opening.   If the reader will refer back to the Fenton and Potter ending, he will appreciate that if, in that line of play, White promotes to a Queen, he is falling into a trap of sorts.   That actually happened in the game.   It was Lasker who discovered the winning move.   But, as has been pointed out, where Black's play is the best in any event (as here) the word trap is out of place.   More consciously a trap is the effort to procure a Stale-mate in the following position where the player with the inferior force does not adopt the logical defence, which, as it happens, fails, but plays so as to give his opponent an oppor-tunity for an error that is not hard to make.   Traps of this type, whether coincident with the best play, or justified by desperation, are the only traps that a good player can be said to set. The proper Chess attitude is that one makes the move that is most adequate in the light of all variations.

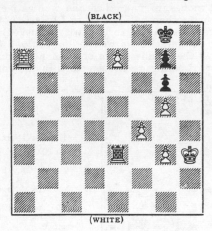

(BLACK)

(WHITE)

A TRAP

In answer to 1. R to R8 Ch. Black's normal move is K to B2, which, however, loses. He therefore tries 1. .... K to R2. If, then 2. P = Q, R × Q. 3. R × R gives Stalemate.

White's best plan is:

1.   K to R4.
2.   P to Kt4.
3.   P to B5.

LEARNING TO SEE.

The reader has now been shown a great number of clevernesses. He may have observed that some of these are, if not exactly similar to, yet suggestive of others. Ideas echo each other. The next diagram for example shows a different manoeuvre from the Bernstein-Kotov cleverness in Chapter II ; but the suggestion is that a player who has experienced a manoeuvre of one type will be ready to apprehend cognate ideas. Study, from examples, and more particularly by experience in play, of the peculiar geometry of the Chess Board makes one familiar with it ; and, given a general factor of perspicacity, the student can become adept at recognising and appreciating the unexpected possibilities. Hard concentration will also bring into being a certain receptivity and at that stage the player will find himself seeing ideas quite a long way ahead.

About the long variations that the reader has seen, there should be no despair. Very few pieces of Chess are as difficult as the Tarrasch Trap. Moreover not all games of Chess involve the same degree of strain. Some games are less combative than others, less closely contested at all stages, less dependent for their outcome on fine points finally perceived. We shall see more of this aspect of the Chess mind in later

Chapters. Meanwhile let it be said that since the processes of Chess are always rational, always explicable, there is nothing, even in the cleverest moves, to make them the prerogative of genius. Or, to put it another way, genius in Chess is not a revelation of mysteries, but a degree of clarity: achieved, as the saying goes, by perspiration as well as inspiration. To regard Chess vision as the manifestation of an innate faculty is to make the error of confusing the simple with the easy,

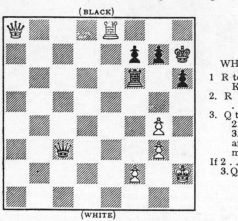

(BLACK)

(WHITE)

WHITE WINS.

1 R to R8 Ch., K to Kt3.
2. R × P Ch. If 2 ...P × R
3. Q to Kt8 Mate. If 2...K × R 3. Q to R8 Ch., and mate next move.
If 2 ... K—Kt4. 3. Q—Q5 Ch. et seq.

the logical with the innate. The mind does not work as directly as its mature capacities seem to indicate. To think that it does, whether in Chess or other processes, is to forget about the variety of forces that underlie the surface of the waterfall.

CHAPTER IV

INTRODUCTION TO STRATEGY AND TECHNIQUE

[The reader is advised to read this chapter in conjunction
with the Illustrative Games]

Obviously a great number of games of Chess are lost by
accident (gross oversight), or by mistake (e.g., the failure to see
a tactical point). And obviously there are many degrees of
error ranging from blunders, through failures of anticipation,
to the failure to discover some really fine, subtle possibility
or method of exploitation available to one side or the other.
At the higher level, one is inclined to say not that a player
has lost through a mistake, but that he has been outplayed
by an opponent whose interpretation of the positions that
arose in the game was better, and whose control of an intrac-
table material was subtler.

Even at that stage, it must be remarked that not all errors
lose. A normal game of Chess very rarely amounts to one
single movement of exploitation. The attack ebbs as well as
flows ; advantages are held and wrested. If that is so, then
why is it predictable, as it is, that the better equipped Chess
player will almost invariably win against the less well equipped,
even at a level where not many mistakes of tactics are likely
to be made ?

One answer consists in a type of error that we have not so
far considered, the strategic error—or, at a higher level, the
failure of one player to control a game dominated and made
difficult by the superior strategy of his opponent. Thus when
we find a position such as we have in the next diagram where
White can win easily, breaking open the position with B × RP, it
is clear that the whole method of play of one of the players
has been better than that of the other. It may conceivably
be the result of a long series of tactical manoeuvres, but it is
more likely that Black's idea of his method of defence has
been generally wrong, rather than that he has made particular
oversights.

In the companion diagram the situation is different. White
is attacking his opponent's King's side with a formidable
array of Pieces, but Black's position is well integrated and
tenable. It is evident that in order to accumulate material
for the attack White has allowed Pawns to be taken—he

WHITE WINS
B × RP
If 1. ... Kt × B
  2. R × KtP.
if 1. ... P × B.
  2. R × Kt Ch.
if 1. ... B × R.
  2. B to B4 Dis. Ch.

INSUFFICIENT ATTACK.
KB to B5 is met by Kt to Kt5.

sacrificed them for what may have seemed gains of tempo—but the expenditure has been ill advised, because when the attack is beaten off the opponent will have a superior endgame. Here again the strategy of one player has been better than that of the other. Of course he had to see a lot of specific tactical points well in advance. As has been said above, tactics and strategy are not separable. The coefficient of strategy runs through series of tactical manœuvres. But given a general plan which is sound, a general framework or layout of the game which is adequate to the processes, then one is not likely easily to become the victim of the kind of attack shown in the first diagram, or of the illusion of attack shown in the second diagram. It is also clear from the diagrams that the question is not one of being on the aggressive or being on the defensive. Both policies can be right and both policies can be wrong. It may be a good strategic decision to prepare an attack; it may equally be a good strategic decision to invite the attack. The question is particularly likely to arise when a tactical operation is being considered. Thus it may be wise to seize a Pawn and endeavour to hold it (or the equivalent) in the teeth of attack; or it may be fatal to do so. Sometimes that decision can be arrived at through clear analysis of all the variations. Sometimes it is a decision made mainly on general principles. But whether it is made for tactical reasons, or made on general principles, it is a strategic decision, because it governs the general pattern of the game as well as the tactical possibilities.

The next two diagrams show the different consequences

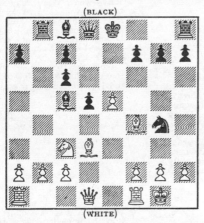

(BLACK)

(WHITE)

MIESES—THOMAS.
Black plays R × P
and loses.

that can follow Pawn-winning excursions. The first is from a game between that famous attacking player Mieses, and Sir George Thomas, one of the leading English Masters of his day. In the diagram position (arising from the Scotch opening) White has the kind of initiative that is normal in the King's Pawn attacks, but Black is sufficiently well co-ordinated not to fear any disaster. However, in order to acquire something out of the opening, so as to compensate for the slight inferiority of general development, or acting in the belief that he had nothing to fear, Black played 10. . . . R × P ignoring the superstition of the fatality that attaches to the QKtP. Also the move has some tactical point, because if White replies 11. Kt to R4 Black has the following pretty piece of play 11. . . . Kt × BP, 12. R × Kt, B × R Ch. 13. K × B, R to Kt5, forking two Pieces and probably winning. However, White had other ideas, and the play went as follows :—

White	Black
10. . . .	R × P.
11. Kt to K2. En route ror Q4.	P to KR4.
12. Q to B1.	R to QKt1. Perhaps inferior to R to QKt3.
13. P to QB3. White has judged that he can afford time to prepare.	B to Q2. In answer to the threat to the QBP, which will arise whether the Kt is left on Q4 or exchanged.
14. Kt to Q4.	Kt to R3. To protect the square KB4—which White may wish to occupy. Note that for the last few moves Castling has been dangerous for Black, because the Knight could always be driven to R3 and captured.
	Note the tremendous effect that is flowing from 12. Q to B1.
15. R to K1.	K to B1. Endeavouring to escape.
16. P to K6. A typical " break ing-up " move. It would have been better for Black to play 15 . . . B × Kt, followed by B to K3, blockading this dangerous Pawn. But then his Queen side Pawns would rapidly have fallen without compensation.	
16. . . .	P × P.
17. Kt × P Ch.	B × Kt.
18. R × B. A heavy Piece, using the open lines, is now in the attack. Black's open file is irrelevant.	Q to Q2. A desperate effort to stop the immediate gain of a Pawn (at least) by B × Kt ; also the move defends the QBP.
19. R × Kt. Sometimes the Exchange does not matter to a good player.	P × R.
20. B × P Ch.	K to K1.

White	*Black*

21. **Q to B4.** A beautiful quiet move bringing the Rook into play. Not every move in an attack has to be Check.

    Q to K3. The only move to save material. B to Q3, e.g., would lose the Rook in two moves by B to Kt6 Ch., etc. The next move holds everything for a very short moment and actually threatens to win a Piece.

22. **Q × P.** Very fine. If in reply R to QB1, then B to Kt6 Ch. picks up two Rooks.

    B × P Ch. Ingenious but inadequate. White is not obliged to take the Bishop and expose his King to R to Kt7 Ch.

23. **K to R1.**

    R to Kt7. As good as any. If R to Q1, B to KKt5 is fatal.

24. **B to KKt5.** Threatening Q to Kt7 followed by B to Kt6. Notice that Q to B2 for Black is met now by B to Kt6, a pretty pin.

    K to B1.

25. **R to KB1.** Immobilizing another Black Piece and, indeed, Black's entire force. Among other things B to R4 is threatened.

    K to Kt1. Unpinning the Bishop.

26. **B to B1.** A very pretty clearance of a square that may be required for the Queen.

    R × RP. The only move that does not lose the Bishop. R to K7 fails after a series of Queen Checks.

27. **Q to Q8 Ch.**   K to Kt2.
28. **Q to Kt5 Ch.**   K to B2.
29. **B to K3.**   Q to B3.
30. **Q × Q Ch.**   K × Q.
31. **B to Q4 Ch.** Resigns.

It is not claimed that Black's capture of the Knight's Pawn on move 10 made this debacle inevitable. But clearly Black was involved thereafter in difficulties. Had he succeeded in solving all his problems and surviving the attack without surrendering material, then Black could have claimed that the strategic decision was right. In view of what happened (the process was logical in a high degree) it may be said that the strategic decision was wrong. It was not so much a failure to see, because the distance was too far for normal Chess vision : it was rather a wrong choice of terrain, an ill-advised invitation to combat ; in other words a wrong strategic decision.

The next diagram shows a position from the second game between Lasker and Marshall, in which Lasker captures a Knight's Pawn and holds off the ensuing attack. That may have been an act of vision by Lasker, who, in his day, was capable of seeing very great lengths of tactical process. But however the decision was arrived at, it illustrates the possibility that the capture of a Knight's Pawn can in some settings be a good decision. If and when the tactical consequences are not immediately discernible, the decision has to be a strategic one. Again it is a decision to invite combat, or not to invite it, in a particular situation. That is typical of strategy as distinguished from tactics.

(BLACK)

(WHITE)

LASKER—
MARSHALL

White goes in for Q to Kt4 Ch., winning K Kt P, but after R to KKt1 (forcing Q to R6) survives the attack.

The next diagram shows the revenge of Thomas against Mieses, a decade later. This is less spectacular, but

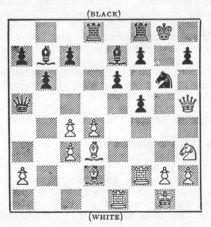

(BLACK)

(WHITE)

MIESES—THOMAS.

21. ... Q to R6 puts pressure on White's centre while he is attacking the King's side.
22. KR to K2, R × P.
23. P × R, Q × B, breaks up White's game.
There followed:
24. P to Q5, Q × BP.
25. P × P, P × P.
26. R × P, B to B4 Ch.
27. K to R1, Q to KKt5, with great advantage.

illustrates the exploitation of a wrong strategic decision. Mieses has committed himself to a King side attack. Thomas demonstrates that this was insufficient justification for leaving certain gaps in the position.

THE FUNCTION OF STRATEGY

Strategy is hard to define, because, as we have seen, the Chess player cannot divide his activities with a clear cut separation between the strategic and the tactical. The strategic decision is hard to abstract from specific lines of play, because no player is content to make a move on the strength of a general principle—if indeed there are any general principles concrete enough to be useful in Chess. It follows that strategy in abstraction is vague ; and the word is only meaningful to the player who has used his vision and found that vision is not enough.

At this stage the student will have discovered, from his experience of the Board, that vision in Chess is restricted by more than human stupidity. The reader has seen enough to realise that good players are not likely to exhaust the Board in their tactical analyses, because the nature of the Board is such that lines of play are apt to end in, or pass through, positions which are either too hard to analyse, or else seem not to require analysis. Psychologically, the foreground of clear vision fades into, is indeed suffused in parts by, the hazier blend of seeing and thinking which is judgment. The effort of concentration gives perhaps a wrong impression of the clarity of the human mind. As the limits of concentration are reached one becomes conscious that the mind economises its efforts ; indeed, that its operations are never as simple as they appear to be when clarity is achieved. When this is realised, then one appreciates that there is scope for, and there takes place, in Chess, activity other than, though impossible to isolate from, what we call pure vision. If any thought can be stated in general terms to help or guide vision, then that guidance gives us strategy to reinforce our tactics.

This aid is necessary, because of the difficulties of the Board, and because so often it would be wasted labour to try and work further through a position where one is reasonably satisfied that there is no danger, or too much danger, in that position, or that progress thereafter will be easy, or too difficult, as the case may be. And nearer to any immediate move there is scope for thinking, judging, and applying strategic notions in positions where clear tactical processes are not yet available. One function at least of strategy is that it equips a player to know what to do when there is nothing immediate to be done. Then one prepares; then one " over-protects " points likely to require defence later on; then one has regard to the general shape of the game; and the strategian differs from the unstrategic player in that he does not, at such a point, endeavour to force processes into the game for which the position is insufficiently developed, or is otherwise inadequate. Whereas the tactician knows what to do when there is something to do, it requires the strategian to know what to do when there is nothing to do.

Strategy, of course, has always existed in Chess and been known to good players. The difference between the players of today and previous generations of Chess players is that now the scope of strategy is known to be wider.

What may be called primitive, or elementary, strategy consists mainly in playing with a view to the endgame; thinking of the general frame of the game as constituted by the Pawn position, and so playing that the tactical efforts shall not result, after conflict, in a hopeless endgame. Modern players have more experience of the endgames, and of the methods and technique that the Masters have perfected. Consequently their appraisal of the endgame from a distance is better. But the difference is one of degree. Where the modern player is mainly superior is in his appreciation of the strategy of the earlier game, the opening and the early middle-game attack.

In the middle nineteenth century, when the Chess world was rich in players of great vision and tactical genius, this strategy of the early game was relatively unnoticed. It existed in a degree, but was particularly hard to isolate, or think about, because, in the kind of game that was played then, with rapid attacks succeeding through great gains of tempo achieved by sacrifice, or through the unbalancing of the position, the strategic skill that was required went naturally, and unobserved, with the capacity for gaining tempo, for achieving an unbalance, and for exploiting these things brilliantly. In that kind of play, the play of the more violent King's Pawn openings, the kind of development that was necessary was always seen as tactical necessity. Only when a greater number of players achieved tactical experience of a high order did the Chess world become aware of other factors in the game. It was the success of Steinitz against the more brilliant Anderssen and Zukertort that made the Chess world strategy-conscious.

SOME PRINCIPLES OF STRATEGY

The first principle of opening and middle-game strategy laid down by Steinitz illustrates excellently well what strategy is. This is the principle of the necessity for adequate development. The principle is that, given the capacity on the part of the players to see what is going on tactically over a reasonably good range, so that they do not make oversights, then tactical operations depend for their ultimate success upon the adequacy of preparation or development. The player whose Pieces are relatively well developed in comparison with his opponent's Pieces is more likely to succeed in an attack than his opponent, and much less likely to fail, when attacked, in achieving a satisfactory defence.

This is really a principle of causation. It amounts to the proposition that there are no miracles in Chess. The majority of successful and devastating attacks that appal their victims and dazzle the spectators are not thunders from a clear sky. It is a condition of their coming into being that adequate forces are available to be used. That does not mean that there should be plenty of Pieces lying about the Board. The Pieces must be functionally well placed ; and, incidentally, modern theorists have improved upon Steinitz by achieving a better notion of development ; effective placing rather than bringing the Pieces away from the back rank. A Piece on the back rank may be functionally better developed than a Piece in the centre of the Board. But, that being said, Steinitz was clearly right. If your Pieces are not adequately mobilised, then you cannot reinforce any expedition that you send out ; nor can you organise, when called upon, your own defence. This principle is easier to adopt in theory than to act upon in practice. The following short line illustrates the facility and speed with which a player who sees some of the tactical points of the game can be led by his ideas into disastrous ventures.

	White	*Black*
1.	P to K4.	P to K4.
2.	B to B4.	KKt to B3.
3.	P to Q4.	P to QB3. Not a good move. It aims at over ambitious play in the centre.
4.	P × P.	Kt × P.
5.	Kt to K2.	Kt × BP. Greedy. Of course the King does not re-take because of Q to R5 Ch. ; but there is a very good alternative.

	White		*Black*

6. O–O.   Kt × Q. A mistake. Necessary
                                     was B to B4, to which White
                                     can reply with B × P Ch. with
                                     advantage. The conclusion of
                                     the game is an object lesson in
                                     the unwisdom of a tactical
                                     excursion from an undeveloped
                                     position.

7. B × P Ch.   K to K2.

8. B to KKt5 Mate.

A worse tactician than the opponent of the late Captain
Mackenzie (the brilliant blind player who was White in this
short game) would not have fallen into such trouble. A
better strategian could never have allowed himself to embark
on such a venture, however clear or obscure his vision of
tactical possibilities. But if the reader will refer to the
chapter of illustrative games he will find a more surprising
example, where the great strategian himself, no less than
Steinitz, suffered, at the hands of the English Master Bird,
the consequences of departure from his own principles.
Steinitz, a brilliant tactician himself, was capable of the kind
of Chess in which the coefficient of strategy seems almost to
disappear (see his game against Von Bardeleben among the
illustrative games) and was capable of being misled into the
pursuit of clever tactical possibilities, in disregard of his own
teaching.

And here let it be explained that the principle of development is not a sort of copy book rule ; nor did Steinitz, in
stating it, invent something new. There were great players
before, and after, Steinitz, players like Morphy and Capablanca,
whose command of the Board was so great that their development was always adequate. To suppose from this that they
acted upon rules is to make the mistake, which Macaulay
ridicules, of supposing that great orators build their speeches
on the rules of grammar and rhetoric. The rules are regulative
principles, laboriously extracted by analysts from their study
of the great performances. What Steinitz imported into
Chess was a discipline, and himself was sufficiently great a
player at times to dispense with it, yet not great enough to
do so with impunity.

SPECIFIC PRINCIPLES

The principle of development being stated, it still remains
a question how to develop. Here too, Steinitz's researches
have been of the greatest utility. He laid it down that the
essence of a good development is control of the centre. Lasker

put the matter epigrammatically when he commented on a certain game that "this player is not well developed enough in the centre to be able to attack on the wings". And the converse was proved true by Steinitz, when, repeatedly in his match with Zukertort, he allowed his opponent to accumulate forces against his castled King, while himself engaged in other undertakings (the creation of weaknesses elsewhere in his opponent's position) knowing that his centralised forces would be adequate to beat off his opponent's eventual onslaught. Zukertort, be it mentioned, was sufficient of a strategian to appreciate the aggressive merits of the centre, (see his game v. Blackburne), but he tended to underestimate its defensive possibilities.

Modern theory and technique have modified and subtilised the conception of the centre ; but it remains true that a sound centre, of whatever type, is a safeguard for the wings. Thus, if you have a Knight situated at Q4, you are proof against the Greek gift sacrifice, the point being that the Knight can return to KB3 to control R7. That same Knight can work its way via K2, or KB5 to KKt3, in case the attack is upon the Knight's Pawn. Similarly a Queen at Q4 enjoys a big defensive range. So does a Bishop on Q3. There are usually squares to which these Pieces can go in order to defend wings. Moreover from the centre they can counter-attack the wings. And, again, a good centre means that the opponent's manœuvring space is limited, either because the holder of the centre is containing most of the opponent's forces in the opponent's half of the Board, or because, when the centre is blocked, the opponent cannot penetrate the closed lines. Then squares like KB4, QB4, etc., are good outposts for defensive and counter aggressive Pieces.

Now once the fact is grasped that reasonably good positions with well centralised Pieces cannot be stormed, then the tactician has to abandon his ideas of quick mating attacks, and must seek other objectives. The slow penetration of the centre is one such objective ; e.g., the pushing through of a Pawn to K5 or Q5 with threats, and the opening up of diagonals. Similarly the establishment of Knights on good squares from which they cannot be driven, is a good purpose to play for. K5 is a good point , K6 or Q6 even better if the Knight stationed there can be held in position.

Other objectives are the obtaining of open files for Rooks. If a Rook controls an open file it becomes very useful in the middle-game, and can be very destructive in the endgame. And there are lesser objectives of importance. Steinitz, and his pupil and conqueror Lasker, were exponents of the aggregation of minute advantages. These advantages might consist in such small matters as the doubling of opponent's Pawns, the isolation of Pawns, the acquisition of a little extra mobility for a Piece, etc. For these they campaigned tactically, leaving the major attack to wait, in the belief that after minor advantages had been acquired the major attack was more likely to be successfully carried out.

Again let it be made clear that Master play is not so slow that laborious undertakings at great length for small advantages occupy the whole of the play. The game is so well integrated that the major attack is always in contemplation. But the logic of the game now is that the attacker's threats include positional movements as well as attacks on Pieces and Pawns ; and the defender is more conscious of the concessions he may be making in moving Pawns. Consequently, more then ever now, the Pawn structure is important ; and the possibilities of the endgame are more constantly present to the majority of players than they were. It follows that only a player who is convinced that his middle-game attack is going to succeed, for strategic and tactical reasons, will disregard the endgame. On the other hand the game is too dynamic for players not to compromise their endgame framework. On the same reasoning a player cannot hope to control every stage of the game, holding only strategic advantages, and having no strategic defects. Players must accept as a postulate of the game the belief that advantage sets off advantage. There is a principle of compensation in Chess. You may have a Bishop against a Knight ; on the other hand you may have some Pawn weaknesses. You have an open file ; your opponent also has an open file. Tactically you must see whether or not you can achieve some exploitation, or can be the victim of some exploitation ; but failing the perception of these things, you must be content if the disadvantages are shared.

Most players achieve a feeling for the balance of the position. This helps to form the judgment. One knows whether one has lost time relatively to one's opponent. One knows, or judges, whether one is generally more restricted or less restricted in movement than one's opponent. If both sides are not wasting time, i.e., not going in for manœuvres that are irrelevant to the progress of the game, or not letting themselves be forcibly retarded in development, by the awkward placing of Pieces ; and if one's own development and one's own power of movement, and one's own few technical advantages, seem to be not less than one's opponent's and not more, then there is in being a balance of position which means that the issue of the game is still open. And on consideration, it is logical, in the light of the margin of draw described in the first chapters, to expect that two sets of forces interpenetrating should bring about and maintain a permanent, though unstable, equilibrium.

When the forces are seriously unbalanced in favour of one side, then there is victory. Thus, given a bigger control of space and a saving of tempo, and no noticeable defect in material, you are justified in expecting to win the game by the exercise of reasonable pressure. A great many Chess victories are strategically explicable in those terms. One player has his forces well organised, mobile, with plenty of squares at his disposal; the other has not used his time so well. His Pieces are cramping each other, are short of space; and he has too many difficulties of development, for purely defensive purposes, to be able to establish any kind of attacking formation. But in a well balanced game it will probably be the case that each player is exerting some pressure against his opponent. If the strategy has been wise, and the tactical play equally good, it is improbable that either side can achieve anything decisive. Then, as material gets exchanged, the game may resolve itself into a Pawn endgame, where each side has to prevent the other from promoting Pawns, or when, alternatively, neither side can be prevented from promotion. Results as far ahead as this are hard to predict in the middle-game; but in general good Chess produces a large percentage of draws.

Victories are achieved in good Chess when the unbalance proves to be decisive, either in the middle-game or the end-game. Very fine points indeed may be sufficient to make a middle-game attack decisive. There may just be available a combinative possibility, which is either carried out, or which, being apprehended by the opponent, compels him to abandon his own projects in order to defend. Then he will have lost time, and his position will be relatively disintegrated. Similarly a very fine point may determine whether the endgame into which the position ultimately resolves itself gives winning chances to one side or the other. On the whole, it may safely be said that if there are winning chances, either in the middle-game or the endgame, it will be because better tactics and/or better strategy have given one player a better control of the total situation. If in the play neither opponent has missed any important tactical point, and if neither player has allowed the other to consolidate any really dangerous strategic advantage—i.e., if neither position suffers a serious weakening—then a draw should be the result.

In the old days when players relied more on their capacity to exploit a slight gain of tempo or a slight advantage in space, then the typical battle was of the Anderssen-Dufresne—or (better balanced) the Zukertort-Blackburne type (see illustrative games). Each player was planning something and carrying it out. The winner was he whose plan could be carried out the more quickly. That kind of Chess is also played to-day, for the reader must appreciate that in every period the styles and talents of players differ, and even at a more advanced stage players recapitulate in their own development, and as part of the development of the Chess world, stages typical of earlier periods ; and always, of course the tactical possibilities may cause any player to depart from the accepted strategy of his period. But allowing for all that, it may be said that the modern player does not embark so easily on his own attack in disregard of his opponent's attack. There tends to be a better general preparation of the whole position ; and the result usually is that neither side achieves a striking preponderance early in the game. When battle is joined it is because one player or the other is determined to complete his development, to make himself free, to occupy a square important in the integration of his game. Then the attack and counter-attack is likely to flare up.

Again the old game was more combative in that players were not only ready to embark on attack quickly, but they were also prepared to face an attack in order to hold sacrificed material. That was a strategy of sorts ; and the strategy of the more cautious players of the older period was to prevent themselves from being attacked. That method was apt to provide advantages, as well as to create dangers, for the good attacking player. Nowadays, strategic experience makes most players chary of undergoing a heavy sacrificial attack in order to maintain the material sacrificed. But they will defend themselves against an attack of reasonable weight in exchange for very slight compensating advantages, if they are satisfied with their general development. That is part of the tendency to attack and to defend, in order to achieve or maintain the smaller advantages. And this again is part of the general recognition that in good Chess overwhelming victories cannot be expected ; that the game is a war rather than a single battle. With that goes the recognition of the Steinitzian truth that what matters in the long run is the framework of the game. Defects in the Pawn structure that seem slight in the middle game bring about defeat in the end game more certainly than an aggressive formation brings about victory in the middle game. What may be added to this is that the framework of the game, even in the middle-game, is more of a factor in victory than the capacity to produce clever tactical threats which, if seen by the opponent, can be refuted. An excellent example of victory, through the better placing of Pawns and Pieces in the frame of the game, is to be found in the game Szabo-Denker in the illustrative games. Some winning attacks can be analysed in order to show that victory followed the lines that a strategian or tactician could expect ; the Szabo-Denker game shows victory more consciously and intentionally gained by technique. Even more striking is the game Nimzowitch-Sämisch ; while for a more understandable strategy the game Lasker-Alekhine (New York 1924) is hard to improve upon.

TECHNIQUE.

If Steinitz made Chess players conscious of the general physics of Chess, modern Masters have developed its methods of engineering ; and in doing that they have also shown the physics of the game to be subtler than was thought by Steinitz's immediate successors. Thus two developments have taken place in Chess in this century. Players have become more conscious of the method of obtaining and holding small advantages. But, more important, they have acquired a better conception of the nature of some advantages and disadvantages. In consequence they have developed important specific methods of playing ; methods which are too concrete to be classed as general principles, and yet, since they belong to the frame of the game, are not apprehended the same way as tactical perceptions. They constitute what, for want of a better word, can be called points of technique. Technique is a middle term between strategy and tactics. It cannot be said that modern Chess has become technological. The vision of modern players is too rich for that. But certainly the modern player is better equipped with knowledge of the technical processes of the game, even if he is no more expert than his predecessors in carrying them out.

POINTS OF MODERN STRATEGY AND TECHNIQUE—
THE CENTRE

From the days of Zukertort onwards players have consciously valued the centre. The King's Gambit itself, the most violent of the openings, starts by gaining a better control

of the centre; and Zukertort saw the possibilities of the
Queen's Gambit for that purpose. For many years, and at
the opening of the twentieth century (after the death of
Steinitz) the conception of the good centre was the centre held
by one's two centre Pawns. Evidently the unrestrained control of the centre by two Pawns can be very effective. Thus
a King's side attack can be launched by the advance P to K5,
opening a line for the Bishop or Queen against R7, driving
the defending Knight from its KB3, and often allowing the
attacker to sacrifice a Piece on that important square in order
to establish a Pawn there as part of a mating attack, or in
order to open the Knight's file, etc. Similarly, the advance
of a Pawn to Q5 can open another diagonal against the King's

(BLACK)

(WHITE)

ATTACK ON THE
CENTRE.

side and can give difficulties to other defending Pieces. Also
the Pawns can be deadly in a central attack, as in the Bird-
Steinitz example. All this is true. But it is not the whole
of the story. Notice for example that if a Pawn goes to K5 a
defending Piece can occupy its Q4. That may create a diagonal
attack; or a Knight may be able to settle there, and to move
from there to its KB5, K6, QKt5, etc. (Incidentally, these
excursions of Knights are quite a feature of modern opening
play, making the game look wilder than it is.) Similarly, the
advance of the P to Q5 gives the defender a square at his K4.
Now if the possession of two centre Pawns has been achieved
through the exchanging of Pawns so that the player with the
central Pawns is lacking one or two Bishop's Pawns, then the

occupancy of the interstitial square is likely to be permanent. If, on the other hand there are Bishop's Pawns in being, then if they move to drive out, say, an occupying Knight, that Knight can, at KKt5 or QKt5, embarrass Bishops at K3 or Q3 respectively, and can have other attacking chances (against B7, R7, etc.). And it requires a great deal of preparation before this can be prevented. Moreover, moves like P to KR3 and P to QR3 in distant support of the centre may also create weaknesses or lose time.

In other words a centre formidable in appearance can be hollow. Modern openings calculated to exploit the potential hollowness of the centre include the Grunfeld Defence and the King's Indian Defence. These are given in the next

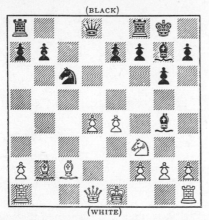

(BLACK)

(WHITE)

HOLLOW CENTRE
(Grunfeld's Defence).

chapter. And it will also be seen that the centre can become hollow in many other openings such as the Moller, the King's Gambit Declined, etc. Conscious of this, many players play slower forms of the Queen's Pawn openings, delaying the pressure on the centre. Then there comes a struggle for K4; and that square may have to be occupied by a Piece, which may be good, or the Pawn on K4 may be blocked by the opponent's P to K4, and that in turn introduces notions that will require to be separately considered.

The idea of blocking the centre is one instance of the general idea of *Blockade*. A dynamic Pawn, that is to say a Pawn that can advance dangerously, like Bird's centre Pawns, or like Steinitz Queen's Pawn which advanced against Von

Bardeleben, or Zukertort's Pawn that advanced to open a diagonal, or a Pawn that can sacrifice itself on a square where it can cause a restriction of the opponent's movement or force the opening of a line, etc., a Pawn like this requires to be blocked. It is important for the opponent to have a

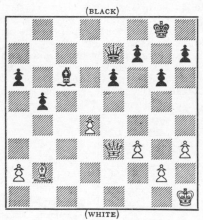

(BLACK)

(WHITE)

NEED FOR BLOCKADE.

If Black does not play B to Q4, P to Q5 gives White an attack and freedom.

Pawn or a Piece (preferably a light Piece) on the square immediately in front of it. That is a Blockade. And the line of thought can be carried further. The blockade of an isolated Pawn is very good preparation for an attack on that Pawn. Otherwise it can advance and sell itself dearly. The modern technician will therefore not hasten to attack an isolated Pawn. If the attack is not immediately decisive he will prepare by putting a Knight or a Bishop on the square in front of it, especially if it is a centre Pawn. Later he will double Rooks behind the Knight, perhaps develop a Bishop on the diagonal of the Pawn. He may even add defences to the square that the blockader is occupying. Later, when the blockader moves, the attack on the isolated Pawn is likely to be decisive.

The notion of blockade, which can be generalised to include the obstruction of the paths of other Pieces (e.g., a chain of Pawns on the same diagonal as a hostile Bishop, or blockade by a Pawn, blocking a diagonal), is very important in Chess—but is particularly relevant to the theory of the Centre. If the opponent's Pawns can be anchored by an interstitial Pawn or Piece, in the position K4Q5, or Q4K5, then though they have their strength, which may be considerable if there is an attack available, yet they also have their weaknesses. They allow the occupancy of the adjacent square on the Bishop's file. Thus, if your opponents Pawns are at Q5 and K4, and you have a Pawn on K4 guarded by a Pawn at Q3, you may be able with the aid of a move like P to QR4 (the tactical effect of which has been seen) to establish a Knight at QB4

(BLACK)

(WHITE)

A STUDY IN
BLOCKADE.
Black's Knight and
KP are holding White
immobilized.
Black wins. B to
KR3 wins a Pawn at
least.

(BLACK)

(WHITE)

BLOCKADE
The Knight on Q4
blockades the iso-
lated Pawn.

which is a very good square. Also you can break up the centre by an eventual P to KB4, incidentally opening your KB file. You can also break the centre by P to QB3, a well-known method of winding up a hostile Pawn chain. You may create by this a weakness at your Q3. Whether that is bad depends on the position. If P×QBP you may be able to liquidate your own QP by a later advance. If the opponent leaves you to capture, then his advanced Pawn is doing both good and harm to your backward QP, but your KP is then very good and with the aid of P to KB4 you will achieve an aggressive centre. (Break-up points can be on any file.)

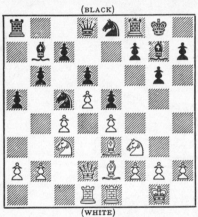

(BLACK)

(WHITE)

A BLOCKED
CENTRE
(Favourable to Black)

The blocked centre and the hollow centre are alike vulnerable to Bishops on the long diagonals. In the case of the blocked Pawn or Pawns it is quite surprising that a Bishop behind its own blocked Pawn is nearly as strong as a Bishop directed against a hostile blocked Pawn. Thus suppose you have a Pawn on Q4, and your Bishop on QKt2. If you later manage to place a Pawn or a Knight on K5 and that is captured, your Bishop's diagonal is lengthened and then there may be a tactical operation possible against your KB6. Also there are other ways in which a diagonal is likely to open : exchanges on your QB4, etc. That is one of the reasons why Fianchetto Openings are quite popular. The Bishop's action on the long diagonal can be directly good ; but if it is delayed it may also be good ; and if the diagonal becomes hopelessly blocked, then the Bishop can find another diagonal.

Incidentally, that involves another feature of modern strategy. The modern player is more apt to recognise when tempo has ceased to be of the essence of the game, i.e., when the position has crystallised and a re-grouping of Pieces is more important than the time consumed in carrying out the re-grouping, and not likely to be penalised. That principle also makes it possible for players to go in for manoeuvres such as the following; allowing the Knight at QB3 or KB3 to be driven back on to the back rank so as to re-emerge in a different direction. Thus, the KKt may go to K1 and emerge at KKt2. The QKt may go to Q1 and then KB2, or back to QKt1 and out via Q2 to K4 or QB4. Modern strategy accepts this process of *Reculer pour mieux sauter*, and it is part of the technical equipment of all good players.

(BLACK)

(WHITE)

A FLUID CENTRE.

Another treatment of the centre that is worth noting is not to try to occupy it with Pawns but to keep a control over it with Bishops and Knights. Typical is the Queen's Indian Defence, or the Nimzo-Indian, in which Black plays Kt to KB3, P to K3, B to QKt5 (pinning the QKt and perhaps exchanging it) then P to QKt3 and B to Kt2, and possibly thereafter Kt to K5 followed by P to B4. Then, even without any blocking movement, the control is a good one. This is a fluid centre for the defender; and of course a centre can be fluid both aggressively as well as defensively.

Aggression usually involves Pawn pressure as well as Piece pressure in the centre. But Nimzowitch has taught the Chess world not to regard Pawns in the centre with Fetichism. Nimzowitch has shown that an attack can be good, particularly against the French Defence, if you allow your Pawn on Q4 to fall, and then allow your Pawn on K5 to be exchanged. All that matters is to have the control of the square K5 by some Piece or other. And that control is very helpful in the mounting of a King's side attack. Of course, it should be added that this, too, can become unimportant in the light of other tactical considerations.

(BLACK)

A GOOD CENTRE for White's attacking purposes.

(WHITE)

In general, then, modern technique, and modern improvements in the strategic equipment, have made a great change in the appearance of the Chess Board during the opening and early middle game. Often the centure is left completely vacant while Fianchetto developments are taking place, and approaches to the centre are made by the Bishop's Pawns before the centre Pawns. Eventually centre Pawns tend to be thrown forward, even if only to be exchanged. But more regard is had to the eventual disposition of Pieces ; and Pieces tend to be placed where they are useful functionally, on squares where they have the most scope (not necessarily immediate threats) or where they can exercise a pressure that is relatively permanent. Again, as has been said, modern players do not object to re-grouping. Indeed, in a famous game, Bogoljubow, who had his Bishop on KB1 and Pawn on K3, with an outlet on the diagonal to QR6, played P to KKt3 in order to have his Bishop on the longer diagonal, even though while doing that he enabled his opponent to pin his Knight on KB3 against the Queen, and, generally, seemed to be wasting time. The important thing was the re-grouping and it was one of a series of manœuvres which brought him victory in that game and in an important tournament.

But in case the reader receives any false impression let it be emphasised that, in general, time is too important to use in giving scope for alternative developments. Before you use time like that you must be clear on all the opponent's tactical possibilities.

Tactics are still the essence and reality of the game. Nor do modern developments make tactics less important. What has happened has been the diminution of uncontrolled play characterised by excessive reliance on isolated threats which, however clever, are not sufficient to determine the game if the opponent sees them.

But at the same time the development of strategy involves the need for good tactical equipment, because strategic purposes can involve some quite extraordinary placings of Pieces, giving scope for tactical exploitation and combative Chess. How two sound strategians can find themselves quite early engaged in speculative combat is illustrated in the game between Capablanca and Fine played in the Avro Tournament (see illustrative games). There White has sacrificed a certain amount of King's side development in order to achieve an early strategic advantage (a Rook well placed on the seventh rank). Against this Black finds the only resource—one cannot judge how far ahead he saw it—which introduces combative Chess of a high order. The moral of such a masterly draw is that, given reasonable strategic ground work, then, when the combat is joined, good tactical ability enables the player to do justice to himself, and not to lose against the strongest opposition.

SACRIFICIAL ATTACK IN THE MODERN GAME

Strategic, or technical, Chess does not, be it emphasised, exclude the combative, the speculative, or any tactical process involving vision. Only the approach is different. The modern Chess player tends to think first in terms of the framework of the game.

Typical terms are ; Open Lines ; Outposts ; Strongpoint ; Blockade, etc. The analyst, looking at a game in which a brilliant combination has been made, finds that there has been an exploitation of these strategic and technical factors. It does not follow that strategy and technique carry with them the capacity for combination ; but a sound strategy and technique is the condition *sine qua non* for the coming into being of a sound combination. That is true. But if one thinks further, it becomes clear that strategy and technique are terms somewhat too abstract in this context. The open lines that matter, the Outposts that matter, the Strongpoints that matter, the Blockades that matter, these are only determinable in the light of combative and combinative possibilities. (The first Diagram on page 161 affords an excellent example of an aggregate of technical advantages—Black has the open lines that matter.)

There was a stage in Chess when players were content to make sure that they had at least as much space as their opponents. This was the period dominated by the geniuses of Capablanca and Rubinstein, players who could exploit very fine shades of advantage on an open Board, or in an end-game, and of course, showing plenty of combinative ability for the exploitation of their strategic advantages.

Later, under the influence of Tartakower, Reti, Nimzowitch, and Alekhine, the conception of space in Chess was altered, as we have seen. And that a more functional type of play could give excellent results was demonstrated in such a game as Samisch-Nimzowitch (see illustrative games).

But that is not the end of the matter. In the new struggle for position there was a greater interpenetration of positions.

The modern openings can, therefore, lend themselves to highly combative complexes. Before the position is crystallized, so that the time factor ceases to be all important, tempo in the struggle for the attainment of the right structure can be as important as it was in the days when Anderssen and Zukertort were annihilating quite strong opponents. Thus there has been a strange reversion in modern times. After Capablanca had declared that he had made Chess safe for, so to speak, the Chess Proletariat, a generation of players arose to make the game as dangerous as it was before. And the Chess of recent generations has been highly combative. Modern Russian Masters with their flair for interesting experiment have completed the refutation of the belief that the resources of the Chess Board have been exhausted. The last game in this book shows that Capablanca realized this himself

It still remains true, however, that much of the combination and sacrifice that has enriched the æsthetic content of Chess has been occasioned by bad strategy. A player allows his opponent to seize important points, to develop on open lines, to put pressure on the defences without there being counter pressure. Then the resulting attack, however beautiful, may even be unnecessary. The intrusion of ideas effects an economy of longer processes of thought and preparation. To win quickly is better than to win slowly, because it reduces the chances of error due to fatigue. Thus it is quite certain that Morphy would have won his game against Paulsen without the beautiful sacrifice seen in the previous chapter, because, from a strategic standpoint Morphy was much better placed. On the other hand, his process of winning without the sacrifice would have been long and laborious and not easy to ascertain. From another standpoint the combination is part of the game, because, without it, Paulsen's previous move would have done much towards relieving the pressure.

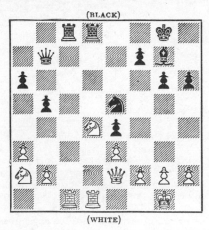

(BLACK)

(WHITE)

ALEKHINE—
GRUNFELD.
CREATIVE CHESS.
28. ... Kt to Q6
29. R × R, Q × R.
30. P to B3, R × Kt.
31. P × P, Kt to B5.
32. P × Kt, Q to B5.
33. Q × Q, R × R Ch.
34. Q to B1, B to Q5
      Ch., with Mate
      next move.
Note, if
31. P × R, B × P Ch
32. K to B1, Kt to B5.
33. Q × P, Q to B5
      Ch.
34. K to K1, Kt × P
      Ch.
35. K to Q2, B to K6
      Ch. etc.

According to modern standards sacrifice in Chess is meritorious when it is the determinant that makes the difference between victory and equality. The sacrifice that matters is that which enables whatever strategic advantage exists to be demonstrated. Indeed, the game may be so close, and the strategy so well balanced, that only rich tactical possibilities make the play of one opponent better than that of the other. Makaganov's victory against Reshevsky and Kotov's win against Yudovitch are excellent examples of this (see illustrative games) and Alekhine has enriched Chess with an Art Gallery of beautiful ideas against opponents who were playing so well that only great subtlety and richness of vision in the stategic tactical complex could have achieved victory. The accompanying examples, showing combinations by Alekhine against Grunfeld and Reti, illustrate excellently the exploitation (if not the creation) of the possibilities that condition victory.

(BLACK)

(WHITE)

ALEKHINE—RETI. White has allowed P to QB5, although he cannot capture the Rook. Now comes :
19. B × P. If then P × B.
20. Q × R, B to Kt2.
21. QR to Kt1, Q × R.
22. Q × R Ch., K × Q.
23. R × Q wins. ; and if—
19. . . . B to Kt2.
20. Q to K5 Ch., P to B3
21. Q to K7 Ch., etc. It was hard to see this at the stage when Black assumed that White could not allow his Bishop to be imprisoned.

There is no advantage in attempting a classification of combinative exploitations. The reader may, however be reminded of some varieties, of which examples are given in this book. We have seen the exploitation of a wrong decision made in a fairly level game (e.g., in the Mieses-Thomas examples). We have also seen exploitations of many types where a clear advantage, whether in the middle game or end game, already exists. In some cases the combination was necessary in order to exploit (if not create) the advantage ; in other cases it was unnecessary. There may be added to this a reference to the frequency of combinative exploitation of defective opening play. This is particularly likely to arise in two sets of circumstances, both illustrated in the illustrative games. One kind of situation arises when one player plays insufficiently incisively, allowing his opponent to prepare a strong attack (Botwinnik-Vidmar and the Morphy examples). The other, more interesting, situation is when one player plays too compromisingly. The game between Botwinnik and Fine is as good an example as any.

Further, interesting combinative play can take place whenever, at any stage, a player endeavours to do too much, gets out of his depth so to speak. In Chess players are destroyed, not only by decapitation as Von Bardeleben by Steinitz, not only by strangulation, as the Duke of Brunswick by Morphy, but by simple drowning. A good example of this is the game between Alekhine and Sterk—an amusing example of a gallant failure to live up to a name (see illustrative games).

(BLACK)

(WHITE)

CLEVER
EXPLOITATION
OF AN EXISTENT
ADVANTAGE

A WIN BY
TARTAKOWER.

1. QB7 Ch., Kt × Q.
2. PK6 Ch., Q × P.
3. KtB5 Ch., KQ1.
4. Kt × Q Ch., KQ2.
5. KtB5 Ch., KQ1.
6. KtKt7 Ch., KQ2.
7. BR3 Ch. wins.

But, more frequent than the actual exploitations, and more important even, are the infinite number of combinations which do not take place. These are the unheard melodies of Chess, the variations that are not played. In an infinite number of Chess positions there are lines of play which can lead to a brilliant exploitation, but, being seen, are avoided. They are part of the tactical strategic complex. A good example is furnished by the position in the game between Makaganov and Reshevsky, where a Queen's sacrifice is contemplated but not actualized. In many games we find clever threats that do not come as near to actuality as this; but their possibility may operate to influence the play over many moves. The onlooker who applauds spectacular moves may never know how near he was to seeing say a Kt's sacrifice on Q5, etc.

F*

Conversely, very often the combination that is played in Chess is a variation that could be avoided. Sometimes, in the best games it is not avoided because it cannot be avoided without some other type of loss developing. Sometimes it is not avoided because it is not seen by the defender. But it is part of the game. It is part, and not the whole. On the other hand it is a much more important part than is believed by those theorists who hold that Chess can be reduced to something like a geometry.

The true approach to Chess is a fusion of the tactical and strategic approaches. One cannot isolate individual lines from the framework, because it is unwise to do so. One cannot isolate the framework from the lines of play because it is impossible to do so. Players looking at the Board are analysing lines of play. When they are playing strategically as well as tactically, their choices of move, and of variations to analyse, are conditioned by their conception of the frame of the game.

(BLACK)

(WHITE)

CLEVER
EXPLOITATION
OF ADVANTAGE
LEVITSKY—
MARSHALL.
Marshall plays Q to
KKt6, and wins.

If they are lacking in Chess genius their strategic technical equipment will preserve them from a certain amount of danger. If the strategic equipment is not allowed to thwart the speculative mind, then very fine Chess results. In Chess as in the arts one must not strive after effects, but the difficulties of exploitation can be so great that the mind must always be open to the reception and appreciation of constructive, even brilliant, possibilities.

VARIOUS EXPLOITATIONS OF STRATEGIC ADVANTAGE

The non-combative method can be as hard as, if not harder than, the imaginative. Rubinstein was a great master of both kinds of exploitation. The diagrams show situations where neat tactical processes are required to turn the accrued strategic advantage into a win : also a few quieter lines.

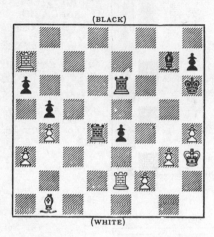

NEAT CAPTURE

White (Rubinstein) wins.
1. B × P, R (either) × B.
2. R × R, R × R.
3. R × P Ch., K to R4.
4. P to B3 wins.

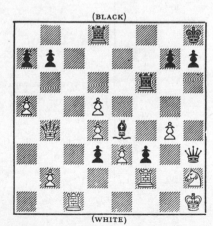

SACRIFICIAL EXPLOITATION.

Black (Rubinstein) cannot play R to KR3, because of Q to K7. Therefore
1. .... P to Q7.
2. Q × P, R to KR3, and Q × Kt Ch. is a fatal threat.
(instead)
If 2. R to Q1
R to QB1 wins.
After 2. Q × P,
R to KR3. 3. K to Kt1, Q to Kt6 Ch.
4. K to B1, R × Kt.
5. R × R, B to Q6 Ch. forces a win.

RUBINSTEIN—
JANOWSKI.

1. B × RP Ch., K × B.
2. P to Kt6 Ch., K to Kt1.
3. Kt × Kt, P × Kt.
4. P to R6, P to KB3.
5. P × KtP, P × Kt
6. R to R8 Ch., K × P.
7. R to R7 Ch., K to Kt1.
8. Q to B5, P to B6.
9. R × Q wins.

A TACTICAL POINT.

White has played B to Q6 and Black gains advantage with K to B2. After R × RP, R to Q6 and, after K to B2, B to B5, the KBP must fall. Then the Black centre Pawns win.

(BLACK)

(WHITE)

SEIZURE OF
ADVANTAGE.
White plays B to
Kt3 and Black
(Rubinstein) plays P
to QKt4, eventually
forcing the B at B3
from the defence of
Q4.

But by contrast the next diagram shows the same player
avoiding what appears to be the most vigorous line and doing
a great deal of preparation in order to make his strategic
advantage greater.

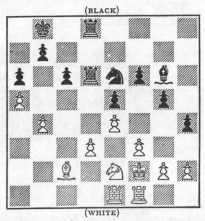

(BLACK)

(WHITE)

SLOW
EXPLOITATION
(by Rubinstein).
Not the obvious . . .
P to QB4 because of
2. P × P, Kt × P
3. P to Q4, P × P.
4. P to K5
and White has a little
freedom. Black plays
first B to K1 !

The style of the soundest Chess Masters tends to consist in
the avoidance of a combinative variation except in two sets of
circumstances. The first requisite is that it shall be **exact**

and completely reliable. The second requirement is that it shall be necessary. More precisely, if the combination is sound and not necessary, the adoption of it is a matter of style. If, however, the combination constitutes something of a strain on the vision, the professional player tends not to rely on it unless this is the only way of establishing a winning advantage. Of this last type, Rubinstein's com-

(BLACK)

(WHITE)

RUBINSTEIN—
CAPABLANCA.

1. B × Kt, Q × B.
2. Kt × QP, Q to R3.
3. K to Kt2, QRQ1.
4. Q to QB1 wins.
The Knight is miraculously un-pinned, and still guarded (by the B).

bination against Capablanca at San Sebastian is noteworthy. There, two far sighted players were involved in an early middle game manoeuvre. Capablanca's very interesting counterplay, or resource, fails against a move which, several moves previously, must have been incredibly difficult to anticipate.

But a great number of games of Chess are won uncombinatively by the nursing of small advantages. Sometimes highly complicated tactical lines have to be considered. On other occasions it is only a question of reasonably logical play and the avoidance of obvious risks.

The next diagram shows an interesting study in the disintegration of a game through the quite clever exploitation by the opponent of a strategic feature. This piece of play, by Keres, shows at once the importance of small strategic features and the skill required in the exploitation; it also shows the emergence, in the middle-game, of endgame considerations.

(BLACK)

(WHITE)

DISADVANTAGE.
White's only advantage is that, owing to the placing of Black's QBP, he is tying Black's Bishop to a short diagonal. It follows that the B. is not a good guard for the Rook. R to QKt1 is played and Black cannot play R × R followed by RQ1. Therefore, a White Rook reaches the 7th rank

TRANSITION TO THE ENDGAME

Possibly the hardest of all phases of Chess occurs at that stage when one has a good position, perhaps with slight material advantage or some space, and it is a question of reducing material, or of some tactical engagements in which material becomes reduced. The most typical transition involves the Pawn chase. Each player with his Rook or Rooks can win one or two of his opponent's Pawns. It can often happen that though you emerge victorious in the Pawn hunt, or without loss, yet your opponent has some compensations. It is particularly important not to leave a compensating advantage on one side of the Board in exchange for an increase in your advantage on the other side of the Board. Thus your opponent's lone Pawn guarded by a Rook can even counter-balance your own united passed Pawns on the other wing. Much of course will depend on the relative position of the Kings; but Kings are surprisingly mobile in the endgame. Rather, then, than liquidate, it is advisable to keep the middle game in being, if you can, and hope that the advantage that ultimately crystallizes will be a solider one, not offset by counter thrusts. The ideal endgame position is one in which only your advantage matters. Then it is a question of forcing the promotion of a Pawn. It can be an advantage then to have blocked Pawns on the other wing, so long as yours are safe. In case you cannot Queen the Pawn that you are working on, you may just gain sufficient tempo in order to win on the other wing after the battle for promotion has caused the disappearance of all other material.

These matters require for their handling a technique of endgame play, which is the subject matter of a later chapter.

Meanwhile the reader is reminded that some at least of the technique and strategy of middle game Chess consists in the accumulation of endgame advantages. These can be hard to assess.

One that is clear is the cutting off of one's opponent King from your own important Pawn or Pawns. If you can emerge into the ending with your own King among the Pawns, and your Rook keeping your opponent's King away, you should win. The defender's task is to bring his King across under cover of the Rook, if he can afford Rook exchanges. If the Pawn is not too far, or if a Pawn that is blocking it occupies time in its removal, this manœuvre can be effected. But in general the cut-off King is an unmitigated disadvantage to the player whose King is the victim.

Other advantages include the superiority of joined Pawns to isolated Pawns facing them. When they are on opposite sides of the Board, the advantage is not so great, because isolated Pawns can hold a King as effectively as joined Pawns. The technique has been shown.

Another well known advantage is present when your opponent has two Pawns held by one of yours. If your Pawn at Q5 holds your opponents at his Q3 and QB2, for example, then he has a bad form of " hanging pawn." There may, however, be a situation where a hanging Pawn has its uses. It can sacrifice itself to remove the Pawn that is obstructing its more advanced companion. Quite a well known endgame situation exists whenever hanging Pawns are obstructed by one Pawn only. If the hanging pawns are blocked by an interstitial Pawn, they are quite strong, because the forward member of them is passed and guarded.

The reader must remember that every Chess construction depends on its context. Groupings of Pieces are ambiguous in their functions. In point is one of the well known Chess advantages, the remote passed pawn. Assume three Pawns facing each other on the King's side with Kings near to them. Now one player has a QBP the other a QRP. The player with the QRP should win, because his opponent's King has to travel further to stop it than his own King has to travel to stop the QBP. Then, when the attack on the Pawn masses comes, the nearer King wins. But to show the difficulty of assessment, Rook-play or a well placed King can offset this advantage. The diagram shows Rubinstein winning against a remote passed Pawn. Similar reflections apply to the " hanging Pawns " (Pawns say at K4Q5, with an interstitial opposition Pawn). This can be a weak formation, because it can be broken up by an undermining of the defending Pawn. On the other hand it can constitute a very strong threat if the forward member of the hanging pawn chain holds the King within the Queening square.

(BLACK)

(WHITE)

BLACK WINS.
40. ... R to R1.
41. R to B3, R to R5.
42. R to Q3 (a typical cramp), ... K to K2.
43. K to Kt3, K to K3.
44. K to B3, K to Q4.
45. K to K2, P to Kt4.
46. R to QKt3, P to B3.
47. K to K3, K to B5.
48. R to Q3, P to Q4.
49. K to Q2, R to R1.
50. K to B2, R to R2. (Tempo play.)
51. K to Q2, R to K2.
52. R to B3 Ch., K × P, and now Black is much better placed and wins.

These matters, be it repeated, are hard to assess. What emerges is the necessity for the player of any middle game to be well equipped for the endgame. Endgame technique is so important that appreciation of it may enable you to choose a winning middle game line which otherwise you would not adopt because of your own uncertainty. The technique of endgame play is sufficiently important to require separate treatment.

PART III

CHESS LEARNING

CHAPTER V

THE GROUND WORK OF THE OPENINGS

The history of the development of Chess is the history of development in Chess. The brilliant players of the middle part of the last century, of whom Morphy was the greatest virtuoso, and Anderssen and Zukertort were great types, were not lacking in any of the capacity for Chess vision that has been possessed by the outstanding players of this century. The only defect in their play consisted in the fact that they were more reliant on vision than are modern players. If one examines their best performances one finds usually that either they won their great victories against bad players—and, incidentally a victory can be brilliant even against a bad player; or else they won their victories in very unbalanced positions. In point, are efforts like that of Morphy against Isouard, a much weaker player, and that of Anderssen against so strong a player as Kieseritsky. They played openings of a combative type, openings in which the game became quickly unbalanced. Skirmishing was early; each player endeavoured to force the pace or to force his opponent to commit himself decisively. Such openings included the King's Gambit, the Evans Gambit, the Scotch Gambit and (later) the Max Lange, Moller, etc. And these openings, from which the play is really quite controllable, tended to be played at too fast a tempo. From them players won by achieving more than their opponents anticipated. But often they lost through trying to do too much.

The generation of Steinitz, having perceived the logical principles that could be extracted from the play of such a one as Morphy, proceeded to make Chess self-consciously strategic where previously strategy had been the unexpressed discipline of the best vision. From the end of the nineteenth century onwards the evolution has been logical. First an emphasis on space, rather than time, on mobilization rather than attack; then, in attack, to play for the centre and lesser objectives rather than, with violences, to attempt to gain considerable material, or bring about mate. Thus we have the period of the Queen's Pawn and the Ruy Lopez, following upon the period of the King's Gambit and the Evans. Then, as we have seen, came a subtilisation. Two tendencies became manifest here. First the majority of players became sufficiently well equipped to appreciate the deeper strategy of Steinitz and Lasker, viz., the merits of defence, and the possibility of planning the movements of Pieces without a slavish adherence to the conventional notions of good development. Second was the change in the notion of the centre. These two tendencies give us " ultra-modern" Chess, characterised by the Nimzowitch, Tartakower, Alekhine experimentalism, and the Fianchetto Defences. Those treatments, having been heresy, are now orthodoxy. The present phase is an acceleration of tempo in the new orthodox modes of development. There is also a tendency to go back to older openings and play them in the light of a maturer strategy. That last fact suggests the thought that the student of Chess is unwise to become obsessed with the pursuit of opening learning. Given a reasonable tactical-strategic equipment it may be said that no opening, rationally played, can be bad.

THE KING'S PAWN OPENINGS

The advantage of P to K4 as the first move is reasonably clear. It gives access to the board, immediately, to two pieces, the Queen and the Bishop, and gives an immediate control over the centre squares. Pressure on the centre from squares like K4 and Q4, or, to a lesser degree from KB4 or QB4, implies that the player exerting the pressure has a certain amount of manoeuvring space, behind the Pawn or Pawns, in which he can mobilize. Also the majority of the King's Pawn Openings attack, more or less directly, the weakness at White's KB7.

There are many answers to 1. P to K4.

There is 1. . . . P to K3, which is the French Defence.

    1. . . . P to QB4, Sicilian Defence.

    1. . . . P to QB3, The famous, and difficult,
                  Caro-Cahn. Much used by Botwinnik.

    1. . . . P to Q4, The Centre Counter.

    1. . . . Kt to KB3, Alekhine's Defence.

to say nothing of other quite playable irregular opening moves such as 1. . . . Kt to QB3, 1. . . . P to KKt3, 1. . . . P to QKt3. But one of the most frequent, and perhaps the best—though it is not now so popular as it was—is the simple move 1. . . . P to K4. After the opening moves 1. P to K4, P to K4, White and Black are exercising equal pressure in the

centre, but White has the slight advantage of tempo. If the
game is well played by Black that advantage will disappear.
If Black plays more weakly than White, White's initiative
will increase. Meanwhile White sets the pace because he can
make the first threat, or the first act of aggression. White can
thrust against the centre on the second move, either with a
Pawn or with a piece. His choice will be determined by the
speed with which he desires to attack his opponent's King's side.

Nineteenth century players favoured the immediate 2. P to
KB4, the King's Gambit. To understand this, and several
other aspects of the King's Pawn openings, the reader must
appreciate that Black, who is being attacked, has his greatest
weakness at KB2 (White's KB7). White can bring to bear
against it a Bishop placed at QB4, a Knight coming quickly
to KKt5, a Queen possibly developing itself, after one or two
Pawn moves, at QKt3. The advantage, then, of a move like
P to KB4 is that it adds to this force the Rook that will arrive
on KB1 when White Castles. Further, if White secures control
of K5 so as to be able to push a Pawn there at will, he will be
able to drive away such a piece as Black's Knight from Black's
KB3. For the rest, the control of the K5 square by the P at
Q4 is an aggressive feature.

That is the simple basis of White's strategy. Of course
Black has plenty of counterplay ; but, since in Chess it is
important to make one's moves with a purpose, and preferably
a purpose characterized by incisiveness, the type of attacking
development that is being described is as good a way of starting
the game as any, subject only to the consideration that this
kind of attack, against good defence, is likely to burn itself
out too quickly, leaving the game a little arid.

There are two main types of Pawn attack on the centre.
There is, as we have seen, 2. P to KB4. There is also 2. P to
Q4, the Centre Game or Gambit, which can be followed up so
as to turn it into the lively but risky Danish Gambit (P to K4,
P to K4 ; 2. P to Q4, P×P ; 3. P to QB3) or which can be
transposed into the Scotch Gambit and several varieties of
later developing attack, such as the Max Lange, etc. In
modern times the most frequent second move for White is
Kt to KB3. This is an immediate attack on Black's King's
Pawn. It is not, as we have seen in an earlier chapter, a
terribly serious attack ; but Black has nothing better available,
by way of development, than to defend the Pawn with Kt to
QB3, or P to Q3 ; or to counter-attack with Kt to KB3.

At this point, it should be observed that a move like 2. . . .
B to Q3 is bad. For obvious reasons the Bishop at Q3 is

not as good a defender as the Pawn would be (against, e.g., an immediate P to Q4). But, what is more important, the B at Q3 is doing much less than it could do at K2 or QB4, and it is blocking the QP, and with it the Queen's side Pieces. The move then, B to Q3, though it cannot be called an immediate cause of loss, is unsatisfactory. In the opening stages it is desirable to play moves which facilitate further development rather than retard it. That indeed is the whole art of opening play. Certain openings do admittedly give what appears to be a cramped game (e.g., Alekhine's Defence), but it will be found that those openings are really based on a plan for later development which cannot be prevented. A move like B to Q3, that we have just considered, retards development without any compensation.

In answer to 2. Kt to KB3, the moves Kt to KB3 (Petroff's Defence) or P to Q3 (Philidor's Defence), will be considered later. The most usual and popular is 2. Kt to QB3.

Then, on the third move, White has a choice of plans of campaign. In the spirit of the King's Pawn's openings is the move B to B4, pointing to KB7. This can be met by 3. . . . B to B4, after which the game can settle down into the Giuoco Piano (slow game) or can be enlivened by 4. P to QKt4 into the Evans Gambit. An alternative move, 4. P to Q4 is an interesting sacrifice, which is not quite sound, but which can yield a promising game (4. P to Q4, B×P; 5. Kt×B, Kt×Kt; 6. P to KB4, P to Q3; 7. 0–0, Kt to K3). But P to Q4 is stronger on move 3, and can either be played as the Scotch Game (recapture of the Pawn) or as the Scotch Gambit—one variety of which can form the Max Lange. Alternatively, Black on the third move (after 1. P to K4, P to K4. 2. Kt to KB3, Kt to QB3. 3. B to B4), can play Kt to KB3 (the Two Knights Defence) which offers White a choice of attacking lines. According to the best opinion the immediate thrust of Kt to Kt5, winning a Pawn (because Black is compelled to play P to Q4 immediately), gives Black good counterplay, if not the eventual advantage. On the other hand a form of Scotch Gambit can now be immediately initiated by 4. P to Q4, or prepared by 4. 0–0, to be followed by P to Q4. In this way again, the Max Lange or the Moller can develop. These are formidable attacks which can, however, be successfully defended. Let it be added that there is no opening attack in Chess which can be said to give ultimate superiority against good defence. That explains why players tend these days to play openings in which the attack can be delayed.

Typical of these is the Ruy Lopez. This develops when

White, on his third move, plays not B to B4 but B to Kt5. This initiates a long process of pressure against the centre and is one of the hardest openings to defend correctly. Also, if defended correctly, it becomes one of the hardest openings for the attack. Hence its popularity among players who believe themselves capable of exploiting, either for White or Black, the finer points of the Chess struggle.

It is not possible in an introductory volume to give anything like an exhaustive analysis of any particular opening. But the following pages contain some pieces of play from which it is hoped the reader will obtain a grasp of the kind of attacks that develop from the main King's Pawn and Queen's Side Openings.

The King's Gambit

After the opening moves, 1. P to K4, P to K4. 2. P to KB4 Black has the option of accepting the Gambit or declining it, 2. . . . P×P constitutes the acceptance of the Gambit. When that is done White usually plays 3. Kt to KB3. The disadvantage of this move is that Black can immediately throw back the Pawn with 3. . . . P to Q4.

In this position Black gets a fairly free development whether or not White captures the Pawn or advances his King's Pawn. The game is quite good, with plenty of scope for both players, but is not characterised by the interesting dangers of the various lines that develop if Black tries to hold the Pawn with 3. . . . P to KKt4.

It is worth remarking at this point, and the reader will be wise to bear in mind, that Black's power to play P to Q4, freeing his game, is the test of equality in most of the King's Pawn Openings. This does not apply, always, in the Ruy Lopez or the Four Knights, where the centre has to be more subtly treated. But in many openings where the attack is against the King's side, e.g., in the Scotch, Giuoco, etc., P to Q4 for Black spells freedom from anxiety. That follows from the general strategic truth that a good control of the centre ensures that one is not likely to be overwhelmed by any attack against either of the wings. On the other hand a good attack in the centre can make possible a quick attack against either of the wings without very much additional preparation.

Sometimes, in order to mitigate the effect of a possible P to Q4 White plays 3. B to B4, instead of Kt to KB3. This is called the King's Bishop's Gambit. In it Black can be tempted into a rapid attack against the King with 3. . . . Q to R5 Ch., followed by Kt to KB3 with chances of bringing that Knight via R4 to Kt6 forking the King (which will have moved to KB1) and the Rook. Suffice it to say that Black's attack can be beaten off. At the proper moment Q to K1 can be played, and the P at B4 captured by the Bishop. White is then left with the kind of centre control that usually occurs when an attack has been successfully beaten off. Black, therefore, is not well advised to pursue his counter-attack too quickly. The move 3. Q to R5 Ch. is not bad ; but after that general development should not be neglected.

That proposition about general development is important in the King's Gambit. Both White and Black have got to consider not only the realities of a sharp attack, and the desirability of keeping material advantage, but the situation that is developing on the parts of the board that are not directly under attack, because they may become important both in connection with the attack, and as the game that remains if and when the attack is beaten off.

Typical of the older forms of the King's Gambit are the following three variations. These constitute respectively, the Allgaier Gambit, the Muzio Gambit and the Kieseritski Gambit.

White	Black
ALLGAIER	
1. P to K4.	P to K4.
2. P to KB4.	P × P.
3. Kt to KB3.	P to KKt4.
4. P to KR4.	P to Kt5.
5. Kt to Kt5.	P to KR3.
6. Kt × P.	K × Kt.
7. B to B4 Ch. (PQ4 is also playable.)	P to Q4.
8. B × P Ch.	K to Kt2.
9. P to Q4. With a lively game. The dangers, to both players, need no stressing.	

White	Black
MUZIO	
1. P to K4.	P to K4.
2. P to KB4.	P × P.
3. Kt to B3.	P to KKt4.
4. B to B4.	P to Kt5.
5. 0—0.	P × Kt.
6. B × P Ch. This is the Double (popular) form of the Muzio. Q × P is quite good instead.	K × B.
7. Q × P.	Q to B3.
8. P to K5.	Q × P.
9. P to Q4.	Q × P Ch.
10. B to K3 with a formidable attack. If White is giving odds of QKt this attack wins quickly !	

White	Black
KIESERITZKI	
1. P to K4.	P to K4.
2. KP to B4.	P × P.
3. Kt to KB3.	P to KKt4.
4. P to KR4.	P to Kt5.
5. Kt to K5.	P to Q3.
6. Kt × KtP. With a sounder position than in the other variations.	

In modern play Black does not try to hold the Pawn.

White	Black
P to K4.	P to K4.
P to KB4.	P × P.
Kt to KB3.	P to Q4 with a free development.

4. P × P followed by P—QB4 (if the Pawn is left) seems good for white.

VIENNA OPENING

A form of King's Gambit can develop on the third move, when White's second move is Kt to QB3 (The Vienna). If Black plays unincisively this attack can be even more vigorous than the normal King's Gambit. The usual play is as follows :—

White	Black
1. P to K4.	P to K4.
2. Kt to QB3.	Kt to KB3.
3. P to KB4.	P to Q4.
4. P × KP.	Kt × P.

and here White has the option of proceeding with either 5. Q to B3 or 5. Kt to B3. In the former case Black can simplify with Kt × Kt followed by P to Q5, after which White maintains something of an attack, but nothing decisive.

Let the reader take note that in this, as in all other openings, an attack is not the same thing as a winning attack. An attack is something to be treated with respect, but very often amounts to little more than a slight initiative allowing the player to develop, and to determine the direction of the game for a few moves, but not for sufficient moves, or to sufficient effect, to prevent a more far seeing opponent from eventually winning.

The alternative line 5. Kt to B3 can be met by more or less any move of the King's Bishop, and there are many other moves available.

Other aspects of the Vienna are worth considering.

The following is a very interesting piece of Chess 1. P to K4 P to K4 2. Kt to QB3 Kt to KB3 3. B to B4 Kt × P. Obviously this is only the loan of a piece because if 4. Kt × Kt P to Q4; and if, instead, one treats the B as Desperado

with 4. B×P Ch. K×B 5. Kt×Kt P to Q4, the exposure of
Black's King is more than compensated by his open development.

There may however, be played (after 1. P to K4 PK4
2. KtQB3 KtKB3 3. B to B4 Kt×P)

White	Black
4. Q to R5.	Kt to Q3.
5. B to Kt3.	Kt to QB3. Modern opinion seems to recommend B to K2.
6. Kt to Kt5.	P to KKt3.
7. Q to B3.	P to B4.
8. Q to Q5.	Q to K2. Q to B3 also has its points.
9. Kt × P Ch.	K to Q1.
10. Kt × R.	P to Kt3.

and Black, although temporarily a Rook down, has a promising counter-attack in the course of which he will regain some
of his material. White will have to play exceedingly well
to avoid the many dangers that will develop ; but he too
will have his chances.

Again, there still sometimes occurs the old fashioned line :—

White	Black
1. P to K4.	P to K4.
2. Kt to QB3.	Kt to QB3.
3. B to B4. Not so good as P to B4.	B to B4.
4. Q to Kt4.	K to B1 ; and Black, although he has moved his King, is at no disadvantage.

For the rest, after 2. . . . KtQB3, the delayed King's
Gambit 3. P to KB4, can be quite effective. If it takes Allgaier
form it is called Hampe-Allgaier.

KING'S GAMBIT DECLINED

In this century the King's Gambit has lost some of its appeal
because it can quite reasonably be declined.

The usual declining move is 2. . . . B to B4 (Black's
Pawn can obviously not be taken immediately because of
the check at R5) ; and this is followed by moves like P to Q3,
Kt to QB3 etc. White can then proceed to try and force
P to Q4, or else, with the Queen's Knight, to get rid of Black's
Black square Bishop, so as to be able to Castle. Black has
counterplay with B to KKt5.

It can then happen, as in other King's Pawn openings,
that White's centre proves to be less formidable than it looks.

The King's Gambit Declined is an excellent example of the
principle that developing move for developing move, coupled

with a guard against immediate attacks, constitutes adequate opening play.

A more aggressive continuation for Black is the Falkbeer Counter Gambit :—

White	Black
1. P to K4.	P to K4.
2. P to KB4.	P to Q4.
3. P × QP.	P to K5.

and Black can make it difficult for White to develop for quite a time, e.g. (to quote one of several reasonable lines) :

White	Black
4. P to Q3.	Kt to KB3.
5. P × P.	Kt × KP.
6. Kt to KB3.	B to QB4.
7. Q to K2.	B to B4.
8. Kt to B3.	Q to K2. With a good development, though not perfect.

THE GIUOCO PIANO AND VARIETIES OF CENTRE GAME

If it is desired to point one's pieces quickly towards Black's King's side, a usual method is the following :—

White	Black
1. P to K4.	P to K4.
2. Kt to KB3.	Kt to QB3.
3. B to B4.	

Now Black has the choice of two principal methods of defence; either 3. . . . B to B4 or 3. . . . Kt to KB3.

EVANS GAMBIT

In answer to 3. . . . B to B4, White's 4. P to QKt4 introduces a magnifiicent specimen of combative Chess, the Evans Gambit. This lost its popularity for some years for a variety of reasons. First, it is rather a strain on both players; second, it has been analysed so carefully that well informed players can be expected to cope with its difficulties; and third, because, as we have seen in a previous chapter, it can be quite successfully declined. Latterly, it has been revived because it is known to be capable of slower treatment, yielding good development.

The reader has already seen the Evergreen Game. That developed from an Evans Gambit ; and it may be studied as an excellent example of the possibilities and dangers of that opening.

1. P to K4   P to K4 2. Kt to KB3   Kt to QB3 3. B to B4 B to B4

4. P to QKt4 B × P 5. P to QB3 B to B4 (or R4) 6. P to Q4 P × P 7. 0–0   P × P 8. Kt × P with a good game.

The general plan of a safer defence to the Evans (the

Accepted Gambit) is for Black to play B to R4, refuse the 2nd Pawn, and endeavour to get in the moves, P to Q3. B to QKt3, B to KKt5 and 0–0. There is always a tactical danger of the loss of a piece by the pin of the QKt and the move P to Q5 ; but Black can prevent this if he keeps a steady eye on the possibility of Q to R4 while his B is at R4.

THE MOLLER ATTACK

If White wishes to attack without sacrificing the Knight's Pawn, a good method commences with 4. P to QB3.

The following is the typical form of the Moller attack.

White	Black
1. P to K4.	P to K4.
2. Kt to KB3.	Kt to QB3.
3. B to B4.	B to B4.
4. P to QB3.	Kt to KB3.
5. P to Q4.	P × P.
6. P × P.	B to Kt5 Ch.
7. Kt to B3.	Kt × KP.
8. 0–0.	B × Kt.
9. P to Q5.	Kt to K4 ; B to B3 is playable.
10. P × B.	Kt × B.
11. Q to Q4, with a strong attack.	QKt to Q3.
12. Q × KtP.	Q to B3.
13. Q × Q.	Kt × Q.
14. R to K1 Ch., etc.	

But Black can avoid this kind of attack in two ways :—

On move 7. he can Castle, leaving White with a hollow centre.

Or earlier, on move 4, he can play Q to K2 ;* and in answer to P to Q4 play B to Kt3 following with P to Q3, Kt to KB3, 0–0, etc.—a Giuoco Piano with advantage to Black. White's development against this involves P—QKt4 and P—QR4.

In contrast, this opening which produces such excitements, can also produce very slow Chess—as the name Giuoco Piano suggests, e.g. :—

White	Black
1. P to K4.	P to K4.
2. Kt to KB3.	Kt to QB3.
3. B to B4.	B to B4.
4. Kt to QB3.	Kt to KB3.
5. P to Q3.	P to Q3.
6. B to K3.	

It is interesting to note that on White's move 6 the apparently safe move of Castles gives Black something of an attack with B to KKt5. In this type of opening that move is bad if played before the opponent Castles, because if the

*This is better than BKt3, because in some variations it gives Black the option of P—QR3 before P—Q4 is played by White.

Bishop is attacked with P to KR3, Black's answer B×Kt can be replied to with P×B, and the opponent has the open King's Knight's file for his Rook, while he Castles on the Queen's side.

The student should also be warned that if he has Castled and the Bishop comes to KKt5, he should not automatically try to drive it with P to KR3 followed by P to KKt4, because it may be that Black will sacrifice the Knight with Kt×KtP, in exchange for a considerable attack.

An interesting pitfall in the Giuoco Piano is the following :—

White	Black
1. P to K4.	P to K4.
2. Kt to KB3.	Kt to QB3.
3. B to B4.	B to B4.
4. Kt to QB3.	Kt to KB3.
5. P to Q3.	0–0 (playable because B to Kt5 can be met by B to K2).
6. Kt to KR4.	

This move, which is not very good, is directed towards the occupation of KB5. What is interesting is that Black cannot win a Pawn by Kt × KP because after

White	Black
7. Kt × Kt.	Q × Kt.
8. B to KKt5. Wins the Queen.	

What makes 6. Kt to KR4 inferior is

White	Black
6. . . .	P to Q4 (the old " Touchstone ").
7. P × P.	Kt × P.
8. Kt × Kt.	Q × KKt., etc.

THE MAX LANGE

If Black on the third move plays Kt to KB3 instead of B to B4 we have seen that the immediate attack by 4. Kt to KKt5 is illusory. But 4. P to Q4 can produce some interesting attacks, of which one is (or can transpose into) the famous Max Lange (which can also arise from the Scotch Gambit).

White	Black
1. P to K4.	P to K4.
2. Kt to KB3.	Kt to QB3.
3. B to B4.	Kt to KB3.
4. P to Q4.	P × P (the best).
5. 0–0.	B to B4. An alternative is Kt × KP, after which may follow—
	6. R to K1. P to Q4.
	7. B × P. Q × B
	8. Kt to QB3. (Canal's attack, which is embarrassing, though defensible.)
6. P to K5.	P to Q4.
7. P × Kt.	P × B.

White	*Black*
8. R to K1 Ch.	B to K3.
9. Kt to Kt5.	Q to Q4. Very important. If

instead—

9. ... Q to Q2.
10. Kt × B wins a piece by reason of the Check at R5.

If again—

9. ... Q to Q3.
10. Kt to K4 wins,
   e.g., if Q to K4.

11. P to KB4.	P to Q6 Ch.
12. K to R1.	P × P.
13. Q × P.	

If then—

13 ... Q to KB4. 14. Kt to Q6 Ch.
                           wins;

If instead—

13 ... Q to KR4. 14. P × P wins;

If, at 11. Black plays Q to KB4 there can follow—

12. P to KKt4.	Q × P.
13. Q × Q.	B × Q.
14. Kt × B Ch., etc.	

10. Kt to QB3.	Q to KB4.
11. QKt to K4.	. . . and White has a very fine attack which is defeasible only by the very best play. With the best play Black threatens to win, because he is likely to emerge with a Pawn superiority.

Although much analysed, this opening is still of the greatest interest and eminently playable. Relatively safe is 11. . . . 0–0–0, and a hard game results from this. Interesting also is—

White	*Black*
11. . . .	B to B1.
12. Kt × BP	K × Kt.
13. Kt to Kt5 Ch.	K to Kt1 (or Kt3)

and White's attack may not be so dangerous as it looks.

If, in this variation,

White	*Black*
12. P × KtP.	B × P.
13. P to KKt4.	Q × P.
14. Q × Q.	B × Q.
15. Kt to B6 double Ch.	K to Q1.
16. Kt × B.	P to KR4 wins back the Piece.

THE SCOTCH GAME

After the opening moves, 1. P to K4, P to K4. 2. Kt to KB3, Kt to QB3 ; White often plays 3. P to Q4. If then Black plays P × P, White can play B to B4, probably arriving at the Max Lange. He can, however, play 4. Kt × P and this constitutes the Scotch game. (The refusal to recapture makes it the Scotch Gambit.) The Scotch game can lead to very logical Chess, e.g.—

	White	Black
1.	P to K4.	P to K4.
2.	Kt to KB3.	Kt to QB3.
3.	P to Q4.	P × P.
4.	Kt × P.	Q to B3. 4. . . . Kt to KB3 is also playable (and after Kt × QKt, KtP × Kt).
5.	B to K3.	B to B4.
6.	P to QB3.	Kt to K2.
7.	B to Kt5.	P to Q3 (not 0–0). If 7. B to K2 P to Q4 with equality.

An interesting, but unconvincing attack can develop in this variation (one of the many Blumenfeld attacks) by—

	White	Black
6.	Kt to Kt5.	B × B.
7.	P × B.	Q to R5 Ch.
8.	P to KKt3.	Q × KP.
9.	Kt × P Ch.	K to Q1.
10.	Kt × R.	Kt to KB3, to take the edge off Q to Q6.

THE CENTRE GAME

1. P to K4, P to K4. 2. P to Q4, P×P. 3. Q×P, Kt to QB3. 4. Q to K3 with later 0–0–0 is too logical to require detailed analysis. A by-product is the Danish Gambit.

This is an attempt to gain manoeuvring space and development in exchange for irrelevant Pawns in the following (not very reliable) attack.

	White	Black
1.	P to K4.	P to K4.
2.	P to Q4.	P × P.
3.	P to QB3.	P × P.
4.	B to B4.	P × KtP.
5.	B × P.	B to Kt5 Ch.

Kt to QB3⎫
Kt to Q2. ⎬ with a dangerous formation.
K to B1. ⎭

In the teeth of danger Black must endeavour to develop and centralise with P to Q4; also to Castle.

Finally, there should be mentioned the fact that White can play B to B4 on the second move, before the Knights develop. There is no particular advantage in this, except that it preserves the option of a King's Gambit for one move.

The reader should avoid adventures like, 1. P to K4, P to K4. 2. P to Q4, P×P. 3. B to B4, B to B4. 4. B×P Ch., K×B. 5. Q to R5 Ch., P to KKt3. 6. Q×B with disadvantage.

RUY LOPEZ

The feature common to most of the openings considered so far is that in them White aims at a quick attack against the King's side, and the slight advantage of tempo that White enjoys is sufficient to cause Black to play carefully and to face difficulties. But in the long run, given good play, the initiative diminishes—even passes, and Black is left with, at least, equality. Consequently, modern players who want to maintain as long as possible White's initiative (granted that this is not a vain undertaking) are more likely to elect for the Ruy Lopez. In this they are reverting to something that was popular before the Masters of the middle nineteenth century introduced a period of quick attack. In Chess, as in many other departments of intellectual activity, there can happen a reversion to the period before last. The relatively immature strategy of the pre-Morphy epoch produced games nearer to some modern styles, with their advanced strategy, than to the intervening stage of tactical brilliance. However, the Ruy Lopez has survived in Chess because of its merits from any standpoint, and continues to exist as modern, notwithstanding its great age. Here indeed, when we consider Russian analyses of the old Spanish opening, are we reminded of the transition of culture from Iberia to Siberia.

The first three moves of the Lopez are already familiar to the reader, 1. P to K4, P to K4. 2. Kt to KB3, Kt to QB3. 3. B to Kt5, with, as we have seen, a sort of attack on the King's Pawn.

At this stage Black has two main methods of defence or counter play. One of these is based on P to Q3 (the Steinitz Defence), the other on Kt to KB3 (the Berlin Defence). Both of these are playable, but nowadays, whichever choice is adopted, Black usually precedes it with 3. . . . P to QR3. This is due to the discovery that White has little to gain, either tactically or strategically, by the immediate exchange the Bishop for the Knight. He retains the initiative for a short time, and has a slightly better Pawn formation, but Black will eventually get equal play. Consequently White usually retreats with 4. B to R4. If, after that, Black plays 4. . . . P to Q3 we have the Steinitz Deferred. If, instead, Black plays 4. . . . Kt to KB3 we have the Morphy Defence, perhaps the most popular, and reminiscent of the fact that a great master of attack was also a great master of defence.

These lines of play have been the subject matter of much experiment, much trial and error. The most popular is the Morphy Defence, because, notwithstanding early difficulties,

Black's eventual counter chances and strategic compensations are evident to those experienced in the opening.

Here is the main line :

White	Black
1. P to K4.	P to K4.
2. Kt to KB3.	Kt to QB3.
3. B to Kt5.	P to QR3.
4. B to R4.	Kt to B3.
5. O–O.	Kt × P.

Here Black has a very important alternative, B to K2, which leads to a rather different type of game, considered below.

| 6. P to Q4. | |

This, the product of much experiment gives a more lasting attack than the plausible 6. R to K1. Viz :

6. R to K1.	Kt to B4.
7. B × Kt.	QP × B.
8. P to Q4.	Kt to K3.

9. P × P and although White has a positive strategic advantage for the endgame, Black has sufficient intervening play to compensate. This plan may be improved by the playing of 6. Q to K2 instead of 6. R to K1.

In this variation incidentally, there is an interesting pitfall—

6. R to K1.	Kt to B4.
7. Kt to QB3.	Kt × B.
	A bad move.
8. Kt × KP.	B to K2.
	Virtually forced.
9. Kt to Q5.	O–O.
10. Kt × Kt.	P × Kt.
11. Kt × B Ch.	K to R1.
12. Q to R5.	Kt to B4.
13. R to K3.	Kt to K3.
14. Q × RP Ch.	K × Q.
15. R to KR3 Mate.	

It is to be observed that the play from move 12 is not completely forced, but Black is in great difficulties ; e.g., if 12. . . . B to K3. 13. R × B is playable, with quick recapture of the exchange and an excellent game.

To revert to the main line :

White	Black
6. P to Q4.	P to QKt4. (For P × P see p. 29.)
7. B to Kt3.	P to Q4.
8. P × P.	B to K3.
9. P to B3.	

This is in order to enable White to preserve his very important

White

White-square Bishop in the event
of Black playing Kt to QR4. The
Russian Master Smyslov has,
however, achieved successes with
9. Q to K2 (threatening R to Q1
and P to B4). Against this Kt to
QR4 is not immediately playable
because of 10. Kt to Q4. Best
is 9 ... B to K2. If 10. R to Q1,
then Kt to QR4, after which
11. Kt to Q4 can be met by O–O.
9. . . .

Black

B to K2.
Again the result of much
experiment. Recently there has
been a revival of the old-fashioned
9 ... B to QB4, which has certain
tactical advantages (e.g., the
pressure on White's KB2), also
some defects, including the strategic danger that after the Bishop
is forced to retreat Black will be
left with a backward QBP against
which White can exert a great
deal of pressure.

After 9. . . . B to K2 White has a choice of several moves,
including possibilities such as P to QR4 and R to K1. In
practice Lopez experts usually play, on the tenth move of this
variation, either B to K3 or QKt to Q2. Both are very good.
In answer to 10. B to K3 Black endeavours to improve his
position with O–O and Kt to QR4, followed, if the White
Bishop moves, by P to QB4, after which he has to defend very
carefully on the King's side, standing quite a considerable
attack, before his endgame superiority becomes a feature of
the game.

The most popular move (after a period in which it was rather
critically regarded) is nowadays 10. QKt to Q2.
The following is a typical sequence :—

White	*Black*
10. QKt to Q2.	0–0.
11. R to K1. B to B2 is also good:	Kt to B4.
best in reply is either P	
to KB4 or BB4.	
12. B to B2.	P to Q5.
13. P × P.	Kt × QP.
14. Kt × Kt.	Q × Kt.
15. Q to R5.	P to Kt3.
16. Q to R6.	Q to KR5, with an equal game.

Within the extent of these few moves there is tremendous
scope for variation. White has possibilities like 11. Q to K2 ;
instead of R to K1. It is not advisable for White to exchange
Knights on move 11, because after

G

White	Black
	White — *Black*
11. Kt × Kt.	P × Kt.
12. B × B.	P × Kt.
13. B to Q5.	Black can sacrifice the exchange with Kt × KP, obtaining a very good game.

If on move 9 of this variation of the Lopez Black plays B to B4, he is making it more difficult to straighten out his Pawns with eventual P to QB4. He is, however, making possible some counter-attack, of which some interest attaches to the possible sacrifice of two minor pieces for a Rook, Pawn, and the attack, e.g. :—

White	*Black*
9. . . .	B to B4.
10. QKt to Q2.	Kt × KBP.
11. R × Kt.	P to KB3, with good attacking chances.

This variation, which was much played among Lancashire "Skittlers" in the 1920's was later analysed by a Manchester player named Dilworth, and has become known as the Dilworth Variation. The Russian masters have analysed its sequences to the 36th move.

It is quite impossible in an introductory book to do justice even to a small part of so big an opening as the Lopez. The reader should however, learn the alternative treatment of the Morphy Defence, observing that in this, as contrasted with the line just analysed, Black's problem of developing his QBP is more easily solved. In the last chapter it has been explained that this can be a very important consideration, since a backward Pawn is a target for Rooks. In the quicker form of the Lopez, one possible process is for White to play Kt to Q4 at a proper time (not too early as in the unsound Breslau attack) and recapture on that square with the BP —then develop Rooks on the open file. This should be prevented.

Slower form of Morphy Defence (sometimes called the Tchigorin: and the other the Tarrasch).

White	*Black*
1. P to K4.	P to K4.
2. Kt to KB3.	Kt to QB3.
3. B to Kt5.	P to QR3.
4. B to R4.	Kt to B3.
5. 0–0.	B to K2. The divergence that gives a less combative but quite difficult game.
6. R to K1. (Q to K2, the Worrall attack is playable.)	P to QKt4.
7. B. to Kt3.	P to Q3. At this point, Black with Castles followed by P to Q4 can introduce the sacrificial Marshall attack which can give

White	Black
	White some difficulty, and should not lose, but is not popular in modern first class play.
	(7. . . . 0–0.
	8. P to B3. P to Q4.
	9. P × P. Kt × P.
	10. Kt × P. Kt × Kt.
	11. R × Kt. P to QB3,
	followed by B to Q3, etc.).
8. P to B3.	Kt to QR4.
9. B to B2.	P to QB4.
10. P to Q4. White often plays P to KR3 here in order to prevent B to KKt5. Black's answer is 0–0.	. . . and now Black has the choice of Q to B2 or Kt to QB3, or (perhaps best) the difficult B to Kt5.
	He may, incidentally, initiate that manoeuvre earlier if he refrains from pursuing the White Bishop.

In this variation, too, there are countless possibilities. It has been discovered by the Russians that Black can dispense with P to QKt4 and can play P to Q3, B to K2, and later B to Kt5, as a variation of Steinitz Deferred. (The possibility of an early Kt to Kt5 has been mentioned.) If in the slow Morphy Defence Black does not get in an early B to KKt5, then White develops with P to KR3, QKt Q2, R to K1, Kt to KB1, P to KKt4, Kt to Kt3, K to R2, R to Kt1, Kt to KB5, a strong attack. Black defends with 0–0, Kt to K1, P to KKt3, P to KB3, Kt to Kt2, etc.

Of other variations the Steinitz Deferred is too logical to require detailed treatment here.

White	Black
1. P to K4.	P to K4.
2. KtK to B3.	Kt to QB3.
3. B to Kt5.	P to QR3.
4. B to R4.	P to Q3.
5. P to B3. (A good alternative is B × Kt Ch., followed by 6. P to Q4 with good development. Black can reply 6. . . . QP × P or (better) P to KB3).	B to Q2.
6. P to Q4.	Kt to KB3.

With a sound game.

On move 5 of this line . . . P to KB4 for Black gives the Siesta variation which is playable.

There are many other defences to the Lopez. Quite hard to refute is the impudent looking " Schliemann's Defence "—

White	Black
P to K4.	P to K4.
Kt to KB3.	Kt to QB3.
B to Kt5.	P to KB4.

Best then is Kt to QB3.

If 4. P to Q4, this may happen :—

White	*Black*
4. ...	P × KP.
5. Kt × KP.	Kt × Kt.
6. P × Kt.	P to QB3.

winning a Pawn through the check at QR4. (But the Q is misplaced.)

Another line in the Lopez upon which it is impossible to pronounce is :—

White	*Black*
1. P to K4.	P to K4.
2. Kt to KB3.	Kt to QB3.
3. B to Kt5.	Kt to Q5.
4. Kt × Kt.	P × Kt.

with no perceptible middle-game disadvantage, but doubled Pawns. (This is Bird's Defence).

So far we have considered King's Pawn Openings giving an Open Game—either with defence of the centre, or unbalance of the centre by acceptance of Gambits. Now there must be considered one or two lines in which Black fights for the centre, but avoids the Ruy Lopez pressure; and some other openings in which Black yields centre space, in the hope of later exploiting the hollowness of White's game—or the tempo he has used in building the centre.

PHILIDOR'S DEFENCE

This is a difficult defence based on P to Q3 instead of Kt to QB3. It only retains its popularity these days among those players whose style it is to invite pressure so as to achieve a subtler kind of development, or an eventually better development, when White has over-expanded.

White	*Black*
1. P to K4.	P to K4.
2. Kt to KB3.	P to Q3.
3. P to Q4.	QKt to Q2. Better than Kt to QB3, after which White could gain tempo by exchanges, including exchange of Queens, leaving Black with his King on Q1.
4. B to B4.	B to K2.
5. 0–0.	P to QB3 or KtKB3.

If the latter, White can go for a quick attack by

White	*Black*
6. B × P Ch.	K × B.
7. Kt to Kt5 Ch.	K to Kt1.
8. Kt to K6.	Q to K1.
9. Kt × BP.	Black should eventually emerge with a slightly better game, since the Knight, having captured the Rook cannot escape. The variation has something in common

White	*Black*
	with an attack that was seen in the Vienna. An alternative method of playing this attack is—
	6. Kt to KK5. 0–0.
	7. B × P Ch. R × B.
	8. Kt to K6, etc.

White, however, has no need for these adventures, and can gain a good game by castling and development on both wings. A·possibly safer approach to the Philidor is the Author's— *i.e.* P—QB3 on the first move—then PQ3, QKt Q2 etc.

PETROFF'S DEFENCE

A variation which avoids the Ruy Lopez, but is not easy.

White	*Black*
1. P to K4.	P to K4.
2. Kt to KB3.	Kt to KB3.
3. Kt × P.	P to Q3.
4. Kt to KB3.	Kt × P.
5. P to Q4.	P to Q4.
6. B to Q3.	B to Q3.
7. 0–0.	0–0.
8. P to B4, and White has a slight initiative.	

Another approach is—

White	*Black*
1. P to K4.	P to K4.
2. Kt to KB3.	Kt to KB3
3. P to Q4.	Kt × P.
4. B to Q3.	P to Q4.
5. Kt × P.	B to Q3.
6. 0–0.	0–0.

and if now—

7. P to QB4.	Kt to QB3, gives Black the attacking chances.

FOUR KNIGHTS

This can develop from the Petroff, if White on move 3 plays Kt to QB3 and Black plays Kt to QB3 ; or it can develop instead of the Lopez if after 2. Kt to KB3 Kt to QB3 White plays 3. Kt to QB3 and Black replies Kt to KB3.

The normal form of this opening (of which there are many variations) is the double Ruy Lopez.

White	*Black*
1. P to K4.	P to K4.
2. Kt to KB3.	Kt to QB3.
3. Kt to QB3.	Kt to KB3.
4. B to Kt5.	B to Kt5. Instead Kt to Q5 gives the interesting but difficult Rubinstein Defence.
5. 0–0.	0–0.
6. P to Q3.	B × Kt.
7. P × B.	P to Q3.
8. B to Kt5.	Q to K2.
9. R to K1.	Kt to Q1. This is the Metger Defence and there are many others.

Observe that White's moves 5 and 6 cannot be transposed, because of 5. P to Q3   Kt to Q5!

DEFENCES TO THE KING'S PAWN OTHER THAN P TO K4

The notion of a subtler treatment of the centre, contemplating the moulding of Black's development on squares left weak in the White field accounts for the prevalence of answers to White's first move P to K4 in the form of 1. . . . P to Q4 (Centre Counter, seen in another Chapter) 1. . . . P to K3, (French Defence), 1. . . . P to QB4 (Sicilian Defence), 1. . . . P—QB3 (Caro-Cahn). 1. . . . Kt to KB3 (Alekhine's Defence). These, between them, cover more than half the King's Pawn openings that are played in modern tournaments. The Sicilian is the most stable of them. The French Defence and Alekhine's Defence give scope to attacking play by White; and Black may wait for White to develop his attack before countering; or else play a flanking attack against the centre. Then it can happen that White's attack breaks down and Black is left with superiority. But the play is far too close to permit of any compendious pronouncement on the merits.

The reader should always remember that it is the player who wins or loses, not the opening. The strategic strength or weakness of any formation is, by itself, usually insufficient to determine the result of a struggle in which there is always scope for ability.

FRENCH DEFENCE

The main variations of this opening commence on the third move :—

White	*Black*
1. P to K4.	P to K3.
2. P to Q4.	P to Q4.

These moves are the most reasonable and usual and now White has the choice of 3. P × P (the Exchange variation), a deceptively simple looking opening; or 3. P to K5 developing quickly a pressure which is not easy to maintain; or 3. Kt to QB3, the most usual line.

Very frequently seen is the following :—

White	*Black*
1. P to K4.	P to K3.
2. P to Q4.	P to Q4.
3. Kt to QB3.	Kt to KB3. An alternative that is popular nowadays, after a period of disfavour, is 3 . . . B to Kt5. (See below.)
4. B to Kt5. (B to Q3 is playable on this or the next move, but is out of fashion : Lasker played it.)	B to K2. 4. . . . B to Kt5 gives the McCutcheon Defence.
5. P to K5.	KKt to Q2.
6. P to KR4. Alekhine's attack.	

And now Black can hardly play to win the Pawn by B × B because White gains considerable space and tempo. Black can play P to KB3, which gives White the opportunity of a dangerous sacrificial attack commencing B to Q3, which Russian analysis has failed either to establish or refute.

The normal method of defence is to aim at counterplay by P to QB4, etc. This move is usually preceded by P to QR3 to prevent an attack (which may look more dangerous than it is) by Kt to Kt5.

If safely played the game resolves itself into a testing of the weakness of White's apparently good centre.

In this and other variations of the French Defence (e.g., when White plays P to K5 on move 3—Nimzowitch's favourite—or on move 4) White allows his Queen's Pawn to fall to Black's QBP but maintains a Pawn or a Piece on K5 and a Bishop on Q3 maintaining a constant threat against the King's side.

A good deal of interesting play can also arise from White's early abandonment of some centre control by P × QBP when the opportunity affords.

WINAWER'S VARIATION

This alternative system is an old defence revived.

White	Black
1. P to K4.	P to K3.
2. P to Q4.	P to Q4.
3. Kt to QB3.	B to Kt5.

This was thought to be refuted by :—

4. P × P, a form of exchange variation in which Black's Bishop does not appear well placed and White appears to have a freer development. That this is not the case was, however, demonstrated by Alekhine in the famous first game of his match with Capablanca. Since that game most players adopt as the fourth move for White P to K5. Then Black can play safely Kt to K2, or, more dangerously, P to QB4— a line much favoured by the Russian Master Botwinnik.

White can then attack with :—

5. Q to Kt4; and it is then doubtful how much attention Black should give to White's King's side attack at the expense of his own Queen's side attack. This is a variation which very often produces exciting Chess of a combative type. Black can, if he wishes, make the game safe with K to B1 at a proper time, but that has not been the usual treatment. Another (typical) sequence is the following:—

White	Black
1. P to K4.	P to K3.
2. P to Q4.	P to Q4.
3. Kt to QB3.	B to Kt5.
4. P to K5.	P to QB4.
5. P × P.	Kt to QB3.
6. Kt to B3.	KKt to K2.
7. B to Q3.	P to Q5.
8. P to QR3.	B to R4.
9. P to QKt4.	Kt × KtP.
10. P × Kt.	B × P.
11. B to Kt5 Ch.	B to Q2.

The reader's attention is directed to the game Fine-Botwinnik (1938) in the illustrative games.

Another good line in the French arises when Black plays 3. . . . P×KP. Then White can make a Gambit of it with P to KB3.

A different, and playable, system is introduced by Whites' 3. Kt to Q2 reserving the option of P to QB3.

THE CARO-CAHN

The defect of the French Defence from the point of view of many players is that Black closes out of play his Queen's Bishop. This is not a complete account of the matter, because if eventually the Bishop develops on QKt2, behind the Pawns, it is in play strategically, on the assumption that White's centre cannot last for ever, and the diagonal will be opened ; and there are other possibilities for the Bishop— e.g. via Q2 and K1 to the King's wing.

Nevertheless this difficulty has made many players favour the Caro-Cahn, which also invites pressure in the centre, but gives more scope to Black's Queen's Bishop.

White	*Black*
1. P to K4.	P to QB3.
2. P to Q4.	P to Q4.

and now White can proceed with 3. P to K5, answered by B to B4 ; alternatively he can exchange Pawns and follow up with 4. P to QB4, getting the kind of game which can arise from the Slav Defence to the Queen's Pawn. White has an initiative and some pressure, but Black should not lose. In general, it may be said that the Caro-Cahn is not an opening to be recommended to anyone beginning Chess ; but, if mastered, can constitute a useful weapon against the KP openings.

SICILIAN DEFENCE

The reader may by now have apprehended a general notion about the King's Pawn Opening ; that is, the possibility and desirability for Black of counterplay against White's centre. If White is operating against KB7, P to Q4 seems to be a desirable move for Black at some stage ; if White is operating against KR7, or occupying K5 strongly, Black seems to need P to QB4 at some stage. Indeed, both the Queen's Pawn and the Queen's Bishop's Pawn seem to become aggressive for Black sooner or later. The strategic motif is the difficulty for White of any wing attack unless his control of the centre is unchallenged and unimpeded.

That kind of thinking has been responsible for the increase, in modern times, in the popularity of the Sicilian Defence. In answer to 1. P to K4, Black plays 1. . . . P to QB4. According to the best opinion this is the only first move for Black that stands comparison with 1. . . . P to K4. Development appears easy for White—deceptively easy ; Black on the other hand, though not perfectly free, can build his game up on logical lines ; and will eventually generate some threats on the Queen's wing.

The two best known systems of development for Black in the Sicilian are the Paulsen Variation and the Dragon Variation. The former, involving P to K3, lets the King's Bishop develop on K2. The latter, involving P to Q3 and P to KKt3, gives the King's Bishop a Fianchetto Development, a method very popular these days, and giving the game some of the characteristics of the modern Queen's Pawn structure. There is a third of some importance called the Scheveningen Variation, in which Black plays P to Q3 as in the Dragon and P to K3 as in Paulsen's Variation. The line is eminently playable. [However the Sicilian be played, Black, at some stage, is wise to play P—QR3, for defence and attack.]

Paulsen's Variation

White	Black
1. P to K4.	P to QB4.
2. Kt to KB3.	P to K3.
3. P to Q4.	P × P.
4. Kt × P.	Kt to KB3. This move is very important. If it is not done immediately, White can play P to QB4 giving the Maroczy attack—a pressure against the centre, and restrictive of Black's space. The same danger has to be avoided also in the Dragon Variation, or indeed, in any way that the Sicilian is played. The loss of space is not fatal ; but Black is much better not to allow the deprivation to take place.
5. Kt to QB3. Some players endeavour, in this and the other main variations to keep the Queen's Bishop Pawn moves open by playing 5. P to KB3. This can lead to highly speculative play after P to K4, sooner or later, by Black.	
5. . .	P to Q3.
6. B to K2.	Kt to B3.
7. 0—0.	B to K2.

G*

White	Black
8. K to R1. White manoeuvres so as to develop his Queen's Bishop on the line from KKt1 to QR7 and to be able, at the same time to avoid any possible exchange of Bishop for Knight that may be threatened. As he also wants to throw forward his KBP, the text both avoids Check and makes KKt1 available for the Bishop.	
8. ...	P to QR3.
9. P to QR4.	Q to B2.
10. P to B4.	0–0.
	And both players have plenty of scope for manoeuvre.

The Scheveningen can give the same position by transposition of moves, viz. :

White	Black
1. P to K4.	P to QB4.
2. Kt to KB3.	Kt to QB3.
3. P to Q4.	P × P.
4. Kt × P.	Kt to KB3.
5. Kt to QB3.	P to Q3.
6. B to K2.	P to K3, etc.

Paulsen's line only differs from the Scheveningen when Black plays (as he can in some lines) B to QKt5.

In the above variations, as in the next—possibly safer— Black must try, either for P—Q4, or to make the Pawn safe at Q3.

THE DRAGON VARIATION

White	Black
1. P to K4.	P to QB4.
2. Kt to KB3.	Kt to QB3. This move can also be played on the second move of the Paulsen.
3. P to Q4.	P × P.
4. Kt × P.	Kt to KB3.
5. Kt to QB3.	P to Q3.
6. B to K2. (Kt × Kt ; P × Kt, P to K5 is interesting, but unsound.)	
6. ...	P to KKt3.
7. B to K3.	B to Kt2.
8. 0–0.	0–0.
9. Kt to Kt3.	In order to avoid a long and hard to calculate series of exchanges that might be initiated by Black's 9. .... KtKKt5.
9. ...	B to K3.
10. P to B4.	Kt to QR4.
11. P to B5.	B to B5.
12. B to Q3.	And White has a slight advantage.

A good deal of variation is possible in the previous play. Some experiment has been made with 6. B to KKt5, Richter's attack, in order to impede the Dragon formation, but the effort does not appear to justify itself conclusively.

The most modern experimentalists are shifting the emphasis of the opening to an early P—QR3 for Black. The great Anderssen used it as a first move for White!

WING GAMBIT.

White has a sacrificial method of side-tracking the Sicilian in order to get control of the centre, reminiscent of the Danish Gambit, but safer—

White	Black
1. P to K4.	P to QB4.
2. P to QKt4.	P × P.

The traditional way of proceeding is 3. P to QR3, which, however, leads eventually to advantage for Black. The author, however, has had some success with

White	Black
3. B to Kt2.	P to Q4.
4. P × P.	Q × P.
5. Kt to KB3. Or 5. P to QB4, speculative, but good.	
3. P—Q4 is also eminently playable.	

ALEKHINE'S DEFENCE.

Of all the openings based on the strategy of retarded development Alekhine's Defence is the most extreme; and its playability, although it is not recommended to the beginner, demonstrates the richness of strategic resource available on the Chess Board.

White	Black
1. P to K4.	Kt to KB3.
2. P to K5.	Kt to Q4.
3. P to QB4.	Kt to Kt3.
4. P to Q4.	P to Q3. The counterplay begins.
5. P to B4.	P × P.
6. BP × P.	Kt to B3.
7. B to K3.	An interesting point. White waits for the Black Bishop to commit itself before moving the King's Knight. If, e.g., White plays 7. Kt to KB3, Black can pin that Knight without loss of tempo.
7. . . .	B to B4.
8. Kt to QB3.	P to K3.
9. Kt to B3.	Kt to Kt5.
10. R to B1.	P to B4. And Black has recovered some of the mobility of which the opening appeared to deprive him.

Of course White is not obliged to play this opening at a fast tempo. White can play e.g. 3. P to Q4 and develop quietly.

Alternatively, White can chase the Knight with 3. P to QB4 and 4. P to QB5 and 5. Kt to QB3. Thus Kt × Kt then gives a remarkable position in which Black will have used up half a dozen moves with a Knight, while White has opened up his game. Yet Black does not necessarily lose.

THE QUEEN'S SIDE OPENINGS

The reader will have observed, while studying the more combative openings, that it is very easy for the player, either of the attack or of the defence, to become pre-occupied with tactical interests on one side of the Board or another to the detriment of general development. He will also have observed that a quick attack is quite likely to burn itself out too quickly.

For practical purposes then it seems desirable to play a type of Chess in which a more general preparation takes place and in which the attack, when it eventually becomes incisive, has more strategic weight behind it. Now there is no opening in Chess in which a good player will find it impossible to develop strategically. Even the varieties of King's Gambit can be played in a balanced way and a subtler way than they were in the past. But they still offer temptations to impetuosity. Consequently there is a tendency on the part of the many to avoid them. That accounts for the immense popularity in modern Chess of the Queen's Gambit and other varieties of Queen's Pawn opening. These (which are far from new), also have their excitements and their speculative excesses ; but, on the whole the Queen's Pawn gives, to White at least, a steadier, less hectic type of game than those openings in which the tactical threats are more quickly generated. The move 1. P to Q4 is not quite so good a developing move, or so incisive an attack on the centre, as 1. P to K4 ; nevertheless it " contains " the centre, and creates space in which White can mobilise ; and even exerts a pressure that Black cannot ignore, and which can become formidable.

There are perhaps more playable replies to P to Q4 than there are to P to K4. Several Pawns, and both the Knights can move in reply, though 1. . . . Kt to KB3 is a very much better reply than 1. . . . Kt to QB3, the reason being, not only that Black is afraid of pursuit, but that in the Queen's Pawn generally Black's Queen's Bishop's Pawn should be free to move either to QB3 or QB4. Notwithstanding the playability of other moves, Black's normal reply to 1. P to Q4 is either 1. . . . P to Q4 or, with a view to one of the modern defences, 1. . . . Kt to KB3. 1. . . . P to KKt3 is also playable.

THE QUEEN'S GAMBIT

The danger of the Queen's Pawn opening, from White's stand point, is that Black can equalise more easily than in the King's Pawn. It therefore behoves White to play with such incisiveness as a relatively slow opening allows. That is why the Queen's Gambit is the normal development, and much more frequent among Queen's Pawn openings than the King's Gambit is among King's Pawn openings. As much as the King's Gambit, the Queen's Gambit is a logical way of generating a pressure on the centre.

In contrast to the King's Gambit, the Queen's Gambit is more usually declined than accepted. Once White is inhibiting Black's P to K4, it is important for Black to inhibit White's P to K4. In the King's Gambit the converse does not hold, because Black can move his King's Pawn away from the centre and still be able to play P to Q4. In modern times there has, indeed, developed a tendency to accept the Queen's Gambit. That entails something of the subtle modern strategy that aims at breaking up White's centre later on, and gaining the occupancy of important squares round the centre. Before considering other lines the reader is well advised to study the orthodox form of the Queen's Gambit declined.

	White	*Black*
1.	P to Q4.	P to Q4.
2.	P to QB4.	P to K3. There is an alternative, 2. . . . P to QB3, which aims at a deferred acceptance after Black has brought some pressure on White's K4. Also playable is 2. . . . P to K4 (Albin's Counter Gambit: see p. 140).
3.	Kt to QB3. More incisive than 2. Kt to KB3, which is good but contemplates a slower development.	
3.	. . .	Kt to KB3.
4.	B to Kt5. Again the incisive line and popularised by the famous Pillsbury. White achieves a good, but different, type of game by keeping his Black square Bishop behind his Pawns.	
4.	. . .	QKt to Q2. The reader has already seen that this move does not lose a Pawn. The only advantage of this move over 4 . . . B to K2 consists, not in the trap, but in the option of developing the Bishop on other squares.
5.	P to K3.	B to K2.
6.	Kt to B3.	0–0.

At this point White has a variety of moves. He is not well advised to exchange Pawns, because that develops Black. He has some slow moves such as P to QR3, or even P to QKt3, which are not unplayable. But they give Black counterplay. White's normal choice is between 7. R to B1 and 7. B to Q3. 7. Q to B2 used to be played, and was indeed used in the Lasker-Capablanca match. It is still good ; but less popular than 7. R to B1 because R to B1 prevents Black's immediate 7. . . . P to QB4, which 7. Q to B2 does not prevent but indeed invites. Of course if after 7. R to QB1 Black plays P to QB4 White can either win a Pawn or gain positional advantage at Black's option :—

White	Black
7. R to QB1.	P to B4.
8. P × BP.	P × P.
9. P to B6.	Kt to Kt3
10. Q × Q.	R × Q.
11. Kt to K5.	

Alternatively :—

White	Black
7. R to B1.	P to B4.
8. P × BP.	Kt × P 8. . . . B × P is obviously no better.
9. P × P.	P × P.
10. Kt × P.	Kt × Kt.
11. R × Kt with a distinct advantage.	

In answer to 7. R to B1 Black usually plays P to B3. At that point White frequently plays the logical B to Q3 and Black, at that point, can take the Gambit Pawn with gain of tempo, and secure sufficient counterplay to neutralise any advantage White may have in the centre thus :—

White	Black
7. R to B1.	P to B3.
8. B to Q3.	P × P.
9. B × P.	Kt to Q4. KtQKt3 is also playable.
10. B × B.	Q × B.
11. 0—0.	

Perhaps the best reply to that is 11. . . . R to Q1 but the following line of play has become popular :—

White	Black
11. . . .	Kt × Kt.
12. R × Kt.	P to K4.
13. P × P.	Kt × P.
14. Kt × Kt.	Q × Kt.
15. P to B4.	Q to K5. And Black should be able to perfect his development.
16. B—Q3 intruduces highly speculative chess.	

To Rubinstein is attributable another popular departure. On

move 8, instead of B to Q3, White plays Q to B2, adding a threat of sorts to the move B to Q3 when it is made.

Against 8, Q to B2, Black has no particularly incisive counterplay, 8. . . . Kt to K5 being of doubtful validity after 9. B×B Q×B 10. Kt×Kt P×Kt 11. Kt to Q2. In answer to 8. . . Kt to K5 the Author also favours P to KR4.

The normal play for Black against Q to B2 is as follows :— P to KR3, followed by P to QR3. Sooner or later, Black will free the Queen's side with the moves P×BP, P to QKt4, and P to B4.

It is worth mentioning that the attacking possibilities of the Q.G.D. were known to Zukertort. He, however, used to play 7. P to QB5, in order to avoid the loss of tempo after B to Q3. Steinitz refuted this by showing how it makes possible P to K4.

The move P to QB5 is playable, however, at about move 11 if Black plays P to QR3 as well as P to QB3.

As for the loss of tempo when the Bishop goes to Q3, this is relatively unimportant. Indeed, Black can play P×P before BQ3 without disadvantage, as was shown in a game Naegeli v. Alekhine.

The above is the orthodox treatment of the Queen's Gambit But, as in the Ruy Lopez (which corresponds to it among King's Pawn Openings) so here, there is a big variety available to Black. He has at his disposal for example the Cambridge Springs Defence (introduced by Marshall at the Cambridge Springs Tournament, 1904).

	White	*Black*
1.	PQ4.	PQ4.
2.	PQB4.	PK3.
3.	KtQB3.	KtKB3.
4.	BKt5.	QKtQ2.
5.	PK3.	PQB3.
6.	KtKB3.	QR4.

and now White cannot play
7. BQ3 because of 7 . . . . KtK5.

Nevertheless, White has good play after 7. B×Kt or 7. B to K2, or 7. P×P, etc. The Defence has been played in World Championship games, but seems to have lost its popularity.

Interesting is the author's treatment of it.

	White	*Black*
7.	B×Kt.	Kt×B.
8.	B to Q3.	B to Kt5.
9.	0–0 sacrificing a Pawn for the attack.	

LASKER'S METHOD

Another useful idea that can be adopted against the Queen's Gambit (B to Kt5 variation) is the following : to play the Bishop to K2 on the fourth move, follow with P to KR3 (this is good because it prevents a counter by P to KR4, but is not strictly necessary) and later Kt to K5. White cannot then win a Pawn on his K4 after the exchange of Bishops because of Black's threat to check with the Queen at QKt5, regaining a Pawn and considerable freedom, thus :

	White	*Black.*
1.	P to Q4.	P to Q4.
2.	P to QB4.	P to K3.
3.	Kt to QB3.	Kt to KB3.
4.	B to Kt5.	B to K2.
5.	P to K3.	P to KR3.
6.	B to R4 (B × Kt is also good).	QKt to Q2.
7.	Kt to KB3.	Kt to K5.
8.	B × B.	Q × B.
9.	Kt × Kt.	P × Kt.
10.	Kt to Q2.	Kt to B3.
11.	Q to B2.	P to K4 with equality.

A better method for White is, on Move 9, to play not Kt×Kt but P×P. This forces Black to play Kt×Kt ; and after the recaptures of Knight and Pawn, White can play B to Q3 with the initiative.

8. P to KR4 (played by the Author) is also worth considering.

THE SLOWER FORM OF THE QUEEN'S GAMBIT; AND SLAV DEFENCE.

The modern orthodox form of the Queen's Gambit Declined has been popular since the days of Pillsbury Before his period the development of the Queen's Bishop at KKt5 was not popular. And subsequently to Pillsbury's time there has been a revival of the Slow form, as it is called, of the Queen's Gambit on the part of players who feel that the tempo of the Pillsbury attack is too fast. They prefer to leave the Queen's Bishop behind the Pawns, in order to develop it eventually on QKt2 or on the K-wing after the KP has moved to K4. This incidentally suggests another point of strategy already mentioned, and of which modern players are more conscious than were there predecessors, namely, that a Bishop on a long diagonal behind Pawns is a well developed Bishop. If, e.g., White has Pawns on Q4 and K5 or a Pawn on Q4 and a Knight on K5 the Bishop is supporting them. Moreover, the Pawns will eventually be liable to liquidation by exchanges and eventually the Bishop is likely to be in the sole control of the diagonal. This, it must be understood, is a possibility that has to be judged in the light of the tactical dynamics of the particular game. In general however, it may be said that, in the modern openings, both for White and Black, the Fianchetto of one Bishop or two Bishops is normal. *Inter alia* it has the advantage of preserving the Bishops against exchanges by Knights. That player gives up his Bishops for Knights who can block the Fianchettoed Bishops successfully.

Notwithstanding its advantages, the voluntary adoption of the slow form of the Queens is rare.

White	Black
1. P to Q4.	P to Q4.
2. P to QB4.	P to K3.
3. Kt to QB3.	Kt to KB3.
4. Kt to KB3.	B to K2.
5. P to K3.	P to QB3. Preparing for the possibility of the Meran counter attack. A good alternative is Castles.

The reason why players do not play the voluntary form of the slow Queens is that most of them do not wish to facilitate P to QB4 for Black. Consequently we find that the slow form of the Queen's is usually played when Black has committed himself to the move P to QB3. This may happen in the following way :

White	Black
1. P to Q4.	P to Q4.
2. P to QB4.	P to K3.
3. Kt to QB3.	P to QB3.

If now White plays Kt to KB3 in order to preserve the option of B to Kt5 he runs the risk of the deferred acceptance of the Gambit by the following

White	Black
4. Kt to KB3.	P × P.
5. P to K3.	P to QKt4.
6. P to QR4.	B to Kt5.
7. B to Q2.	P to QR4.
8. P × P.	B × Kt.
9. B × B.	P × P.
10. P to QKt3.	B to Kt2. Obviously P to Kt5 is unplayable for the moment.
11. P × P.	P to Kt5.
12. B to Kt2.	Kt to KB3. With a good game. (Black's play from 5 onwards is known as Abrahams' Defence.)

If on move 4, White plays P to K3, Black can play P to KB4 —the Stonewall Defence—which has never been refuted

White	Black
1. PQ4.	PQ4.
2. PQB4.	PK3.
3. KtQB3.	PQB3.
4. PK3.	PKB4.
5. KtKB3.	BQ3.
6. BQ3.	KtKR3. (In order to ensure that BP × P can be met by KP × P.)
7. QB2.	0—0, etc.

The Slav Defence introduces P to QB3 for Black on the second move, viz :

White	*Black*
1. P to Q4.	P to Q4.
2. P to QB4.	P to QB3.

This is very popular nowadays. It has the advantage of giving Black's Queen's Bishop more freedom than in the orthodox Q.G.D. Thus

White	*Black*
3. Kt to QB3.	Kt to KB3.
4. Kt to KB3.	B to B4: or 4. . . . P × P a playable variation of Queen's Gambit Accepted; but the main line is popular, because it is wise for Black to control White's K4.

However, there are dangers in the quick development of Black's Queen's Bishop. White, with or without the exchange of Pawns, can get a quick development on the Queen's side, with some endgame advantages. e.g., by P × P, followed by Q to Kt3. Also White can, after much preparation, force P to K4 with advantage.

Consequently, and rather paradoxically, Black frequently abandons that particular advantage of the Slav and on the fourth move plays not B to B4 but P to K3.

At this point B to Kt5 for White is not generally recommended, because again Black can carry out the deferred acceptance of the Gambit by 5 . . . P × P—a difficult game for both sides. Normal, therefore, is the following main play :

White	*Black*
1. P to Q4.	P to Q4.
2. P to QB4.	P to QB3.
3. Kt to QB3.	Kt to KB3.
4. Kt to KB3.	P to K3.
5. P to K3.	And we have the Slow form of the Queen's, which is a very good opening.

Play may continue as follows :

White	*Black*
5. . . .	QKt to Q2.
6. B to Q3.	B to Q3. Many authorities regard B to K2 as safer against the possible 7. P to K4 ; but it is now generally thought that 7. P to K4 is a drawing line. That may or may not be a reason for allowing it.
7. 0–0	0–0.

White	*Black*
8. P to K4.	P × BP. Not, however :

	Black
8. . . .	P × KP.
9. Kt × P.	Kt × Kt.
10. B × Kt.	P to K4.
11. P × P.	Kt × P.
12. Kt × Kt.	B × Kt.
13. B × P Ch.	K × B.
14. Q to R5 Ch. wins a Pawn.	

White	*Black*
9. B × P.	P to K4. With a tolerable game

THE MERAN COUNTER-ATTACK

At move 6 in this variation (which can be reached by transposition from the (voluntary slow Queen's) Black has the option of P × P, and that can be followed up by the Meran counter-attack.

White	*Black*
6. . . .	P × P.
7. B × P.	P to QKt4.
8. B to Q3.	P to QR3.
9. P to K4.	P to B4.
10. P to K5.	P × P.
11. Kt × KtP.	Kt × KP. Better, perhaps, is
	11. . . . P × Kt.
	12. P × Kt. Q to Kt3.
12. Kt × Kt.	P × Kt.
13. Q to B3.	B to Kt5 Ch.
14. K to K2.	R to QKt1 with many excitements to come.

Complete analysis of this and other variations is of course beyond the scope of an introductory volume. Enough has been shown, however, for the reader to realise that even in the so called slow openings there is scope for tactical lines that raise the tempo and style of the game from piano to forte.

Modern strategians, both as Black and White, are quite likely to take early steps to prevent the game from reaching crescendo too early. This accounts for the modern popularity of the Catalan System for White. After 1. P to Q4. P to Q4. 2. P to QB4. P to K3 (or P to QB3), White instead of playing Kt to QB3 plays Kt to KB3. This move, in answer to P to K3 makes the eventual B to KKt5 a little more difficult because it is unsupported by the attack on the Queen's Pawn ; and Black with P to KR3 can virtually force an exchange of pieces. (1. P to Q4 P to Q4 2. P to QB4 P to K3 3. Kt to KB3 Kt to KB3 4. B to Kt5 P to KR3. If 5. B to R4 P to KKt4 6. B to Kt3 Kt to K5 7. P to K3 P to KR4 with advantage.) But when White plays 3. Kt to KB3 he can elect not for eventual B to KKt5 but for P to

KKt3 followed by B to KKt2 and he can combine that with P to QKt3 and B to QKt2. In this way White gets a good control of the centre squares, but Black, playing carefully, can prevent White's attack from becoming too strong. At the proper time Black will have to play vigorously in the centre in order to free his game.

White	Black
1. P to Q4.	P to Q4.
2. P to QB4.	P to K3.
3. Kt to KB3.	Kt to KB3.
4. P to KKt3.	B to K2.
5. B to Kt2.	0–0.
6. Kt to B3.	And now Black has to prepare P to K4 or P to B4 in order to get counterplay in the middle of the board.

If Black has started with a Slav, the Catalan is better for White because P to B4 for Black will waste a tempo. In that case Black has to play for the possibility of P×BP followed by P to K4.

RETI-ZUKERTORT. ENGLISH OPENING, ETC.

The Catalan leads us logically away from the Queen's Gambit to the set of openings loosely known as the Queen's Pawn Openings. These include some openings in which the move of the Queen's Pawn is long delayed, so that they might more properly be called Queen's side openings or Slow openings than Queen's Pawn openings.

Typical is the Reti-Zukertort system. The combination of names—a classical master and a modern master—indicates that old experiments have been perfected in modern strategy. White's first move is Kt to KB3. Whether Black replies with Kt to KB3 or P to Q4 White's second move can be P to QB4. (If P to QB4 is White's first move—and it is eminently playable—we get the English opening, which, achieving continental appearances, comes to resemble the Reti-Zukertort). If Black plays slowly against the Reti-Zukertort, what happens may be as follows—

White	Black
1. Kt to KB3.	Kt to KB3.
2. P to QB4.	P to QB4.
3. Kt to QB3.	P to KKt3.
4. P to K4.	P to Q3.
5. P to Q4.	P×P.
6. Kt × P.	

And White has the Maroczy Attack in the Sicilian. If Black plays more vigorously with 1 .... P to Q4, White, as has been pointed out can play P to QB4. If then Black plays P to Q5 he is engineering a premature attack. If he plays P to K3, we have the English by transposition (P to QB4, P to K3, Kt to KB3, P to Q4). At that point, or later, White can adopt the P to KKt3 system.

It is even possible for White to play P to KKt3, or P to QKt3, on the second move (Kt to KB3 being the first). This method, which would in the past (late 19th century) have been regarded as dreadfully unenterprising, is now quite orthodox.

MODERN VARIATIONS OF THE QUEEN'S PAWN

From the point of view of Black, particularly, it is in the Queen's Pawn rather than the King's Pawn Openings that most of the experiments of modern opening strategy have taken place ; because, since the tempo of White's attack in the Queen's Pawn is slower at the outset of the game, Black has got more leisure in which to carry out his own purposes.

There are many aspects of modern theory—which must not be thought of as a simple formula. One of these aspects consists in the recognition that a centre development is not a good thing in itself, Grunfeld's Defence illustrates this truth.

GRUNFELD'S DEFENCE

The reader will appreciate that after the moves 1. P to Q4, P to Q4. 2. P to QB4, Kt to KB3 is not a very good move for Black. That is to say that Black cannot immediately recapture on his Q4 (in the event of White playing 3. P × P) because of the immediate loss of tempo.

Now consider the Grunfeld system—

White	*Black*
1. P to Q4.	Kt to KB3.
2. P to QB4.	P to KKt3.
3. Kt to QB3.	P to Q4. The following will show why this is playable.
4. P × P.	Kt × P.
5. P to K4.	Kt × Kt.
6. P × Kt.	

And now Black with B to Kt2 and P to QB4, etc., gets excellent command of the diagonal, or forces White to weaken the centre (The Hollow Centre) by advancing one of the Pawns leaving weak squares around it for Black to occupy.

On reflection the reader will recognise that this is precisely the reasoning that takes away value from some of the Giuoco

Piano lines; the apparently formidable centre turns out to be insubstantial.

In the Grunfeld, White is well advised not to attempt to play any quick Pawn advance in the centre. The best treatment is as follows:—

White	Black
	B to Kt2.
4. B to B4.	
5. P to K3.	0—0.
6. Kt to B3.	P to QB4.
7. B to K5.	And White's development is solid as well as aggressive. Notice that now White is threatening to win a Pawn.

King's Indian Defence

At first sight this is a more surprising system than the Grunfeld because it permits White more activity in the centre.

White	Black
1. P to Q4.	Kt to KB3.
2. P to QB4.	P to KKt3.
3. Kt to QB3.	B to Kt2.
4. P to K4.	P to Q3.
5. P to B4.	0—0
6. Kt to B3.	P to B4. Black commences to weaken the centre.

If now White captures the Pawn, Black gets a good free game with·Q to R4. If, instead, White advances the Queen's Pawn then Black has several strategic possibilities to consider. With moves like P to K3 and Pawn exchanges followed by Q moves he can exploit White's weak Queen side and weak diagonals, while White attempts a King's side attack. Alternatively, the Pawn position now being crystallized, Black can prepare to play P to QKt4 or P to K4 and P to KB4 liquidating or undermining the centre. White has counterplay to this; but both sides have chances.

Here, again, the better practice for White is not to overdevelop the centre. Instead of 5. P to KB4 there is much to be said for P to KB3 or Kt to KB3. The former leads to a development with P to KKt4, Kt to Kt3, etc., not unlike a possible development for White in the slow form of the Morphy Defence to the Ruy Lopez.

The reader may be reminded by this opening of the temptation given to White to develop the centre excessively against Alekhine's Defence.

Also playable is 5. B to K2 followed by 6. P—KR4 (the Author's method).

THE NIMZOVITCH SYSTEM

One of the most popular modern methods, backed by the authority of one of the greatest players of this century, consists in a different method of undermining, or blocking the centre.

	White	*Black*
1.	P to Q4.	Kt to KB3.
2.	P to QB4.	P to K3.
3.	Kt to QB3.	B to Kt5. This obviously prevents P to K4 ; and against it P to K4 is surprisingly hard to force, P to KB3 being slow.

One popular reply is 4. P to QR3, which is replied to by B × KtCh. White loses a tempo, and gets a development in which the Pawn at QB4 is not very helpful. On the other hand he has strengthened the defensive aspect of his centre and got rid of one of Black's good pieces. It is not advisable. thereafter, to try and force P to K4 because Black can occupy his own K4 (P to Q3 being played first) blocking the centre.

Other methods of treating the Nimzovitch Defence consist in 4. Q to B2 which can be replied to with P to Q4 giving Black a not unsatisfactory form of the Queen's Gambit.

Also White can play 4. Q to Kt3 to which Black can reply P to QB4 coupled with eventual Kt to QB3. This is typical of the system ; and the following line is instructive :

	White	*Black*
1.	P to Q4.	Kt to KB3.
2.	P to QB4.	P to K3
3.	Kt to QB3.	B to Kt5.
4.	Q to Kt3.	P to QB4.
5.	P × P.	Kt to QB3.
6.	Kt to KB3.	Kt to K5.
7.	B to Q2.	Kt × QBP.
8.	Q to B2.	0–0.
9.	P to QR3.	B × Kt.
10.	B × B.	P to QR4.
11.	P to KKt3.	

White can also elect to ignore Black's 3rd move, assuming that the Black Bishop is not placed on its best possible square.

Thus 4. P to K3. This is sometimes coupled with 5. K KtK2, and P to KB3, a slow process, because it does not avoid the need for P to QR3. Reasonable is P to KKt3 at move 4 or 3.

Exciting is the Budapest—1. P to Q4 KKt to B3, 2. P to QB4 P to K4, 3. P × P Kt to Kt5 (or K5) with play. In answer to 3. . . . Kt to K5 4. P to QR3 is recommended.

QUEEN'S INDIAN DEFENCE

In order to control a fluid centre it is quite a desirable thing for Black to develop his Queen's Bishop at Kt2. This is most usually played when White develops his King's Knight before his Queen's Knight. Black's first three moves are usually Kt to KB3, followed by P to K3 and P to QKt3. To dispense with the second of these is possible ; but if P to K3 is played, then Black can combine his B to QKt2 with B to QKt5. He must be careful about order if White on the third move plays the Queen's Knight to B3. Thus,

White	*Black*
1. P to Q4.	Kt to KB3.
2. P to QB4.	P to K3.
3. Kt to QB3.	P to QKt3.
4. P to K4.	B to Kt5.
5. P to K5.	Kt to K5.
6. Q to Kt4.	Kt × Kt. Black is in trouble.
7. P × Kt.	B × P Ch.
8. K to Q1.	K to B1 (best).
9. B to R3 Ch.	K to Kt1.
10. R to QKt1.	B to Kt2.
11. R to Kt3.	B to R4.
12. Q × KtP Ch. with a mating attack.	

However, if the Bishop is played to Kt2 before B to Kt5 this situation cannot come about. Nor does the danger exist if White's third move is Kt-KB3. Normally the Queen's Indian is played without B to QKt5. If B to QKt5 is played it is with the intention of exchanging that Bishop, because evidently the Pawn formation is incompatible with the comfort of the Bishop on the Queen's wing.

The Queen's Indian and the Nimzo-Indian (Q.1. with B to Kt5) are too logical to require detailed treatment. They are usually met by a King's Fianchetto on the part of White. White will eventually endeavour to play P to K4 and Black will play to block the centre with P to Q3 and K4, the Black Queen's Knight being developed at Q2.

OTHER Q.P. OPENINGS

Of other openings that are worth mentioning, not least is the Dutch Defence 1. P to Q4, P to KB4.

White also can open with 1. P to KB4, but it is not so advantageous to White as to Black, since, early in the game, the move is defensive rather than aggressive.

The Dutch Defence can be met by a Gambit 2. P to K4, (or even P to KKt4) which requires no special treatment. Otherwise it is likely to transpose itself into the Stone Wall Defence.

In conclusion, it may be said of the Queen's Pawn Openings generally, that once their strategy is grasped they do not require learning. That consideration, together with the less

intense nature of the early struggle accounts for the prefer-
ences that are shown among modern players for the Queen's
Pawn over the King's Pawn systems.

It may also be added, as a final note on the Openings,
generally—

1. That even good openings do not win games. All they
create is an initiative—which passes as both sides develop.

2. It is therefore, important for Black not to regard himself
as at any disadvantage. If truth be told, he may even have
the advantage.

3. It is more important to concentrate on seeing good
moves than on learning them.

4. There are fashions in Opening choices. These may
produce surprise, but should not produce alarm. In point is
a recent (1961) resuscitation of an old move—1. . . . P to
KKt3 in answer to 1. P to K4 (or Q4) and the impressive label
Kotov-Robatsch. But this is precisely the kind of play that
gives to the player that meets it every opportunity for doing
well on his own resources.

AFTER THE OPENING

As you emerge from the opening you will find, if you are
playing intelligently, that you have no occasion to ask yourself,
What shall I think about now ? As the game proceeds, two
processes are going on. You are developing your pieces, and
you are attacking or defending. These processes are really one
process. You will find that no attack on a specific object is
worth while if it involves you in difficulties of development,
and no defence is good, if it cramps your development. Again
you will also find that if your pieces are coming into play,
e.g., Rooks getting on to Open Files, etc., then you are also
generating plenty of specific threats and parrying threats.
Your opponent is, from his side, doing likewise. The problem
for both of you is to secure Control and Freedom. As the two
sets of forces integrate the position itself will indicate to you
the proper direction of your thoughts. Then the important
thing will be to miss as little as possible of what the Board
reveals to those who can interpret it.

CHAPTER VI

SOME RESOURCES AND REFINEMENTS
IN THE ENDGAME.

We have seen that the endgame is the beginning of Chess. It is also the end—the latest stage and the most advanced. It calls for vision in the highest degree, and in addition to vision, or in necessary support of it, a considerable technique.

Of basic elementary endgame technique, the reader has already been told a great deal in the second and subsequent chapters. In an introductory volume, it is not possible or desirable to undertake an exhaustive account. All that is aimed at here is the demonstration of a few of the resources and refinements that characterise the ending. The appreciation of these should help to equip the reader for the endgame, as acquaintance with some of the tactical processes may have equipped him for the middle-game.

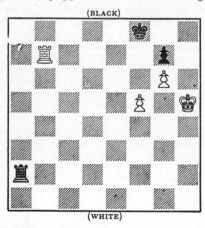

(BLACK)

(WHITE)

AN ERROR.
White can lose.
1. R to Kt8 Ch., K to K2.
2. R to Kt8, K to B3.
3. R to B8 Ch., K to K4.
4. R to B7, K to B5! and White cannot avoid Mate.

Fundamental to the endgame is, of course, vision. In the endgame it is possible to lose by an oversight as easily as at any other stage. The first diagram illustrates an easy error to make.

That is an error of vision at a reasonably elementary level. But it is much easier to go wrong, through, for example,

missing points of tempo. Here is a great endgame player
(Spielmann) missing the best move in the diagram position.
He can win by 1 ... K to B6. He actually played 1 ... K × P
and there followed 2. P to Kt6, K to Q6. 3. R to Q7, P to Q5.
4. P to Kt7, R to Kt3. 5. K to Kt2, R to Kt8. 6. K to Kt3.
Black was wrong to allow the White Pawn to advance to Kt6,
because after that he cannot move his King usefully without
allowing a Rook threat followed by P to Kt7, and then Black's

(BLACK)

(WHITE)

Black to play.

Rook is relatively immobilized, so that nothing can be forced.
Had Black not been greedy and played 1 . . . K to B6 he
would have won as follows : 1. . . . K to B6, 2. R to B7 Ch.
K × P. Now 3. R to KKt7 is forced because if 3. R to QKt7
there follows R × P, 4. R × P Ch. K to B6 winning the Rook
or mating. Therefore, 3. R to KKt7 (Black has already gained
a tempo) K to B6, 4. R to B7 Ch., K to Q6 (another gain of
tempo), 5. R to KKt7, P to Q5. 6. P to KKt6, R to QB7 Ch.
7. K to Kt1 (the effect of K to Q1 is worse) R to B3. 8. R to
Kt8, K to B6 (cleverly protected against the tempo gaining
check) 9. P to Kt7, R to B2 and White must move and lose.

It was said earlier in the book that strategy consists, in some
part, in the preparation for the endgame, in so playing as to
have a good endgame structure. That is true, but " negatively "
true. You must rather play so as not to have a bad endgame
structure. But to guarantee the endgame structure for victory
is an impossible requirement. One enters the actual endgame
fighting ; and at that stage the Board is full of resource.

A very fine example is furnished in a game of Alekhine's (Reshevsky-Alekhine, 1938). Black drew this apparently hopeless ending by play involving a brilliant manoeuvre.

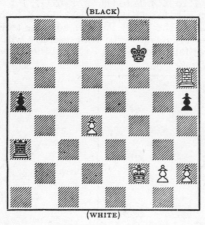

(BLACK)

(WHITE)

RESHEVSKY—
ALEKHINE (1938).
Black draws.

	White	Black
44.	. . .	R to Q6.
45.	R × P.	P to R5.
46.	P to Q5 (R to R5 is not demonstrably better).	P to R6.
47.	R to R7 Ch.	K to B3.
48.	R to R7.	K to K4.
49.	R to R5.	R to Q7 Ch.
50.	K to B3.	R to Q6 Ch.
51.	K to K2.	R to QKt6.
52.	K to B2.	R to Kt7 Ch.
53.	K to Kt3.	R to Kt6 Ch.
54.	K to Kt4.	R to Kt7.
55.	K to R3.	P to R7.
56.	P to Q6. Ch.	K × P.
57.	P to Kt4.	K to B3.
58.	K to Kt3.	K to Kt3.
59.	R to R8.	K to Kt4.
60.	P to R3.	K to Kt5.
61.	K to B4 (threat was R to Kt6 Ch. and R to R6).	R to QB7—threat repeated.
62.	R to Kt8 Ch.	K to B6.
63.	R to B8 Ch.	K to Kt5.
		Draw by repetition of moves.

And here is a position reached between Botwinnik and Euwe at a tournament in 1946 in which the Russian Master gained a draw resourcefully in a position where his opponent had a clear endgame advantage.

BOTWINNIK
—EUWE.

Black to play.
37. ... P to B5.
38. P × P, P × P.
39. P to R4, P to R3.
40. P to Kt5, P to R4.
41. K to K3! K to K4.
42. R to B2! P to B6.
43. K to Q3, R to Q1 Ch. (K to B5 is probably better.)
44. K to K3, R to Q5.
45. R × P, R × P Ch.
46. K to B3, R × P.
47. R to B6! R to B5. Ch.
48. K to K3, R to K5 Ch.
49. K to B3, K to B4.
50. R to B6 Ch., K × P.
57. R × P Ch. Drawn.

A number of diagrams at the end of this chapter illustrate something of the infinite variety of clever Chess that the endgame affords. Meanwhile it may be useful to mention a few points of endgame technique that are sufficiently difficult for an intelligent player to have difficulty in discovering them unaided.

(BLACK)

(WHITE)

OPPOSITION PLAY
1. If P to B6 Ch. P × P Ch.
2. K to B5. If 2 ... K to B1.
3. K × P Wins. If 2 .. K to Q1.
3. K to Q6 wins. Therefore 1 ... K to B1.
2. K to Q6 K to Kt1.
3. K to Q7 P × P!
4. K × P K to B1 draws.
To win, White plays
1. K to K5 K to B3 (best).
2. K to Q4 K to Q2.
3. K to Q5 with Opposition.

The reader has already seen the technique of play by King and Pawn against King (see Chapter II). The basis of that is the move in hand that the player with the Pawn must try to keep. Thus, if a King is situated at K1 opposite a King at K1 and the Pawn is at K2, the technique is to play the King to Q2, K3, K4 as quickly as possible, preserving the Pawn moves. The Pawn move preserves the opposition to the dominant King, so that eventually the position that is reached is King at K6, Pawn at K5, opponent's King it matters not where, and the player with the Pawn must win. This is tempo play and opposition play, of which other examples have been given. Let the reader now work out why K at K5, P at K4 : Black K at K2 is not a win if White to move.

Incidentally, two Pawns against one are more favourable to the attacker than a lone Pawn. He may be able to choose his time to exchange.

(BLACK)

(WHITE)

DISTANT
OPPOSITION

(Modern analysts describe this, also, as a study in RE-LATED SQUARES)

More difficult is the *distant opposition*. There are Pawns on both sides and possibly on both wings. The Kings are distant from each other, but when they approach each other, the opposition will determine which player (if any) breaks through in order to capture the Pawns. How then to gain the opposition at a distance ? This is not always possible ; but the diagram illustrates the problem tackled. White has to keep the King in such a position relatively to the other that when they approach there shall be a distance of three squares between them, and the King to move shall have to leave the square of the same colour as the opposing King, or else retreat. In either case the dominant King will penetrate the Pawn position.

In the diagram the process is made possible by the configuration of the Pawns, which is slightly favourable to White.

Obviously if the White King tries to go straight through, either on the Queen's wing or on the King's wing, he will find the Black King barring his entry ; and this inevitability is only removed by ensuring that the Black King will not have the opposition when the two Kings are next square but one to each other. It so happens that White can take advantage of the restriction in the Black King's space. 1. K to Kt1, K to Kt2. 2. K to B1, K to B2. 3. K to Q1, K to Q2. 4. K to B2, K to Q1. 5. K to B3, K to B2. 6. K to Q3 ; and now if Black plays K to Q2 in apparent opposition, White plays K to B4. [If at move 4. . . . K to B1. 5. K to Q2, K to Q2 (or 1). 6. K to B3!]

If, however, in the diagram position it were Black's turn to move, Black could draw by 1. . . . K to Kt2. 2. K to Kt1, K to R2. If then the White King goes to Kt2, Black plays K to R1 ; if 3. K to B1, K to Kt2 ; if K to B2, K to Kt1 ; and Black's King can always remain an odd number of squares away from the White King on the same colour squares.

In an elementary book all the variations cannot be analysed ; but the student is invited to experiment for himself. A very simple method of learning how to handle the distant opposition is the following : place the two Kings each on their KR1. Let White then endeavour to reach either of two squares for victory, QR8 or QB8. The process is 1. K to R2, K to Kt1. 2. K to Kt2, K to B1. 3. K to B2, K to K1. 4. K to K2, K to Q1. 5. K to Q2, K to B1. 6. K to B2, K to Kt1. 7. K to Kt2, K to R1. 8. K to B3. (The last two moves amount to triangulation ; White still has the distant opposition.) 8. . . . K to Kt2. 9. K to Kt3, K to R2. 10. K to B4, K to Kt3. 11. K to Kt4, K to R2. 12. K to B5, K to Kt2. 13. K to Kt5, K to R2. 14. K to B6, K to Kt1. 15. K to Kt6, K to R1. 16. K to B7, K to R2. 17. K to B8.

More practically important than the distant opposition is the notion of triangulation which we saw in that example. The King with three squares to manoeuvre on can defeat the King with two squares. This kind of manoeuvre is seen in the position in the next diagram. Black has fewer squares. Yet if White were to play immediately, K to K3, Black would reply K to K4 with advantage. But White can waste a move with K to Q2 or K to B2. Then if Black plays K to K4 White becomes dominant with K to K3, and if Black plays K to B3 or Q2, instead, White simply wins the Pawn with K to K3.

The opposition and the distant opposition can be the occasion of neat play of a tempo-losing character. Thus imagine Pawns at R4 and R5, and an opposition Pawn at Kt2; Kings facing each other among Pawns elsewhere on the Board. Then White forces Black to move by playing P to R6 P×P 2. P to R5. It is noteworthy that, whereas in the middle game one usually wishes to gain tempo, in the

(BLACK)

(WHITE)

Purposive Loss of Tempo.

WHITE WINS
(by Triangulation).
1. K to Q2 (not K to K3).
If 1. . . . K—K4, then 2. K—K3.

endgame one often requires to lose tempo. This is the only phase at which Chess technique resembles that of Draughts.

When other Pieces are present with King and Pawn or King and Pawns the possibilities become too great for compendious description.

Some points are worth observing.

Observe the power of a Knight to sacrifice itself for a Pawn. Thus if you have a Pawn at say KB7, and a hostile Knight is guarding the Queening square, you can never force the Pawn home with the aid of your King. Thus suppose your King goes to K7 attacking the Knight on its Q2, the Knight goes to its K4. Then, if you Queen the Pawn, Kt to Kt3 forks King and Queen. Again if you attack the Knight with K to K6 the Kt plays to its B1. If then K to K7, Kt to Kt3 ; and so forth. Therefore it can come about that King, Pawn and Knight can draw with King, Rook and Pawn. With your Pawn on the seventh you hold the hostile Rook, and with the Knight you play against the King and Pawn. The Knight sacrifices itself for the Pawn, and you win the Rook in exchange for your own dangerous Pawn. That of course assumes a fortunate placing of the Pieces ; but it is a feature to be borne in mind.

Another important feature of endgame play is the virtual impossibility of winning with a Pawn majority when each side has a Bishop, and the Bishops are of opposite colour. The reasoning is that given a King barring the path of one or two Pawns, those Pawns cannot be forced (with B check) to a square not controlled by their Bishop. Alternatively if the position reduces itself far enough, the Bishop cannot be prevented by the opposing Bishop from sacrificing itself for the Pawn. The most favourable situation in these circumstances is to have a majority of two Pawns and for Pawns to be on both wings. Then you may be able with the aid of the King to force the Bishop to sacrifice itself for one or two of your Pawns while you still have a Bishop and a guarded Pawn on the Board. Then (usually) Bishop, King and Pawn will defeat King and Pawn.

And this brings us to another consideration, which is of the first importance in endgame play ; that Bishop and Rook's Pawn cannot win if the defending King can place itself in front of the Pawn and if the Bishop does not control the final Queening square. This, be it emphasized, only applies to the Rook's file. On any other file the King can arrive at a seventh square adjoining the Pawn ; this cannot be done when the hostile King is on a Rook's file and the Pawn is the Rook's Pawn, because stalemate occurs first.

However, there is a special case. If you can get your Bishop on R7 and your Pawn on R6, the King cannot reach its R1—and can be headed off by your King, while the Pawn gets promoted.

ROOK AND PAWN ENDGAMES

But far and away the most important feature of endgame technique is the play of the Rooks against the Pawns. The reader has already seen that two or three well-placed Pawns can defeat a Rook. That is a tactical occurrence which is relatively easy to see. What causes difficulty is the fact that a majority of endings are characterised by Rook or Rooks on each side, and a Pawn majority on one side. The keystone of this type of ending is the situation where King, Rook and one Pawn are against King and Rook. This can be extremely difficult.

To emphasise the difficulty let it be mentioned that King, Rook and two Pawns do not necessarily win against King and Rook. The diagram shows such a position. Obviously here Black cannot attack and capture the Bishop's Pawn because the

H

backward King could not stop the Knight's Pawn. But similarly White can do nothing. If he checks, the King can then capture the Pawn, because it so happens that White cannot thereafter save the Knight's Pawn. On the same reasoning the White Rook cannot leave his rank. Even if he goes to R8 and subsequently defends the Pawn from QKt8, it will fall.

(BLACK)

(WHITE)

DRAW.
1. R to R8 K × P.
2. P to Kt5 K to B5.
3. P to Kt6 R to K2!
   (not the 'normal'
   R to QKt8 because
   of the check on the
   file).
4. R to QKt8 K to B4
5. K to K6 R to KR2.
6. P to Kt7 K to Kt3
   Draws.

The diagram position is unusually favourable to Black. It is more favourable to the defender when the two Pawns are Rook's Pawn and Knight's Pawn on the same side of the Board ; and there can also be great difficulty when the Pawns are separated by one file or even two files. When they are separated by more the likelihood is that the defending King will prove inadequate to the task of co-operating in the gain of one Pawn and then in the stopping of the other.

Fundamental in the last diagram position is the fact that when one Pawn falls the other cannot be Queened. But that need not be the case. It follows that the fundamental consideration for endgame play is the possibility of Queening a Pawn with the aid of a Rook against a Rook.

Now obviously the most favourable circumstances exist when the King is playing a causative part in the Queening of the Pawn. A typical position is the Lucena position in the diagram. Here White wins neatly by playing R to B5. The threat is then R to K5 Ch. followed by K to B7. If then R to B7 Ch. K to Kt6 and after R to Kt7 Ch. R to Kt5. The Rook has, as it were, built an arch under which the King can operate. If the Black King were less dominant than in the diagram, obviously the process would be easy, because a Rook is not adequate to controlling a King that is helping a Pawn to Queen (except in the solitary case of the Rook's Pawn, where perpetual check is possible). But even where

(BLACK)

(WHITE)

WHITE WINS
The Lucena Position
1. R to B5 (See Text)
   If 1. . . . K to K2.
2. R to K5 Ch. K to B3.
3. K to B8 wins.
(1. R—K1 Ch. followed by R—K4 also creates an archway for the King.)

the Pawn is a Rook's Pawn, then if the hostile King is sufficiently far away the dominant Rook can execute the kind of protective manœuvre that we have just seen.

That line of thought amounts to one reason among others why it is an advantage to cut the hostile King off from the critical Pawn context; and it is not easy to keep a King cut off. The King can always pass a file with the aid of a Rook, provided that he has time after the exchanges of Rooks to prevent the promotion of the Pawn.

In short then, if both Kings are on the scene of action the win is unlikely. This with one reservation; that if the defending King is on the back rank faced by Pawn with adjacent King, then mating threats become a factor, and it is very important that the defending Rook shall be able to drive away the threatening King.

Most difficult of all is where the attacking King has an option. At K6 it is facing a King on its K1. The Pawn is at Q5. If the King is checked on the rank the Pawn may be able to advance, creating a mating threat; if the King is checked on the file its position when it goes to Q6 is dominant, because then it is probable that the defending King can be driven from the back row, and the Lucena position may easily come into being.

The second main class of Rook and Pawn against Rook endings is when the Kings are not in the battle but the Rooks are.

Then if the dominant Rook is behind its Pawn and the Pawn is sufficiently advanced, the defending Rook, in front of it, is at a great disadvantage; and it is a question of which King can arrive at the scene of action first. It is quite likely that the freer Rook can cut off the defending King along the rank for sufficiently long to enable the attacking King to arrive in time to force the Queening of the Pawn. This class of position is relatively easy. More difficult is the situation where the attacking Rook is in front of its Pawn, and the Pawn is on the sixth or the seventh. Then the position is delicate indeed. Then it may not pay the defending King to be too near. Obviously on the third rank the defending King is at a clear loss because it cannot keep out of Check. Let White King be at K3, R at QR8; P at QR7; Black Rook at KR2, King at Q3. Black's only available move is R to Q2. There follows 2. K to K4. If then R to K2 Ch. White plays either K to Q4 or K to Q3. 3. . . . R to Q2 is then forced and White plays K to B4 and cannot be stopped from taking a decisive part; thus K to B4, R to B2 Ch. 5. K to Kt5, R to B4 Ch. 6. K to Kt4, winning.

If the Black Rook were not on the second rank Black's situation would be worse.

(BLACK)

(WHITE)

White to move, wins. If the Black King were on the third rank (other than QB3 QKt3 or QR3) the win would be even more obvious.

The Diagram on the opposite page is of great technical interest. White to move wins and Black to move draws. White has only to play R to KB8 or KKt8, or KR8 ; and obviously the Pawn cannot be captured or stopped. It follows that unless the Black King can move a square nearer to the Pawn it is worse off than if it were further away. Now further down the file is no use because of the file checks, giving a tempo for Queening. The correct position, and one rather hard to find by the light of nature, is the position in the following diagram.

(BLACK)

DRAW.

(WHITE)

If the Black King stays on its KKt2 or KR2 the game is a draw. The Black King is proof there against file checks or rank thrusts. The White King can never be useful because it can be driven away by an endless series of checks. Therefore, it is useless for the White King to work its way to QKt2 and then up the file. Similar technique applies even if the Pawn is not on the Rook's file. More difficult is the position when the Pawn is at R6. If at the moment the defending King is near enough to reach its QB2 then the game is a draw because the Pawn is forced on to R7 and the King reaches QB2 and QKt2. But if the King is at that moment on the King's file it must rush back to KKt2, because of the threat of P to R7. However, the White King can be prevented, by a combination of file and rank threats, from reaching R7 while the Rook is still at R8. There are checking possibilities on the QB file to cope with the situation.

If, however, the Pawn instead of being at R6 were at Kt6

with the two Rooks at their respective Kt8, then the situation would be uncontrollably difficult for Black, though it would require the greatest delicacy for White to win. The reader is left to work out the process for himself.

Enough has now been said to give the student an idea of the nature of endgame technique and to communicate to him a few of its important principles. To do more would require a

(BLACK)

(WHITE)

WHITE WINS.
(An ending by Kubbel)

1. Kt to K3 Dis. Ch., K to Kt6.
2. Q to Kt4 Ch., K to B7.
3. Q to B4 Ch., K to K7 (best).
4. Q to B1 Ch., K to Q7.
5. Q to Q1 Ch., K to B6.
6. Q to B2 Ch., K to Kt5.
7. Q to Kt2 Ch., Kt to Kt6.
8. Q to R3 Ch., K × Q.
9. Kt to B2, Mate.

(BLACK)

(WHITE)

WHITE WINS.

1. Kt to K2, K × Kt.
2. B to Q1 Ch., K × B.
3. P = Q wins, by 4 Q to Kt1 Ch.
If 2. . . . K to K6, etc.
3. B to B3, K × B.
4. P = Q wins by 5 Q to R8 Ch.
[After 5. . . . K to Kt7 the Q. wins because Black's other pawns prevent stalemate.]

much larger, indeed a special, volume. To conclude the chapter here are a number of endgame compositions by famous composers—and a few from play. Between them they illustrate several of the resources of the Chess Board and some of its beauties.

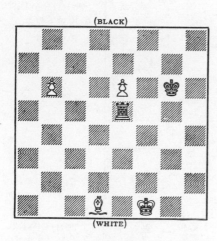

WHITE WINS.
1. P to Kt7, R to QKt4.
2. P to Q7, K to B2.
3. P to Q8 Ch., K × Q.
4. B to R4, wins.

WHITE WINS.
1. R to K1.

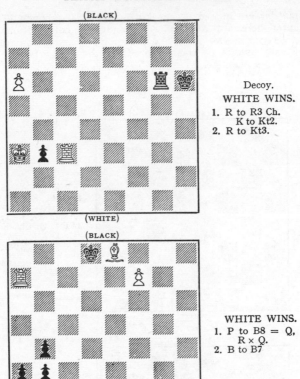

(BLACK)

Decoy.
WHITE WINS.
1. R to R3 Ch.
   K to Kt2.
2. R to Kt3.

(WHITE)

(BLACK)

WHITE WINS.
1. P to B8 = Q,
   R × Q.
2. B to B7

(WHITE)

A NOTE ON CHESS PROBLEMS, CHESS COMPOSITIONS AND
THE AESTHETIC IN CHESS

It is not proposed in this book to consider the rather special
aspect of Chess which is the Chess problem. At one time
problems were studies in difficulty, and were solved by
unexpected captures and spectacular sacrifices. Nowadays
the problem that is seen in the newspapers and the magazines
is a special thing. It is characterised by a certain difficulty :

but normally, the essence of the problem is that the solution and the variations illustrate and express some geometric theme which is intellectually satisfying and may be quite beautiful. The interest, however, is specialized. For the purposes of the student of Chess it should be said, then, that problems are not very helpful. Nevertheless they are not valueless.

In the typical two move or three move problem you have to Mate in the specific number of moves. Usually the position given would not be difficult to win. But to Mate in two or three moves can, from that position, be extraordinarily difficult. The problem may be what is called a Waiter. That is to say if Black moved you could Mate him, but any move you make seems to take away your capacity to Mate him. You therefore have to find an ingenuity which preserves the possibilities, or substitutes possibilities for those that it takes away (Change Mate). Alternatively, you may have to find a way of mating that is unexpected, and threaten it—or prevent a defence to a threat that is in being. These are Threat problems. Very neat can be those in which the defence to one threat reciprocally interferes with the defence to another threat. In the case of three moves the processes involved may be really difficult, and there may be clever Chess in the very short range over which you are thinking ; but they, too, are specialized. The utility of problems for a Chess player consists in this, that in solving them you have to visualize the Mate or the manœuvre that the composer has in mind ; to do that is an exercise of imagination, and imagination is the soul of Chess. The reader is therefore well advised to endeavour to solve problems. In doing so he is well advised to remember that it is not a question of winning but of doing a special task ; and the solution is not likely to be a forceful move such as check or a capture. And when he comes from solving problems to practical play he must not spend his time imagining possible Mates too improbable to be important.

Here in notation are two well known Chess problems to illustrate what ideas Chess problems express and to show how the problem mind works.

6K1, 8, 4p 1 k p, 7p, 4PR 1P, 8, 6 B1, 8.

MATE IN THREE—

White	*Black*
Solution :	
1. B to B1.	P to K4.
2. B to Q3.	P × R.
3. P to K5 Mate.	

The Mate is pretty, and that Mating idea has to be conceived for the problem to be solved.

H *

Harder and even prettier is the following :—
8. 7Q, 4k 3, 4P3, 8. 2Kt 1 p Kt 2, K7, 8.

MATE IN THREE

White   *Black*

Solution :
  1. Kt to QR4 (threatening Kt
     to Kt6 followed by QQ7).
  1. . . .   K to Q4.
  2. Q to KB7 Ch.
  2. . . .   K to K5.
  3. Kt to B5 Mate.
If 2. . . .   K to B3.
  3. Kt to Q4 Mate.

These show clever mating ideas. Problems can also express decoys, batteries, avoidance of stalemate, etc., etc., but with the idea abstracted from the reality of the game.

The reader will also have noticed other compositions, especially in the last chapter, which can only be described as elegant. These (endgame compositions) are much more useful than problems because they show not only elegances of the Board, but interesting methods of play, and resources that may be of practical value.

Again the reader has seen some combinations in actual play that can be described as beautiful. These suggest the reflection that Chess is not only a Science, but may also possess the appeal to the spectator, real or imaginary, which is the essence of art. Nevertheless, let it always be remembered that the beauty of a piece of Chess is accidental, relatively to its effectiveness. Chess is a science and the good Chess move is the effective Chess move, as the good scientific process is the one that carries a result. The formal beauty of an idea is as irrelevant in Chess as, in Science, the aesthetic pleasure provided by colours that may occur in chemical experiments. Yet perhaps Chess gives something greater than the aesthetic. If the student of Chess comes to a stage where he can see a neat, elegant, or beautiful idea, and reject it because there is a better move available, then he has arrived at a high stage of Chess, and is approaching the attainment of that intellectual integrity which is the contribution of any science to culture.

CHAPTER VII
ILLUSTRATIVE GAMES

White	*Black*
MORPHY	DUKE OF BRUNSWICK

1. P to K4. — P to K4.

2. Kt to KB3. — P to Q3. Philidor. A good move, but one that involves the need for very careful play very early.

3. P to Q4. — B to Kt5. A mistake, of which the worst consequences are hard to see.

Black is losing tempo ; best is Kt to Q2 which enables Black reply to P×P with P×P. Black would subsequently develop with P to QB3, B to K2, Kt to B3.

4. P×P. — B×Kt. Almost forced. Black has to fear—

4. . . .	P×P.
5. Q×Q Ch.	K×Q.
6. Kt×P.	
4. . . .	Q to K2

is playable, but " difficult."

5. Q×B. — P×P.

6. B to B4 with immediate pressure. — Kt to KB3. Black is already in difficulties. The text gives him an immediate defence on which Morphy puts great pressure. Possibly better was 6 . . . Q to B3 followed by 7. Q to Kt3, Kt to Q2 losing (or sacrificing) a Pawn but getting some counterplay.

7. Q to QKt3 with double attack. — Q to K2. The best available effort.

8. Kt to QB3. Not Q×KtP because then 8 . . . Q to Kt5 Ch. forces exchanges of Queens and Black has a little freedom to compensate for his Pawn. — P to B3. Defending the Kt Pawn, but leaving the game very cramped. Better was Kt to Q2, letting the Pawn go.

9. B to KKt5. Maintaining the pressure. At this point the game is not yet lost for Black, but his disadvantage is clear. If, e.g., he plays P to KR3 there might follow—
B×Kt   P×B.
and later, the establishment of a Kt on KB5. — P to QKt 4. A desperate effort for freedom which fails disastrously Black has not seen all that his opponent can do.

10. Kt × KtP. — P×Kt.

11. B × KtP Ch. — QKt to Q2.

12. 0-0-0. — R to Q1. Apparently good enough.

White	*Black*
13. R × Kt, showing how little the values of the Pieces matter when there is a decisive process available.	R × R.
14. R to Q1.	Q to K3, necessary in order to enable the Kt to recapture.

At this point White can win simply by B × KKt and if then, P × B either B × R ch. or Q to R4, but the win will not be such a rapid one.

What Morphy does is immediately decisive, and very pretty—

White	*Black*
15. B × R Ch.	Kt × B.
16. Q to Kt8 Ch.	Kt × Q.
17. R to Q8 Mate.	

Observe that White's entire force is B and R against Q, R, B and Kt.

A companion study in strangulation is afforded in Modern Chess, where players are better equipped strategically than was the Duke of Brunswick, but where a keen player still surpasses a dull player, and does so the more strikingly in that what he has to see may be the exploitation of a finer difference in development than was usually exploited in the past.

White (ALEKHINE)	*Black* (BÖÖK)
1. P to Q4.	P to Q4.
2. P to QB4.	P × P. The Queen's Gambit Accepted. A difficult opening.
3. Kt to KB3.	Kt to KB3.
4. P to K3.	P to K3. Slow.
5. B × P. White achieves this without losing the tempo that is usually lost in the Q.G.D.	P to B4
6. 0–0.	Kt to QB3. Awkward. The Kt should go to Q2—the reason appears later. The point of the text is to try and get in Kt to Kt5 after the B has been driven.
7. Q to K2. Offering a Pawn.	P to QR3, (Safer than P × P).
8. Kt to B3. Better than R to Q1, which is met by 8. ... P to QKt4. 9. B to Kt3, P to B5. 10. B to B2, Kt to Kt5.	P to QKt4.
9. B to Kt3.	P to Kt5. Bad because it is a premature attack. More specifically bad, because it does not cope with the (admittedly brilliant) tactical possibilities that Alekhine finds. Better (but not very good) was P to QB5 followed by B to Kt2, losing, at least, no tempo.
10. P to Q5. Vigorous and good. White is commencing on excellent combination.	Kt to QR4. If ... P × Kt, B to R4 is excellent for White. If P × P, Kt × P followed by R to Q1 etc.

White	Black
11. B to R4 Ch.	B to Q2.
12. P × P.	P × P. B × B would lose at least a Pawn by P × P Ch. K × P Kt × B, but is playable.
13. R to Q1. Pinning the Bishop and attacking in a way reminiscent of the Morphy game.	P × Kt.
14. R × B. This and the following moves had to be seen quite clearly, at the latest on move 13, but in order to make move 10 sound, it had to be seen then.	Kt × R.
15. Kt to K5.	R to R2.
16. P × P. This gives the game its hall-mark. White had to see when he sacrificed that, after this quiet move, Black has nothing to stop the attack.	K to K2. A horrible expedient, but it has to be done sooner or later, because of the number of Pieces that White can mobilize against the pinned Kt. If P to Kt3, e.g., 17. Q to Q3 stops any idea of Castling.
17. P to K4. White has seen that he can still attack if the Kt is temporarily unpinned.	Kt to KB3.
18. B to KKt5.	Q to B2. Attempting to get in P to K4.
19. B to B4	Q to Kt3. The brilliance of the attack may be judged on the assumption that White had seen 19. . . . Q to Kt2. 20. R to Q1, Kt × P. 21. Q × Kt, Q × Q. 22. B to Kt5 Mate. Easier to see but less decisive is 19. . . . Q to Kt2. 20. R to Q1, Q × P. 21. Q to Q2, Kt to Q4. 22. B to Kt5 Ch., with a prolonged and convincing attack.
20. R to Q1.	P to Kt3.
21. B to KKt5.	B to Kt2.
22. Kt to Q7.	R × Kt.
23. R × R Ch.	K to B1.
24. B × Kt.	B × B.
25. P to K5.	Resigns. After all the simplification, Black cannot escape.

A splendid example of strangulation carried out on other than the weakest.

The next example is of quick suffocation, occasioned by a great master's decision to incur pressure.

RUY LOPEZ

White (BIRD)	Black (STEINITZ)
1. P to K4.	P to K4.
2. Kt to KB3.	Kt to QB3.
3. B to Kt5.	Kt to B3. Berlin Defence.
4. P to Q4.	P × P.

White (BIRD)	*Black* (STEINITZ)
5. P to K5.	Kt to K5.
6. Kt × P.	Kt × Kt.
7. Q × Kt.	Kt to B4.
8. 0—0.	B to K2.
9. P to KB4.	P to QKt3. Too aggressive. Black is trying to exploit White's bold 9th move. The idea is ingenious, but unwarranted.
10. P to B5.	Kt to Kt6.
11. Q to K4.	Kt × R.
12. P to B6. At move 9 . . . Black had probably expected 12. Q × R.	B to B4 Ch.
13. K to R1.	R to QKt1.
14. P to K6 wins.	

From the 1890's an example of combative, rather than positional play; typical of the attack based on advantage of tempo, in which the positional differences are hard to state. It is an example of neat decapitation, rather than strangulation. It was played by the winner, when he was past his prime, in the famous Hastings Tournament of 1895.

White (W. STEINITZ)	*Black* (C. VON BARDELEBEN)
1. P to K4.	P to K4.
2. Kt to KB3.	Kt to QB3.
3. B to B4.	B to B4.

These moves constitute the Giucco Piano (or Italian) opening. The name implies that it is a slow game; but the variation here played does not support that description.

White	*Black*
4. P to B3. Endeavouring to control the centre.	Kt to B3. Counter attacking towards, rather than defending, the centre.
5. P to Q4.	P × P.
6. P × P.	B to Kt5 Ch. A good move giving Black a breathing space in which to attend to the centre, but developing White's game as well. The opening is becoming tactically rich.
7. Kt to B3. The Moller attack. If now Black plays Kt × P, he lies open to a dangerous albeit speculative attack commencing with P to Q5 or Q to Kt3, or 8. 0—0 (followed possibly by B × Kt. 9. P × B, P to Q4. 10. B to R3 with a vigorous game).	P to Q4. Also playing dangerously. Black was anxious to avoid the main lines of the Moller attack and adopts a method of development which requires the most careful handling.
8. P × P.	KKt × P.
9. 0—0.	B to K3. White was threatening to win a Piece; and the best defence was hard to find.

For Black to win a Pawn by Kt×Kt, P×Kt, B×P, would be wrong because of White's Q to Kt3 to follow, initiating a winning attack against the Black King. There were, however, other playable moves, e.g., 9. . . . . B × Kt followed by O–O or BK3. Also 9. . . . Kt to KB3 was playable. Both of these moves leave White with the attack; but, given good defence, the attack would not be fatal. The text move, which looks safe, proves, in a subtle way, to have lost tempo.

White	*Black*
10. B to KKt5. Good and unexpected. It was hard for Black to see what a control of the Board this gives his opponent.	B to K2. At this point choices are becoming limited. If e.g., 10. Q to Q2 there follows 11. B × Kt, B × B. 12. R to K1 Ch. with a considerable attack. If, on the other hand 10 . . . P to KB3. 11. R to K1 is disruptive. If 10 . . . KKt to K2, 11. P to Q5 seems to win a Piece. If 10 . . . QKt to K2, a variation similar to the text ensues. In any event, it was hard for Black to see, through the exchanges, how formidable White's attack was going to prove.
11. B × Kt.	QB × B. If KB × B there might follow B × B, P × B, Q to Kt3 winning at least a Pawn.
12. Kt × B. Continuing the forcing sequence.	Q × Kt. If B × B White has options like Kt × B forcing Q × Kt(Q4) R to K1 Ch. K to B1 ; or Kt × BP Ch., winning a Pawn but not fatal ; or R to K1 Ch. with similar pressure on the King's file to what happens, but with Black having lost a tempo less.
13. B × B. Much better than R to K1, P to B3. Simplification that helps the attack.	Kt × B. Had Black anticipated the resources that White was to call out of the position, he might have played K × B, which gives him a better chance of eventually mobilizing his Rooks. The position is more critical than Black imagines.
14. R to K1. Stopping Black from immediate Castles, and as it turns out, from ever Castling.	P to KB3. Evidently the move on which Black had relied in order to emancipate himself from the pin and in order to mobilize the Rook.
15. Q to K2. More force being exerted.	Q to Q2.
16. QR to B1. A subtle move, inducing a weakness.	P to B3. Black was afraid that after K to B2, there might follow 17. Q × Kt Ch., etc

White   *Black*

giving White at least two Pawns for the exchange. That, however, would not have been so destructive.

17. P to Q5. A brilliant sacrifice a Pawn in order to obtain a square.   P × P.

18. Kt to Q4.   K to B2. Evidently necessary.

19. Kt to K6. White obtains, with this move, a wonderful command of the squares on which he wishes to attack.   K R to QB1. To prevent, among other things, R to B7. The King's Rook is chosen to avoid the possibility that the Black King may be compelled to go to the back rank, shutting off K R square.

20. Q to Kt4. Threatening Mate among other things.   P to Kt3. White's next move shows why Kt to Kt3 was impossible.

21. Kt to Kt5 Ch.   K to K1. Forced in order to save the Queen. That Queen, incidentally, is now in an awkward position because it is guarding the Rook rather than the Knight.

22. R × Kt. Ch. Taking excellent advantage of the fact that the Queen is tied. But Steinitz has also seen that the King cannot take. If the King could take, White would be left the exchange and a Pawn to the bad. Moreover, it was also necessary for Steinitz to see the effect of Black's refusal of the exchange because, after Black's next move, every Piece of White's is under attack and White is threatened with Mate.   K to B1. If K × R, there follows, 23. R to K1 Ch. If, then, K to Q1, Kt to K6 Ch. wins the Queen quickly. If, instead, K to Q3. 24. Q to Kt4 Ch., K to B2, Kt to K6 Ch. K to Kt1, Q to KB4 Ch. wins.

23. R to B7 Ch.   K to Kt1. Obviously this Rook could not be captured. Black's reply still leaves White with the problem arising from the attack on his Pieces.

24. R to Kt7 Ch. An idea that White must have entertained for a long time. This Rook cannot be captured by the Queen because Black will be left a Piece down at least, whereas the King's capture allows Q × Q Ch.   K to R1. If K to B1, 25. Kt × P Ch. is fatal, because if K × R, Q × Q Ch. and if K to K1, Kt × BP Ch. etc.

25. R × P Ch. And wins.

At this point Von Bardeleben is reported to have made no comment but to have put on his hat and quietly walked home, leaving his opponent to win by effluxion of time. That was a

Teutonic way of showing that he knew what was coming. If, now, K to Kt1, there follows R to Kt7 Ch. Now the King cannot go to B1 or take the Rook for reasons that we have seen. But in answer to 26. . . . K to R1, there follows a beautiful and long mating process, viz. :

	White	*Black*
26.	...	K to R1.
27.	Q to R4 Ch.	K × R.
28.	Q to R7 Ch.	K to B1.
29.	Q to R8 Ch.	K to K2.
30.	Q to Kt7 Ch.	K to K1. (Best.)
31.	Q to Kt8 Ch.	K to K2.
32.	Q to B7 Ch.	K to Q1.
33.	Q to B8 Ch.	Q to K1.
34.	Kt to B7 Ch.	K to Q2.
35.	Q to Q6 Mate.	

The reader will observe that White is still threatened with R × R Mate.

The next example shows the significance of a clear superiority in development.

A good specimen of exploitation of a cramped game. Stabbing the insufficiently agile. Giuoco Piano (in effect).

	White (HERMANN)	*Black* (HUSSONG)
1.	P to K4.	P to K4.
2.	Kt to KB3.	Kt to QB3.
3.	B to Kt5.	P to QR3.
4.	B to B4. Changing to Giuoco Piano with loss of a move.	Kt to B3.
5.	P to Q3. The Pianissimo Variation.	B to B4.
6.	B to K3.	P to Q3.
7.	QKt to Q2.	B to K3.
8.	B × KB.	P × B.
9.	B × B.	P × B. These exchanges are not to White's advantage. The doubled Pawns are not easy to exploit without Bishops.
10.	Kt to B4.	Kt to Q2.
11.	P to QR4.	Q to B3.
12.	P to B3.	0–0.
13.	0–0.	QR to Q1.
14.	P to R5.	Kt to K2. Starting a long trek to the King side.
15.	Q to Kt3.	Kt to KKt3.
16	Q × P. Unwise.	Kt to B5.
17.	Kt to K1. From excessive rashness to excessive caution. Kt to K3 was better.	Q to Kt4.
18	K to R1.	R to B3.
19.	Kt to K3.	QR to KB1. (If R to R3 21. Kt to B3).
20.	Q × BP. Nero in reincarnation !	QR to B2.
21.	Q to B8 Ch.	Kt to B1.

White (HERMANN)   *Black* (HUSSONG)

	White (HERMANN)	*Black* (HUSSONG)
22.	Q × BP.	Q to R4. Black's agressive formation is excellent. White's next move perfects it and allows a pretty finish, which is the better because of White's counter sacrifice.
23.	R to KKt1.	Q × P Ch.
24.	K × Q.	R to R3 Ch.
25.	K to Kt3.	Kt to K7 Ch.
26.	K to Kt4.	R to B5 Ch.
27.	K to Kt5.	R to R7.
28.	Q × Kt Ch.	K × Q.
29.	Kt to B3.	P to R3 Ch.
30.	K to Kt6.	K to Kt1.
31.	Kt × R.	R to B4.
	Resigns.	

A game in which both sides fight well, and a stroke of genius decides the issue.

ENGLISH OPENING.

	White (ZUKERTORT)	*Black* (BLACKBURNE)
1.	P to QB4.	P to K3.
2.	P to K3.	Kt to KB3.
3.	Kt to KB3.	P to QKt3.
4.	B to K2.	B to Kt2.
5.	0—0.	P to Q4.
6.	P to Q4.	B to Q3. B to K2 is safer for Black in this type of game.
7.	Kt to B3.	0—0.
8.	P to QKt3.	QKt to Q2.
9.	B to Kt2.	Q to K2.
10.	Kt to QKt5—gaining a slight advantage.	Kt to K5.
11.	Kt × B.	P × Kt.
12.	Kt to Q2.	QKt to B3. Black plays boldly to invite White's attack. Safer was P × P followed by P to Q4 and Kt to Q3.
13.	P to B3.	Kt × Kt.
14.	Q × Kt.	P × P.
15.	B × P. Strategic decision.	P to Q4.
16.	B to Q3.	KR to B1. The interest of this game derives from the fact that Black as well as White has an aggressive plan.
17.	QR to K1.	R to B2.
18.	P to K4.	QR to QB1.
19.	P to K5.	Kt to QB1.
20.	P to B4. A typical King's side attack of the QP order.	Kt to K1.
21.	R to K3.	P to Kt3.
22.	P × P e.p.	P to B4. (In defence of R2).
23.	P to B5. One of the points of move 17.	Kt × P.
24.	B × Kt.	Kt to K5. White has seen the distant consequences of this.
		P × B.

White (ZUKERTORT)	Black (BLACKBURNE)

25. P × KtP.   R to B7. Black's attack is also looking formidable, in view is a possible R × Kt P Ch.

26. P × P Ch.   K to R1.

27. P to Q5 Ch.   P to K4. Apparently, a sound defence.

28. Q to Kt4. One of the best moves in the history of Chess, and certainly the only one to win here.

QR to B4. If Q × Q—
29. B × P Ch.   K × P.
30. R to R3 Ch.   K to Kt3.
31. R to B6 Ch.   K to Kt4.
32. R to Kt3 Ch.   K to R4.
33. R to B5 Ch.   K to R3.
34. B to B4 Ch. and Mate next move.

29. R to B8 Ch. An additional beauty.

K × P. If Q × R. 30. B × P Ch. initiates a rapid winning process.

30. Q × P Ch.   K to Kt2.

31. B × P Ch.   K × R.

32. B to Kt7. Ch. Pretty finish.   K to Kt1. Of course, if Q × B. Q to K8 Mate.

33. Q × Q.   Resigns.

The other pole of Chess. A study in position play—" Judo " rather than " All-in."

White (SÄMISCH)	Black (NIMZOWITCH)

1. P to Q4.   Kt to KB3.

2. P to QB4.   P to K3.

3. Kt to KB3.   P to QKt3. The Queen's Indian. this move cannot be played if White plays 3. Kt to QB3, because then, P to K4 is playable for White with advantage.

4. P to KKt3.   B to Kt2.

5. B to Kt2.   B to K2.

6. Kt to QB3. Good now that the Black Bishop has committed itself.   0—0.

7. 0—0.   P to Q4. Black now feels the necessity of putting a stronger hold on the centre. The fact that this Pawn is on the line of the Bishop does not amount to a limitation on the Bishop according to the modern conception. This point is made more striking by Black's next move.

8. Kt to K5.   P to QB3.

9. P × P. Not the best. White ought to prevent Black from choosing his own method of liquidating the centre. A better move for White was probably P to QKt3.   BP × P. A very shrewd choice. Many players would play KP × P and eventually push the QBP forward. Black sees a better method.

White (Sämisch)

10. B to KB4.

11. R to QB1.
12. Q to Kt3. Not a good move in the light of subsequent play. Better was an immediate challenge by P to QR4.

13. Kt × Kt.

14. P to KR3. With a view to King's side development. This is inconsistent with White's 12th move. There is no good Knight move available for White. Nevertheless, Kt to K4 is better than the text.
15. K to R2. P to KKt4 is better.

16. B to Q2. In order to prevent an unfavourable exchange.

17. Q to Q1. With a view to counter play against the King's side which proves to be inadequate.
18. Kt to Kt1.

19. R to Kt1. Unpinning the Pawn.
20. P to K4. The move on which White had relied in order to save the game. Black refutes this manoeuvre by sacrificing the Knight for two Pawns, or more, and a

Black (Nimzowitch)

P to QR3. This is the beginning of an attempt to seize the square at Black's QB5. The reader will remember earlier comments on the use of the Rook's Pawn.

P to QKt4.
Kt to QB3. A very good move threatening to bring the Knight into play on the Queen's wing. The move is tactically good because Black can reply to the immediate Kt × QP with Kt × QP. (If 13. Kt × KtP Kt to QR4).

B × Kt. Black has gained tempo by this exchange, but White has got rid of one danger.
Q to Q2.

Kt to R4. Black's original intention has been to work this Knight over to the Queen's side, but now that a King's side weakness presents itself he revises his plan.
P to KB4. Black's game being now better integrated, he proceeds to play vigorously into his opponent's territory. The fact that he is leaving a backward Pawn is unimportant in the light of the strength of the attack that he can develop.
P to Kt5. Seizing the opportunity of further immobilizing White's Pieces.

B to QKt4. Bringing pressure to bear on a point that may become weak, and improving the position of the Bishop. Note how the Bishop comes to life on an unexpected diagonal.
B to Q3. Strengthening the attack against the King's side.
BP × P.

White (Sämisch)   *Black* (Nimzowitch)

considerable attack. The open lines that become available to Black are almost sufficient in themselves to warrant the expenditure of material.

21. Q × Kt.   R × P.
22. Q to Kt5. Because, inter alia,   QR to KB1. This Piece too is
    to move the Bishop would   finding its way into the game;
    cost another Pawn.   also this move prevents
                                     B to KB4.

23. K to R1. In order to prevent   R (B1) to B4.
    QR to KB6.
24. Q to K3.   B to Q6. A most cramping move
                                     from White's point of view,
                                     preventing (at move 26.) B to
                                     B1. Undoubtedly the im-
                                     mediate R to K7 would have
                                     been very good for Black but
                                     it is not conclusive. The text
                                     is conclusive Now R to K7
                                     threatens to win the Queen and
                                     to White's only reply Black has
                                     an extraordinary answer.
25. QR to K1.   P to KR3.
26. Resigns.

Black's 25th move creates one of the most remarkable Zugzwang positions in the history of Chess. White to move must lose. He can delay things with P to QR3 (met by P to QR4) and P to KR4 met by any non-committal move on Black's part, but eventually he has to move a Piece or the Pawn at KKt3.

Now evidently the B on Q2 cannot move because that costs White a Knight (the point of move 24); the King's Rook cannot move without loss of a Piece, the Queen's Rook cannot move because of R to K7 winning the major exchange, and neither the King's Bishop nor the King's Knight Pawn can move because of R to KB6; and that move in any event can be played by Black as soon as he likes because the Queen has no escape (the point of move 25).

As a whole the game is a remarkable example of reliance on positional factors. At all stages there were lines of play to consider; but the difference of degree is remarkable between the emphasis on combinative threats in some of the games that have been shown, and the emphasis on strategic and technical features in this game.

It is an amusing footnote to this game that a greater player, Alekhine, some years later inflicted a remarkable Zugzwang on Nimzowitch himself.

The " Zugger " " Zugged."

FRENCH DEFENCE

White (ALEKHINE)	*Black* (NIMZOWITCH)
1. P to K4.	P to K3.
2. P to Q4.	P to Q4.
3. Kt to QB3.	B to Kt5.
4. P to K5.	P to QB4. Safer is Kt to K2, followed, if B to Q2 is played, by P to QR3. The text, however, is playable because the Kt excursion is speculative.
5. B to Q2.	Kt to K2.
6. Kt to Kt5.	B × B Ch.
7. Q × B.	0–0.
8. P to QB3.	P to QKt3. Slow—or else artificial —White's Kt is strengthened on Kt5 by this process, not weakened.
9. P to KB4.	B to R3.
10. Kt to KB3.	Q to Q2.
11. P to QR4.	QKt to B3.
12. P to QKt4. A move of Alekhinian vigour.	P × KtP.
13. P × P.	B to Kt2. An admission that his policy has been wrong. White has a big control of space now.
14. Kt to Q6.	P to B4. A good move to get in while it can be done, but not helpful to the general situation.
15. P to R5.	Kt to B1.
16. Kt × B.	Q × Kt.
17. P to R6. A restrictive move, made without loss of tempo.	Q to KB2.
18. B to Kt5	KKt to K2. QKt to K2 may be a trifle better, but the pressure is severe.
19. 0–0.	P to KR3. To stop Kt to Kt5 if it be contemplated and with a view to P to KKt4 if Black lasts long enough.
20. KR to B1.	KR to B1.
21. R to B2.	Q to K1. Not good : but there is only a choice of evils, of which Black chooses all. Better was Kt to Q1, but that is met by 22. QR to B1 with tremendous pressure. A possible line would be—

	22. . . .	R × R.
	23. R × R.	R to B1.
	24. R × R.	Kt × R.
	25. Q to B2.	

| 22. QR to QB1. | QR to Kt1. Contemplating move 27 with the R at Kt1, but White does not allow this formation to come into being. |
| 23. Q to K3. | R to B2. |

White (ALEKHINE)	*Black* (NIMZOWITCH)
24. R to B3.	Q to Q2.
25. QR to B2.	K to B1.
26. Q to B1.	QR to B1.
27. B to R4.	P to QKt4.
28. B × P.	K to K1.
29. B to R4.	K to Q1.
30. P to R4. Waiting for a guard to be removed from the R at C7.	Q to K1. Black is in Zugzwang. The next move relieves it by an increase of the pressure to breaking point.
31. P to Kt5.	Resigns.

Now a study in technique.

QUEEN'S INDIAN DEFENCE

White (SZABO)	*Black* (DENKER)
1. P to Q4.	Kt to KB3.
2. P to QB4.	P to K3.
3. Kt to KB3.	P to QKt3.
4. P to KKt3.	B to Kt2.
5. B to Kt2.	B to K2.
6. 0—0.	0—0.
7. Kt to B3.	Kt to K5.
8. Q to B2.	Kt × Kt. This loss of tempo is justified because it makes possible Black's treatment of the centre. An alternative was P to KB4.
9. Q × Kt.	P to Q3.
10. Q to B2. Slow. Threatens KtKt5, but Black's reply meets this and equalizes.	Kt to B3.
11. KR to Q1.	B to B3.
12. P to Q5.	KP × P.
13. P × P.	Kt to Kt5. Typical, in conjunction with the next few moves, of modern technique. Black has much to counterbalance White's apparent gain of space.
14. Q to Kt3.	P to QR4.
15. B to K3.	R to K1.
16. QR to B1.	Kt to R3.
17. Kt to Q4.	Kt to B4. Incidentally, a blockade of the White Rook.
18. Q to B2.	Q to Q2.
19. P to KR4. Sound, but not well followed up.	R to K4. Initiating a King's side attack.
20. B to B4. Kt to B6 is better.	R × QP. Giving the Exchange for good consideration.
21. B × R.	B × B. Note Black's control of the White squares.
22. P to Kt3. Saving a Pawn at too much expense. K to R2 was necessary.	Q to R6.
23. Kt to B3.	B to K5. Note how Black is able to defend his Piece without loss of tempo.

White (Szabo)	Black (Denker)
24. Q to Q2.	Kt to K3. The Kt having done its work on the Queen's side now joins in the King's side attack. P to KKt4 is being prepared.
25. Q to K3.	P to Q4.
26. R × BP. Hoping to disract Black from the attack by surrender of the Exchange.	B × P. A neat little combination. If P × B, Q Kt5 Ch. Then B to Kt3 is forced and Kt × R is playable.
27. R to Kt7.	B to Q1.
28. R to QB1.	P to KKt4. Decisive. Obviously, the Pawn cannot be captured.
29. B to B7.	B to B3. B × B followed by P to Kt5 was sound, but unnecessarily complicated. White is deprived by the text of any counterchance.
30. B × QKtP. To get as much material as possible in exchange for what is going to be lost.	P to Kt5.
31. R to Q1.	B to Kt4. Very good. The threat is the 33rd move
32. Q to B3.	P × Kt.
33. P × P.	Kt to B5. P to Q5 also wins, but the text is a more rapid process.
34. P × Kt.	B × P (B6).
35. Q × B.	Q × Q.
36. R to QB1.	B × P.
37. R to K1.	P to Q5.
38. R (K1) to K7.	Q to Kt5 Ch.
39. K to B1.	P to Q6.
Resigns.	

An object lesson in the development of a good attack from technically correct chess.

White (Alekhine)	Black (Sterk)
1. P to Q4.	P to Q4.
2. Kt to KB3.	Kt to KB3.
3. P to B4.	P to K3.
4. Kt to B3.	QKt to Q2.
5. P to K3.	B to Q3.
6. Kt to QKt5. Doubtful, but inexpensive.	B to K2.
7. Q to B2.	P to B3.
8. Kt to B3.	0–0.
9. B to Q3.	P × P.
10. B × P.	P to B4. A good move, since there is not much pressure on the QB file.
11. P × P.	B × P. Perhaps Kt × P is preferable, since PQKt4 creates weakness for White.
12. 0–0.	P to QKt3.
13. P to K4.	B to Kt2.

White (ALEKHINE)	*Black* (STERK)
14. B to KKt5.	Q to B1.
15. Q to K2.	B to Kt5.
16. B to Q3. A clever reply.	B × Kt. Here Black starts going beyond his depth. White's pin of the Bishop is too logical and consistent with development to be escaped combinatively.
17. KR to QB1.	Kt × P.
18. B × Kt.	B × B.
19. Q × B.	Kt to B4.
20. Q to K2.	B to R4. The awkwardness is forced. This is the only move to stop PQKt4.
21. QR to Kt1.	Q to R3. Very ingenious, but inadequate.
22. R to B4. A dominating move.	Kt to R5. Still being ingenious.
23. B to B6. More than ingenious : deep and sound.	If 23. P to QKt4 Kt to B6! KR to QB1.
24. Q to K5. If Black takes the Rook, then after QKt5, there is no escape for the K via B1, K1, Q2, because of White's Kt and Rook.	R to B4.
25. Q to Kt3. If R × R P × B.	P to Kt3.
26. R × Kt.	Q to Q6.
27. R to KB1.	Q to B4.
28. Q to B4.	Q to B7.
29. Q to R6.	Resigns.

A case of drowning in depths.

White (ALEKHINE)	*Black* (LASKER)
1. P to Q4.	P to Q4.
2. P to QB4.	P to K3.
3. KKt to B3.	KKt to B3.
4. Kt to B3.	QKt to Q2.
5. P × P. Relieving Black of a problem.	P × P
6. B to B4.	P to B3.
7. P to K3.	Kt to R4.
8. B to Q3.	Kt × B. A good exchange.
9. P × Kt.	B to Q3.
10. P to KKt3.	0-0.
11. 0-0.	R to K1.
12. Q to B2.	Kt to B1.
13. Kt to Q1. Aiming at the K side, but the process is slow.	P to B3. A far seeing move. Black wants KB2 for a Bishop.
14. Kt to K3.	B to K3.
15. Kt to R4.	B to QB2. Slow, but effective. The Bishop is directed against a weakness at White's Q4.
16. P to QKt4.	B to Kt3.
17. Kt to B3.	B to KB2. And this Bishop can operate from KR4. Black has arranged his Bishops so as to exercise their maximum functions.

White (Alekhine)	Black (Lasker)
18. P to Kt5. Logical counter-play—a "minority attack" to reduce Black's Q side Pawn advantage.	B to KR4. Well timed. The QBP is guarded by the potential R to QB1.
19. P to Kt4.	B to KB2.
20. P × P.	R to B1.
21. Q to Kt2.	P × P. Better than R × P for tactical reasons (e.g., defence of QP).
22. P to B5.	Q to Q3.
23. Kt to Kt2. To prevent Q to B5.	B to B2.
24. KR to K1. White is on the defensive and wishes to reduce material.	P to KR4. The point of many previous moves.
25. P to KR3.	Kt to R2.
26. R × R Ch.	R × R.
27. R to K1.	R to Kt1. One of the points of move 21.
28. Q to B1.	Kt to Kt4. This Knight's path into this game is a study in the exploitation of weak squares.
29. Kt to K5. A desperate endeavour to close lines.	P × Kt. Black can afford now to give up his Kt.
30. Q × Kt.	P to K5.
31. P to B6. Hoping to cause Queen exchanges.	P to Kt3.
32. P to B4.	RP × P. Avoiding unnecessary difficulties.
33. B to K2.	P × P.
34. B to R5.	R to Kt7.
35. Kt to R4.	Q × P.
36. Q × Q.	B × Q.
Resigns.	

Very rarely has a great master been so outplayed and so deprived of control. The game is a study in the use of open lines and useful squares.

FRENCH DEFENCE (Winawer Variation)

White (Fine)	Black (Botwinnik)
1. P to K4.	P to K3.
2. P to Q4.	P to Q4.
3. Kt to QB3.	B to Kt5.
4. P to K5.	P to QB4.
5. P × P. A method which relies on the strength of White's King's side, and allows some weakness on the Queen's side.	Kt to K2.
6. Kt to B3. Better than P to KB4 ("always too early") which leaves the centre hollow.	QKt to B3.
7. B to Q3.	P to Q5.
8. P to QR3.	B to R4.
9. P to QKt4.	Kt × KtP. Attempting too early to take advantage of a tactical complex.

	White (FINE)	*Black* (BOTWINNIK)
10.	P × Kt.	B × P.
11.	B to Kt5 Ch.	Kt to B3. B to Q2 is better, **because** after exchanges, B × B, Q × B White cannot play R to R4.
12.	B × Kt Ch.	P × B.
13.	R to R4. A development worth the material invested.	B × Kt Ch.
14.	B to Q2.	P to B3. A desperate attempt to loosen White's grip.
15.	0–0.	0–0.
16.	B × B.	P × B.
17.	Q to K1. White has control of much more of the board than his opponent.	P to QR4.
18.	Q × P.	B to R3.
19.	KR to R1.	B to Kt4.
20.	R to Q4.	Q to K2.
21.	R to Q6. A good restrictive move.	P to R5. An attempt to exploit Black's only counter-chance.
22.	Q to K3.	R to R2.
23.	Kt to Q2. In this type of game the Knight finds a big choice of squares (K4,Q4 etc.).	P to R6
24.	P to QB4.	B to R5.
25.	P × P.	Q × P.
26.	R × RP.	R to K1. Q to Kt7 leads to nothing after Q × P Ch. and R to K3.
27.	P to R3.	QR to R1.
28.	Kt to B3.	Q to Kt7.
29.	Kt to K5. Much better play than the capture of the KP.	Q to Kt8 **Ch.**
30.	K to R2.	Q to B4.
31.	Q to KKt3.	Resigns. R to KB3 cannot be prevented. Black is only half a Pawn down, but White can carry out any attack he wishes to prepare, e.g.—

31.		R to R2.
32.	R to KB3.	Q to R4.
33.	Kt to Q7.	K to R1.
34.	R × KP,	R × Kt.
35.	Q to Kt5 et seq.	

Q.G.D. (in effect)

	White (BOTWINNIK)	*Black* (VIDMAR)
1.	P to QB4.	P to K3.
2.	Kt to KB3.	P to Q4.
3.	P to Q4.	Kt to KB3.
4.	B to Kt5.	B to K2.
5.	Kt to B3.	0–0.
6.	P to K3.	QKt to Q2.
7.	B to Q3.	P to B4.
8.	0–0.	BP × P.
9.	KP × P.	P × P.
10.	B × P.	Kt to Kt3.
11.	B to Kt3.	B to Q2.

White (BOTWINNIK)	Black (VIDMAR)
12. Q to Q3.	QKt to Q4.
13. Kt to K5.	B to B3.
14. QR to Q1.	Kt to QKt5. Up to this point Black has developed quite soundly, though without embarrassing White. The text is, however, unwarrantable, losing tempo.
15. Q to R3.	B to Q4. Unnatural.
16. Kt × B.	QKt × Kt.
17. P to B4. White has a definite advantage now.	R to B1.
18. P to B5.	P × P?
19. R × P.	Q to Q3. Missing a point.
20. Kt × KBP. A fine exploitation, the analysis of which is not easy.	R × Kt.
21. QB × Kt.	B × B. If Kt × B, R × Kt is good enough. Observe R " hanging."
22. R × Kt.	Q to B3.
23. R to Q6. Pretty.	Q to K1.
24. R to Q7.	Resigns.

An excellent exploitation of uninspired play.

Q.G.A.

White (KOTOV)	Black (YUDOVITCH)
1. P to Q4.	P to Q4.
2. Kt to KB3.	Kt to KB3.
3. P to B4.	P to K3.
4. B to Kt5.	B to Kt5 Ch.
5. Kt to B3.	P × P.
6. P to K4.	P to B4.
7. B × P.	P × P.
8. K × tP.	Q to R4.
9. B × Kt.	B × Kt Ch.
10. P × B.	P × B. A tribute to the land where midnight oil is unrationed. It is hard to see that Q × P Ch. loses. After K to B1. Q × B Ch. K to Kt1. P × B. R to B1 is decisive. If, instead of 12. . . . P × B 0–0 is played, White has a strong King's side attack.
11. 0–0.	Kt to Q2.
12. K to R1. Preparation for opening of lines that may never be opened.	Kt to Kt3. If Q × BP 13. Kt to Kt5.
13. B to Kt3.	B to Q2.
14. Q to B3.	K to K2.
15. Q to K3.	QR to QB1.
16. QR to B1.	Kt to B5. Planless.
17. Q to K2.	Kt to Kt3.
18. Q to Q3.	R to B4.
19. P to KB4.	KR to QB1.
20. P to B4.	B to K1 with a view to P to K4.

	White (Kotov)	Black (Yudovitch)
21.	P to K5. Initiating a brilliant piece of play.	P × P.
22.	P × P.	R × KP.
23.	QR to Q1.	Q to B4. To guard Q3.
24.	Q to Kt3.	R to K5. To stop Q to R4 Ch.
25.	R to B5. A stroke of genius.	P × R.
26.	Kt × P Ch.	K to B3.
27.	R to Q6 Ch.	K × Kt.
28.	Q to B3 Ch.	R to B5.
29.	Q to R5 Ch.	K to K5.
30.	B to B2 Ch.	K to K6.
31.	R to Q3 Ch.	Resigns. If K to B7 or K to K5, R to Q2 Ch. is fatal.

GRUNFELD DEFENCE (in effect).

	White (Makagonov)	Black (Reshevsky)
1.	P to Q4.	Kt to KB3.
2.	P to QB4.	P to KKt3.
3.	Kt to KB3.	B to Kt2.
4.	Kt to B3.	P to Q4.
5.	Q to Kt3.	P to B3.
6.	B to B4.	P × P.
7.	Q × BP.	B to K3.
8.	Q to Q3.	Kt to Q4. Misconceived. Better, either at move 7, or here, was QKt to Q2 aiming at QKt3, Q4, etc.
9.	Kt × Kt.	Q × Kt.
10.	P to K4.	Q to R4 Ch.
11.	B to Q2.	Q to Kt3.
12.	B to B3.	0–0. Now White has very slightly the advantage, but Black has counterplay.
13.	B to K2.	R to Q1.
14.	0–0.	P to QR4. A far fetched idea for developing the QKt. Nevertheless White's reply comes as a surprise.
15.	Kt to Kt5. A beautiful move, involving a long and clever line of thought. White is sacrificing his Queen.	B × QP.
16.	Kt × B.	P × Kt. Observe, Black can win the Queen with—

But there follows :

16. ...		B × P Ch.
17.	R × B.	R × Q.
18.	B × R.	P × Kt.

But there follows :

19.	B to B4.	P to B4.
20.	QR to KB1.	Kt to Q2.
21.	R to B7.	Kt to B3.
22.	R × KP and wins easily.	

One of the "unheard melodies" of Chess.

| 17. | Q to R3. Now White, having had his sacrifice refused, has a big advantage. | P to B4. |

	White (Makagonov)	*Black* (Reshevsky)
18.	B to KKt4.	K to R1.
19.	B × KP.	Kt to R3.
20.	K to R1.	Kt to B2.
21.	B to KKt4.	P to R5.
22.	P to R3.	B × B.
23.	P × B. An interesting decision implying an aggresive intention on the QKt file.	P to B5.
24.	QR to QKt1.	Q to B4. The most vigorous.
25.	R × P.	R (R1) to Kt1.
26.	R × R.	R × R.
27.	Q to Kt3.	R to Kt6. Loss of tempo.
28.	R to Q1.	R to Kt3. To defend the Kt on B2, if necessary, and so as not to let the B in at K6.
29.	R to Q8 Ch.	K to Kt2.
30.	P to R4.	R to Q3.
31.	R to QB8.	P to K4.
32.	P to R5.	R to Q6.
33.	Q to R4.	P to R3.
34.	P × P.	Q to Q3.
35.	R to KR8. Another move of great beauty, notwithstanding that there were many good alternatives.	Q × KtP.
36.	B to B5.	Resigns, because White has a decisive attack.

Finally, a fighting draw.

Q.P. (Nimzowitch D.)

	White (Capablanca)	*Black* (Fine)
1.	P to Q4.	Kt to KB3.
2.	P to QB4.	P to K3.
3.	Kt to QB3.	B to Kt5.
4.	Q to B2.	P to Q4.
5.	P × P.	Q × P. Counter aggressive; choosing a Queen's Fianchetto for the Bishop. The disadvantage is the loss of B for Kt on move 7 to save tempo.
6.	Kt to B3.	P to B4.
7.	B to Q2.	B × Kt.
8.	B × B.	Kt to B3. Kt to K5 would be met by P × P, winning a Pawn.
9.	R to Q1.	0–0.
10.	P to K3.	P to QKt3.
11.	P to QR3.	B to Kt2.
12.	P × P.	Q × P.
13.	P to QKt4.	Q to KR4.
14.	B × Kt. An interesting decision. Logical was B to Q3 or B to K2. The text is an attempt to cash an immediate advantage. Black's brilliant counter-play shows that the posi-	P × B.

	White (Capablanca)	Black (Fine)
	tion was not ready for it. On the other hand, given slower play, Black would have equalized with QRQ1.	
15.	R to Q7.	QR to B1. Defending the Bishop indirectly, viz: 16. R×B Kt×KtP. with a formidable counter-attack.
16.	Q to Kt2.	KR to Q1. This, in conjunction with the following moves, amounts to a brilliant defence.
17.	R×B.	Kt to K4. Of course, Kt cannot take Kt because of the Mate at White's Q1.
18.	B to K2.	Kt×Kt Ch.
19.	B×Kt.	Q to K4.
20.	Q×Q.	R to B8 Ch.
21.	B to Q1.	QR×B Ch.
22.	K to K2.	QR to Q7 Ch.
23.	K to B3.	P×Q.
24.	R × RP. After a combinative middle-game, a typical transition to endgame.	P to K5 Ch.
25.	K to Kt3.	R to R7.
26.	R to R6.	KR to Q7.
27.	R to KB1.	KR to Kt7. A typical endgame situation. White cannot hold his Pawn.
28.	R×P.	R×RP.
29.	P to Kt5.	K to Kt2. There is no hurry for the attack on the Pawn.
30.	P to R4.	QR to Kt6.
31.	K to B4.	R×KtP.
32.	R×R.	R×R.
33.	P to Kt4. Obviously if K × P. R to Kt5 Ch.	R to Kt5.
34.	R to B1.	R to Kt7.
35.	K to Kt3.	K to B3. A mistake.
36.	R to B4.	K to K4.
37.	R to B8. The point.	K to B3.
38.	R to KKt8. A strong move which should win. The King is "cut off".	P to R3.
39.	P to Kt5 Ch.	P×P.
40.	R×P (P to R5 appears to win easily). If 40. . . . R to Kt8 41. K to Kt2, etc.	R to Kt5.
41.	K to R3. If R moves along the rank, the Black K can place itself at Kt3. If R moves on the file, then R to Kt8 for Black embarrasses White: if then K to Kt2. R to Kt4 and so to KR4.	P to K4.

White (Capablanca)
42. R to Kt1.

Black (Fine)
K to B4. Keeping the White King out of the game. The Rook alone cannot force the Pawn forward. If now 43. P to R5, R to Kt3, or R to Kt1 or even P to B3 draws.

Drawn.

A well-fought game, rich in examples of attack and counter-attack.

List of Games

[Some very short games are to be found on pp. 29, 46, 136, 138, 151.]